AN[?]
REVEALED

THE BATTLE OF ANTIETAM AND THE MARYLAND CAMPAIGN AS YOU HAVE NEVER SEEN IT BEFORE

by
DENNIS E. FRYE

Dennis E. Frye
10-9-2[?]

Collingswood
C. W. HISTORICALS, LLC
2004

ISBN 0-9637745-7-3

Printed in the United States of America

First Edition

10 9 8 7 6 5 4 3 2 1

C.W. Historicals, LLC
PO Box 113
Collingswood, NJ 08108
e-mail: cwhist@erols.com
offices: 856-854-1290

Front cover: "Antietam Sunrise" (The New York State Monument on the Antietam Battlefield) Photograph by Marsha B. Wassel.
Back cover: Luminaries around the Dunker Church, 1994. Courtesy of Valley Studio, Hagerstown, Maryland.

To Sylvia
My Texas Rose

Contents

Maps by Blake A. Magner

Gen. Robert E. Lee (*USAMHI*)

discovery, even though the material had been before me for years. Researching *Antietam Revealed* forced me to slow down, read everything with fresh eyes, and separate facts from analysis. I gained a great deal of satisfaction each time I uttered: "I didn't know that." Hopefully, you also will find something in these pages that will make you say: "I didn't know that either." Readers—please enjoy!

Dennis E. Frye
Burnside's Headquarters
Antietam Village, Maryland
May 2003

Maj. Gen. George B. McClellan (*USAMHI*)

Notes and Acknowledgements

Many different sources were used to obtain the information in this volume. The bibliography lists the sources, and in numerous instances, the entry appearing in the main text identifies the source by name. For example, one entry (1161) explains that General Hancock received directions from General McClellan to defend, and not attack, the Bloody Lane sector: "My instructions were to hold that position against the enemy," Hancock noted *in his official report*, written twelve days after the battle. The key reference here is the general's official report.

Because this book is not a Ph.D. dissertation, it does not follow the conventional style of endnotes. I will save the reader from the laborious and often time wasting chore of flipping back and forth between the entries and the endnotes. Hence, to ease the reader's burden, a simple reference will appear at the end of many entries. Not every entry will be referenced, simply those limited primarily to original and contemporary sources, and direct quotations. Specific "battle-action" information is often derived from a combination of sources, and endnotes sometimes will not appear because the note would stretch longer than the entry.

Battle times, battle locations, and battle lines are often gleaned from the 15 detailed maps prepared by the Antietam Battlefield Commission in 1904 (corrected in 1908). These maps, researched and prepared by veterans, offer the best source of the ebb and flow of the battle on September 17, but the maps are not listed as notes. For those of you who prefer a narrative discussion of battles, you should refer to James Murfin's *The Gleam of Bayonets* and Stephen Sears's *Landscape Turned Red*.

In cases where specific numbers are mentioned, along with superlatives—such as the *most* casualties, the *largest* brigade, the *highest* number of killed, or the *smallest* regiment—endnotes will usually not appear. The author is responsible for the superlatives and the comparative analysis in most cases, but the basis for many of these numbers are compilations in the appendix of John Priest's *Antietam: The Soldiers Battle*.

Information in the final chapter, which deals with The Maryland Campaign from 1890 to the present, is primarily pulled from four sources. Entries dealing with the establishment and administration of Antietam are drawn from the park's administrative history. Information concerning Antietam's monuments are derived from the works of John Schildt and Charles Adams. Data concerning modern preservation issues come from the personal experiences of the author.

In a way of thanks and acknowledgements, I must start with the staff of the Antietam National Battlefield—the national park where I launched my NPS career—who rendered invaluable assistance in this project. The portly pair of Ted Alexander and Paul Chiles eagerly opened their files, boxes, and books, and provided many valuable clues and suggestions. "Cannonball Chiles" possesses enormous expertise, and "Elvis" Alexander—a fine military historian whose knowledge surpasses the boundaries of 1861-1865—has garnered acclaim in the 20 years that have passed since I first hired him for his inaugural ranger position at Harpers Ferry Park. I also express my gratitude to a fellow Shepherd College alumnus, Ranger Keith B. Snyder, who also began his NPS career working for me. Special kudos must be given to Superintendent John Howard, who, as a manager, has a passion for Antietam that is inspiring and unequaled.

Good friends at Harpers Ferry National Historical Park also contributed to this study. Nancy Hatcher, the guardian of the library (and on a personal note, the maid-of-honor at my wedding) answered my calls with enthusiasm and alacrity. Supervisory Ranger Todd Bolton, between our discussions on baseball and politics, tracked mundane sources that I remembered, but could not locate. Marsha Starkey's vivacious enthusiasm always provided encouragement. And the ladies of the Harpers Ferry Historical Association—Debbie Piscitelli, Becky Sollars, and Sue Baker—always welcomed me with a hug and offers of cookies. Accolades must go to Superintendent Don Campbell, whose vision, persistence, and resolute stand for preservation during his 22-year tenure at Harpers Ferry has placed the park among the nation's premier historical sites.

Publisher Blake Magner has outstanding Civil War credentials. As a writer, editor, and reviewer himself, Blake brings creative and technical understanding to a project of this magnitude. Blake aspires for perfection in presentation and contents, and his determined marketing skills will promote optimum exposure. Blake is another long-time Civil War associate, and I'm pleased our paths intersected to produce this volume, and a long tough row to hoe it was.

John Frye, curator of the Western Maryland Room of the Washington County Free Library, helped not because he is my father, but because he has spent over 35 years building the collection of the Western Maryland Room. Any serious student who is researching this region must utilize the vast resources of the Western Maryland Room. I do have one advantage over other researchers, however—I can call upon Dad anytime!

A host of historians have assisted me, some very recently, and many over long years of collegial friendship. Dr. Tom Clemens is my Maryland Campaign sparring partner, and we've enjoyed many spirited debates. Rev. John Schildt has written more about Antietam subjects than any other historian. Dr. Joseph Harsh of George Mason University is the unchallenged master of the details of the Maryland Campaign. Michael Musick of the National Archives and Dr. Richard Sommers of the US Army Military History Institute have guided me to countless sources—always with good cheer. Dr. James I. "Bud" Robertson of Virginia Tech has constantly championed my efforts, and Dr. Gary W. Gallagher of "Mr. Jefferson's University" has remained a guiding beacon. Dr. Mark Snell of Shepherd College's Center for the Study of the Civil War has become an enthusiastic partner. Former NPS Chief Historian Edwin C. Bearss never misses or forgets a detail, and Robert K. Krick, former Chief Historian at Fredericksburg & Spotsylvania National Military Park, unfailingly instills the value of research. I cannot close this section on historians without remembering the late James V. Murfin, whose 1964 book on Antietam and the Maryland Campaign helped inspire my studies in this field.

Saving the most important "thank you" for last, I wish to express my heartfelt gratitude to my beautiful wife Sylvia. She has witnessed me spending endless hours with books and stacks of papers, or glued to a keyboard and monitor. Her lovely smile returns me to the warmth of the present—and for her presence, I am especially grateful.

Main Street, Village of Sharpsburg (*USAMHI*)

Lutheran Church on Main Street in Sharpsburg (*USAMHI*)

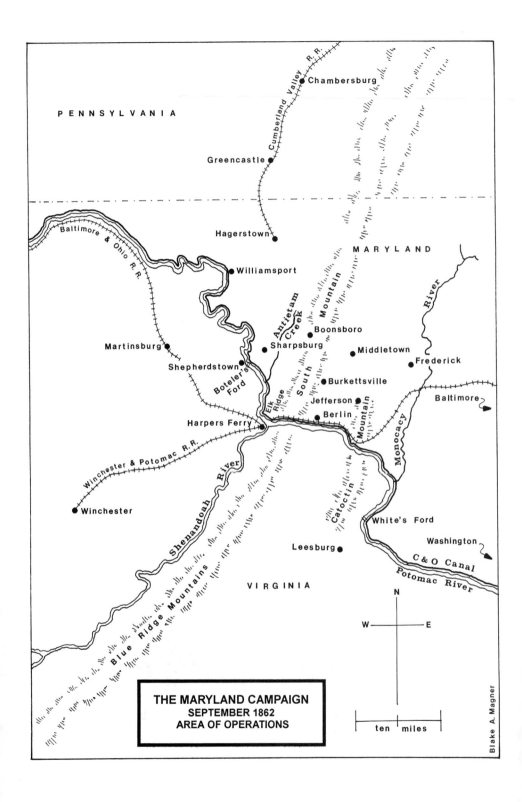

PENNSYLVANIA

Chambersburg

Greencastle

MARYLAND

Hagerstown

Williamsport

Baltimore & Ohio R.R.

Boonsboro

Martinsburg

Sharpsburg

Middletown

Frederick

Shepherdstown

Boteler's Ford

Burkettsville

Jefferson

Baltimore

Harpers Ferry

Berlin

Winchester & Potomac R.R.

Winchester

Shenandoah River

White's Ford

Washington

Leesburg

C & O Canal

VIRGINIA

Potomac River

Antietam Creek

South Mountain

Elk Ridge

Catoctin Mountain

Monocacy River

Cumberland Valley R.R.

Blue Ridge Mountains

N

W — E

THE MARYLAND CAMPAIGN
SEPTEMBER 1862
AREA OF OPERATIONS

ten miles

Blake A. Magner

Early September
The Invasion of Maryland

1. Antietam is a Native American word that translates as "the swift current."
2. Antietam Creek flows from north to south with its headwaters in Franklin County, Pennsylvania, just north of the Mason-Dixon Line. It empties into the Potomac River at the village of Antietam, Maryland, four miles south of Sharpsburg.
3. The battle of September 17, 1862 is known in the North as the battle of Antietam, while Southerners refer to it as the battle of Sharpsburg.
4. September 17, 1862 marked the 75th anniversary of the signing of the Constitution of the United States—at the time, the destiny of the nation was never in more doubt.
5. Antietam's 23,110 casualties—in only 12 hours—defines it as the bloodiest single day in American military history.
6. Pacifists owned much of the land over which the battle took place. The "Dunkers," as they were known, farmed along Antietam Creek and adamantly opposed all war. The "Dunkers" (also spelled Dunkards) are a religious sect officially named the German Baptist Brethren.
7. Sharpsburg is the oldest town in Washington County, Maryland. Established in 1762 by Joseph Chapline, the town is named after Colonial Governor Horatio G. Sharp.
8. The population of Sharpsburg in 1862 was approximately 1,300 residents.
9. Washington County, the unfortunate host of the battle of Antietam, was established on September 6, 1776, as the *first* county in the United States named after George Washington.
10. President Abraham Lincoln adopted slave emancipation as a necessary military measure in July 1862. His cabinet urged him not to announce such a profound proclamation without backing it up with a battlefield victory. Lincoln agreed and held off issuing his draft of the Emancipation Proclamation.
11. International attention was focused on a divided America in the late summer of 1862. Foreign intervention in the Civil War by Great Britain and France became problematic for the North and more hopeful for the South.
12. Two former US senators were Confederate brigadier generals in Robert E. Lee's Army of Northern Virginia—Howell Cobb of Georgia and Robert Toombs of Georgia.
13. Two future US presidents, both from Ohio, were serving in the ranks of a single regiment (the 23rd Ohio) in the Union Army of the Potomac—Rutherford B. Hayes and William McKinley.
14. The Maryland Campaign began when the Confederate Army of Northern Virginia, commanded by Gen. Robert E. Lee, starting crossing the Potomac River on September 4, 1862.
15. The Maryland Campaign closed with a battle along the west bank of the Potomac River just below Shepherdstown, [West] Virginia, on September 20, 1862.

16. The Maryland Campaign included four separate engagements: Harpers Ferry on September 12-15; South Mountain on September 14; Antietam on September 17; Boteler's Ford near Shepherdstown on September 20.

17. Twenty-seven Medals of Honor were awarded to Union soldiers for distinguished valor during The Maryland Campaign. They were distributed as follows: Harpers Ferry— 1; South Mountain—4; Antietam—21; Boteler's Ford—2. Six of the Medals of Honor were awarded for artillery-related actions.

18. The first invasion of the North by a Confederate army in the Eastern Theater of the war climaxed with the battle of Antietam. Two more Confederate invasions later occurred: the Gettysburg Campaign in June and July 1863; and Lt. Gen. Jubal A. Early's advance toward Washington in July 1864.

19. Confederate President Jefferson Davis, in his September 7, 1862 proclamation outlining the "motives and purposes" of the Confederate entry into Maryland, referred to Lee's army as an "invading army." He also implored the people of Maryland to pressure the United States for peace, "to put an end to this invasion of their homes." (*Official Records*, Vol. 19, pt. 2, p. 598. Hereafter cited as *OR*)

20. Very little of the battle of Antietam occurred along the creek itself. The creek is invisible from most areas where the fighting took place.

21. The Confederate army was *retreating* from Maryland and heading back to Virginia when it stopped to rest at Sharpsburg on the night of September 14-15, 1862. Lee initially did not intend to make a stand along Antietam Creek.

22. Robert Edward Lee was 55-years-old during The Maryland Campaign. His opponent, Maj. Gen. George Brinton McClellan, was 35. Lee's home was Arlington House, located just across the Potomac River from Washington D.C., while McClellan lived in Cincinnati, Ohio, at the beginning of the war.

23. Both Lee and McClellan attended the United States Military Academy at West Point. Lee graduated in 1829, finishing second in his class. McClellan graduated in 1846, also ranking second in his class.

24. Both Lee and McClellan served as engineers in the antebellum Regular Army. Lee and McClellan served together on the Engineer Staff of General Winfield Scott at Vera Cruz during the Mexican War.

25. Lee remained in the Regular Army until the outbreak of the Civil War. Although offered chief command of US forces assembling in Washington, D.C., Lee refused and resigned from the army on April 20, 1861 to fight with his native Virginia.

26. In 1855, Secretary of War Jefferson Davis appointed Capt. McClellan as the military's commissioner to Europe to study and report on the latest martial developments in Great Britain and on the continent.

27. McClellan left the army in 1857 to become chief engineer of the Illinois Central Railroad. At the outbreak of the war, he was president of the Ohio and Mississippi Railroad.

28. McClellan's sobriquet was the "Young Napoleon."

29. Gen. McClellan's first victories of the war occurred in western Virginia during the summer of 1861—a theater of operations soon to be under Robert E. Lee's supervision. Lee did not meet McClellan on the battlefield in western Virginia. The Confederate defeats resulted from the failures of subordinate generals.

30. McClellan replaced Winfield Scott as general-in-chief of United States forces on November 1, 1861. Lincoln relieved him of this position when McClellan embarked on the Peninsula Campaign in March 1862. McClellan retained his position as commander of the Army of the Potomac.

31. In the course of eight weeks, Lee's summer offensives shifted the war from the doorstep of Richmond—where McClellan had his army poised within seven miles of the Confederate capital the last week of June 1862—to the front door of Washington, constituting one of the most remarkable military turnabouts in history.

32. General Lee's resounding victories at Second Manassas (August 28-31) and Chantilly (September 1) defeated Union forces in northern Virginia and sent them scurrying back behind the defenses of Washington. The path was now clear for Lee to conduct offensive operations north of the Potomac.

33. McClellan was posted within the environs of Washington's defenses during the Second Manassas battle. The sulking general—whose campaign against Richmond was terminated in mid-August when he and his army were called back to the capital—blamed the Lincoln administration for not reinforcing him while on the Peninsula.

34. McClellan's letters to his wife survive and are housed in the manuscript collection of the Library of Congress. These frank epistles provide historians with the primary source of information on McClellan's innermost thoughts, as well as insights into his character and personality.

35. McClellan's disrespect for the President is epitomized by his characterization of Lincoln as "an idiot . . . nothing more than a well meaning baboon." (Sears, *Landscape Turned Red*, p. 22)

36. Lincoln was a Republican. McClellan was a Democrat. McClellan paraded his politics and boisterously pronounced his differences with the Lincoln agenda. While firm against secession, McClellan sought a limited war and a return to the status quo of 1860.

37. McClellan opposed any plan of emancipation, placing him in direct conflict with the Lincoln administration.

38. The Union Secretary of War, Edwin M. Stanton, detested McClellan and charged him with disobedience for failing to aid Maj. Gen. John Pope at Manassas. At the beginning of September, Stanton circulated a petition to other cabinet members calling for the President to dismiss "Little Mac."

39. President Lincoln was perturbed with McClellan's lack of cooperation during the Second Manassas Campaign. "The President was very outspoken in regard to McClellan's present conduct," wrote Lincoln's secretary John Hay. "He said it really seemed to him that McC. wanted Pope defeated." (Sears, *Landscape Turned Red*, p. 8)

40. McClellan labeled Washington, D.C., "that sink of iniquity." (Sears, *Landscape Turned Red*, p. 31)

41. Washington hosted 450 houses of ill repute in the fall of 1862 and at least 7,500 prostitutes.

42. A desperate Abraham Lincoln, facing demoralization, disorganization, and disintegration of his armies around Washington, asked McClellan to take command of all federal troops defending the capital—including all those in Pope's defeated Manassas army—on September 2. McClellan accepted.

43. Lincoln informed his cabinet on September 2 that he had appointed McClellan to command the joint armies defending Washington. Secretary of War Stanton's petition to relieve "Little Mac" was not presented. The President stated he would rescind his decision if a better candidate than McClellan could be found.

44. President Lincoln exhibited extraordinary humility in turning to McClellan—an avowed enemy of the president—for help. Lincoln's logic prevailed over his emotions. The president reasoned he needed McClellan because: 1) his engineering skills would prepare the capital's defenses; 2) his organizational abilities would mesh two armies and return order out of chaos; and 3) McClellan had the confidence of the soldiers. (Sears, *Landscape Turned Red*, p. 16)

45. McClellan later claimed that the President limited his command only to the defenses of Washington, and that he did not have jurisdiction over the Army of the Potomac operating in the field. McClellan's own orders appear to clarify this "confusion," as all orders from September 6 onward were labeled "Headquarters, Army of the Potomac."

46. In his opening sentence in a letter to President Jefferson Davis from his headquarters near Dranesville, Virginia, on September 3, General Lee declared: "The present seems to be the most propitious time since the commencement of the war for the Confederate army to enter Maryland." (*OR* 19 (2): 590)

47. The Union General-in-Chief, Henry W. Halleck, predicted Lee would move north. In a dispatch to McClellan on September 3 he warned: "There is every probability that the enemy . . . will cross the Potomac, and make a raid into Maryland or Pennsylvania." (*OR* 19 (2): 169)

48. General Halleck was McClellan's immediate superior in Washington. Halleck was sarcastically known as "Old Brains."

49. The first official mention of Pennsylvania as a target of the Confederate invasion occurred on September 4 when Lee informed President Davis: "Should the results of the expedition justify it, I propose to enter Pennsylvania, unless you should deem it unadvisable upon political or other grounds." (*OR* 19 (2): 592)

50. Maryland was a border state. Although a slave-state and considered by most to harbor strong Southern proclivities, Maryland could not secede—primarily because Abraham Lincoln suspended *habeas corpus* and placed the state legislature under house arrest before it could determine the secession question.

51. The first attack upon Union infantry in the war occurred on April 19, 1861, when a mob of pro-secession citizens rioted in Baltimore and assaulted the 6th Massachusetts Infantry while it was marching through the city en-route to Washington. Confederates had not forgotten Baltimore's proclivity. The Confederate Congress passed a resolution on

December 21, 1861, stating: "[N]o peace ought to be concluded with the United States, which does not insure to Maryland the opportunity of forming a part of the Confederacy." (*OR* 4 (1): 806)

52. Marylanders fighting for the Confederate army considered Lee's initiative their best chance to rescue the state from Lincoln's domination. General Lee viewed his army as liberators, and informed President Davis on September 3 his advance into Maryland would "afford her an opportunity of throwing off the oppression to which she is now subject." (*OR* 19 (2): 590)

53. Lee decided to launch into Maryland for the following reasons: 1) keep US forces out of Virginia and thus protect the forthcoming harvest; 2) free Maryland from Union occupation and recruit "Old Line Staters" to the Confederate cause; 3) supply his army from the bountiful foodstuffs north of the Potomac; 4) influence upcoming congressional elections against the Lincoln Republicans and in favor of the "Peace Democrats"; and 5) enhance the Confederacy's reputation with European nations—especially Great Britain—and encourage British mediation or possible diplomatic recognition of the Confederacy. (*OR* 19 (2): 590, 593)

54. In the border-state of Kentucky, Confederate invasion armies under General Braxton Bragg and Major General Kirby Smith were moving north at the same time Lee was entering Maryland. President Davis proclaimed in both campaigns, the design was not conquest, but self defense.

55. General Lee proposed to President Davis in his September 3 letter announcing the Maryland invasion, that General Bragg's army—should it fail in Kentucky—be transferred into Virginia to help oppose the "overwhelming numbers" the federals were concentrating around Washington. (*O R* 19 (2): 590)

56. A Confederate move into Maryland would sever the Baltimore & Ohio Railroad—a major east-west link for the North, capable of supplying 10,000 troops daily.

57. The hardship economics of the "Cotton Famine" in Great Britain—caused by the Union blockade of the South and the Confederacy's initial embargo on cotton exportation—idled 80,000 textile workers and reduced 370,000 more to half-time work by July 1862. This forced British leaders to consider some form of intervention in the war. (Sears, *Landscape Turned Red*, p. 40)

58. British Prime Minister Viscount Palmerston recommended European intervention following the disastrous Union debacle at Second Manassas. Convinced by a succession of Confederate military victories, Palmerston suggested to Foreign Secretary Lord John Russell: "[W]ould it not be time for us to consider whether in such a state of things England and France might not address the contending parties and recommend an arrangement upon the basis of separation?" (Murfin, *The Gleam of Bayonets: The Battle of Antietam and the Maryland Campaign*, p. 394)

59. The Army of Northern Virginia moved north from its bivouac at Leesburg, Virginia, and began crossing the Potomac River at White's Ford on September 4. It would take three days for the army to complete its crossing.

60. A US Signal Corps station on Sugar Loaf Mountain sent the first report of the Confederate invasion at 4:00 p.m. on September 4. The two signalmen, Lt. Brinkerhoff Miner and A. H. Cook, later abandoned the lookout and during their escape captured a courier bearing dispatches from Jefferson Davis to Gen. Lee. Miner and Cook were captured by Confederates before they could deliver the errant messages to a federal command. (*OR* 19 (1): 815; Fishel, *The Secret War for the Union*, pp. 211-212)

61. White's Ford is located just over 39 miles from Georgetown (on the outskirts of Washington, D. C.) along the towpath of the Chesapeake and Ohio Canal. It witnessed three major crossings of Confederate forces, the first being Lee's army advancing north on September 4-7, 1862; second, J.E.B. Stuart's cavalry moving south on October 12, 1862, following its ride around McClellan's army in Maryland and Pennsylvania; and third, Jubal Early's Second Corps returning across the ford to Virginia on July 14, 1864, after threatening Washington.

62. White's Ford was named after Colonel Elijah V. White, a resident of Poolesville, Maryland, and commander of the 35th Virginia Cavalry, also known as "the Commanches."

63. By crossing the Potomac at White's Ford, Lee made no effort to disguise his invasion. Federals operating a signal station atop nearby Sugarloaf Mountain witnessed the initial Confederate crossing. This bold maneuver worked to Lee's advantage, initially freezing the Union army into a defensive posture around Washington. (*OR* 19 (2): 604-605)

64. The 10th Virginia Infantry was the first Confederate infantry regiment to cross White's Ford. Bands blared *Maryland, My Maryland,* a wartime lyric written by poet James Ryder Randall, accompanied by the tune *Oh Tannenbaum.*

65. Stonewall Jackson's quartermaster, John Harman, cursed wildly while driving wagon trains across the Potomac. The pious Jackson quietly disapproved of the profanity, but Harman explained: "There's only one language that will make mules understand on a hot day that they must get out of the water." (John D. Imboden, "Incidents of the First Bull Run." In *Battles and Leaders of the Civil War*, edited by Robert U. Johnson and Clarence C. Buel, 1:238)

66. The Confederates commandeered a barge full of melons on the Chesapeake & Ohio Canal near White's Ford.

67. Reinforcements bolstered Lee as he invaded Maryland. Twenty thousand Confederates—including three divisions commanded by Lafayette McLaws, D. H. Hill, and John G. Walker—arrived from Richmond.

68. D. H. Hill's column began crossing the Potomac on September 4 at the mouth of the Monocacy River, three miles upstream from White's Ford. (*OR* 19 (1): 1019)

69. White's Ford became so crowded with the Confederate crossing that Lafayette McLaws was directed to take his division and cross the Potomac elsewhere. He moved upstream and splashed across the river at Cheek's Ford. (Trimpi, *The Maryland Campaign Diary of Henry Lord Page King*, p. 30. Hereafter cited as King diary.)

70. Confederates under D. H. Hill attempted to destroy the Monocacy aqueduct on the night of September 4 and 5, but failed "for want of powder and tools." Hill did destroy a lock and canal boats near the point where he crossed the river. (*OR* 19 (1): 1019)

71. Emboldened by the advance into Maryland, and confident of continued success, Gen. Lee recommended to President Davis that the Confederacy propose ending hostilities in exchange for independence: "Such a proposition, coming from us at this time, could in no way be regarded as suing for peace; but, being made when it is in our power to inflict injury upon our adversary, would show conclusively to the world that our sole object is the establishment of our independence and the attainment of an honorable peace." (*OR* 19 (2): 600)

72. Gen. Lee entered Maryland riding in an ambulance. A frightened horse caused Lee to fall on August 31, and as a result, Lee broke a small bone in one hand and badly sprained the other. Both of Lee's hands remained in splints throughout much of the campaign.

73. Maj. Gen. James Longstreet arrived in Maryland with a badly blistered heel and throughout much of the campaign he avoided his boot in favor of a carpet slipper.

74. Thomas J. "Stonewall" Jackson was jolted and bruised at the outset of The Maryland Campaign when he was thrown from a young mare presented to him by a reception committee of Southern sympathizers.

75. Two of Lee's generals were under arrest as the army approached Maryland. Maj. Gen. Ambrose Powell Hill was arrested by Stonewall Jackson for perceived delinquencies and improprieties during the march preceding the August 9 battle of Cedar Mountain. Brig. Gen. John Bell Hood refused to yield some captured wagons to the "titular authority"—Brig. Gen. Nathan "Shanks" Evans—over his division. Both men, without commands, rode in the rear of their respective divisions.

76. George McClellan loved his army, and his soldiers adored him. McClellan once proclaimed to his men: "I am to watch over you as a parent over his children." Vociferous cheers greeted McClellan whenever he reviewed or passed by his admiring ranks. (Sears, *Landscape Turned Red*, p. 21)

77. The Army of the Potomac was an all-volunteer army in 1862. No draft was initiated in the North until the following year.

78. President Lincoln issued a call for 300,000 nine-month volunteers in the summer of 1862. New regiments were formed within the states, and 35 had arrived in Washington by the first week of September—all well equipped and well uniformed, but with virtually no training.

79. General Lee's intelligence informed him that 60,000 new recruits had arrived in Washington as of September 3. (*OR* 19 (2): 590)

80. Robert E. Lee, while serving as Jefferson Davis' military advisor, recognized the Confederacy's manpower shortage in the ranks and he became the advocate of a military draft for the entire South. The first conscription act in American history was passed by the Confederate Congress on April 16, 1862. It drafted men between the ages of 18 and 35, and it extended the current twelve-month enlistment term to three years.

81. Lee's first target in Maryland was the city of Frederick. Good roads from every direction of the compass originated in Frederick. To the southeast, 40 miles distant, was Washington D. C.; Baltimore is 40 miles due east, while Pennsylvania is directly north some 25 miles. Hagerstown and the great Cumberland Valley lay just 20 miles to the west.

82. Lee occupied Frederick and its environs with no opposition on September 6. The same day, the Confederate commander established his headquarters in a field east of the Monocacy River and near Monocacy Junction on the Baltimore & Ohio Railroad.

83. The precise location of Lee's headquarters remains unknown, but historians assume the general's tents likely stood in a grove of oak trees upon the Tran Farm, two miles south of Frederick.

84. Since the federals did not know Lee's intentions, his very presence at Frederick presented a threat to Washington and Baltimore.

85. Allan Pinkerton, a well-known Chicago private detective, was responsible for McClellan's army intelligence. Pinkerton always overestimated the strength of the enemy—sometimes doubling or even tripling Confederate numbers—however, McClellan accepted his intelligence as fact.

86. McClellan believed, based upon Pinkerton's estimates, that the Confederate Army invaded Maryland with 100,000-125,000 men—more than double Lee's actual numbers, even when accepting the lower estimate. He reported to General-in-Chief Halleck on September 9 that "Jackson and Longstreet have about 110,000 men of all arms at Frederick." (*OR* 19 (2): 219)

87. "Little Mac" ignored intelligence regarding Confederate troop strengths gleaned from deserters, slave informants, or newspaper accounts. He also failed to utilize his cavalry as an intelligence-gathering arm. McClellan depended exclusively upon Pinkerton and his spies for all intelligence.

88. A fatal flaw for McClellan was his incessant, unyielding belief that he was outnumbered. The odds against him, by Pinkerton's mathematics, were always two or three in favor of the enemy. At no time during McClellan's tenure as commander of the Army of the Potomac did his opponent equal or surpass his strength.

89. Washington, D. C., was the most heavily fortified city in the world in September 1862. At the outset of the invasion, Lee wrote President Davis: "I had no intention of attacking him [the federals] in his fortifications, and am not prepared to invest them." (*OR* 19 (2): 590)

90. The physical condition of Lee's army was wretched. "[T]he men are poorly provided with clothes," Lee advised President Davis on September 3, "and in thousands of instances are destitute of shoes." Lee asked Davis to pressure the Quartermaster's Department to "furnish any shoes[;] it would be the greatest relief." No shoes arrived during the campaign. (*OR* 19 (2): 590-591)

91. Lee reported to President Davis on September 12 that he had procured 1,000 pairs of shoes in Frederick, 400 in Hagerstown, and 250 in Williamsport. "They will not be sufficient to cover the bare feet of the army," he concluded. (*O R* 19 (2): 605)

Confederate Troops marching through Frederick, September 1862
(*Courtesy of the Historical Society of Frederick County, Maryland*)

92. At least 900 Confederate soldiers who were barefooted did not cross the Potomac, but instead eventually gathered at Winchester in the Shenandoah Valley. (*OR* 19 (2): 614)

93. The odor of the Confederate army did not impress the Marylanders. "I have never seen a mass of such filthy, strong-smelling men," uttered a potential recruit who decided not to join the Southerners. "Three of them in a room would make it unbearable, and when marching in column along the street the smell was most offensive." (Gordon & Gordon, *Frederick County, Maryland: A Playground of the Civil War*, p. 61)

94. The appearance of the Rebel soldiers also deterred enlistments. "They were the roughest set of creatures I ever saw," observed a reporter with the New York *Herald*. "[T]heir features, hair, and clothing matted with dirt and filth, and the scratching they kept up gave warrant of vermin in abundance." (Gordon & Gordon, *Frederick County, Maryland: A Playground of the Civil War*, p. 64)

95. Whenever a Unionist met a secessionist in the streets of Frederick following The Maryland Campaign, the Unionist would commence to scratch, symbolizing lice-infested Confederates.

96. Lee expressed to President Davis disappointment that Marylanders did not join his army. "I do not anticipate any general rising of the people in our behalf," he informed the President on September 7. All totaled, the number of new recruits did not exceed 200. (*OR* 19 (2): 596)

9

97. Gen. McClellan shifted his headquarters from Washington to Rockville, Maryland, about 12 miles northwest of the capital, on the road leading north toward Frederick on September 7. (*OR* 19 (1): 38)

98. Not knowing Lee's intentions at Frederick, McClellan divided his army into three wings to protect all the approaches to Washington and Baltimore. (*OR* 19 (1): 25)

99. Maj. Gen. Ambrose Burnside, in his first assignment with McClellan's army, commanded the north or right wing, protecting the approaches to Baltimore. Burnside's wing included the Ninth Corps and the First Corps—nearly 27,000 men. (*OR* 19 (1): 25)

100. The middle wing guarded the roads leading from Washington to Frederick, and was commanded by Maj. Gen. Edwin V. Sumner. The Second Corps and Twelfth Corps comprised this wing, and numbered over 27,000 men. (*OR* 19 (1): 25)

101. The south or left wing fell under Maj. Gen. William B. Franklin, and included his Sixth Corps and Maj. Gen. Darius Couch's division of the Fourth Corps, totaling about 17,000 men. Their mission was to cover the roads along the Potomac River. (*OR* 19 (1): 25)

102. Nearly half the federal troops in the Washington, D. C. vicinity—72,500—remained behind within the capital's defenses while McClellan ventured into the field with the Army of the Potomac.

103. McClellan and the Union army remained on the defensive from September 7 to September 12, showing little offensive initiative in their respective wing formations, but instead cautiously watching and waiting, attempting to determine Confederate intentions. (*OR* 19 (1): 255-257)

104. The Army of the Potomac had about one "public animal" for every four soldiers— or nearly 22,000 horses and mules.

105. Providing logistical support to the Army of the Potomac were 3,000 wagons and an estimated 600 ambulances.

106. Campaigning with the Army of the Potomac were 57 artillery batteries, each accompanied by between 120 and 160 horses.

107. Lee's army was destitute, badly needing food provisions. Confederates referred to this as the "green corn and green apple" campaign because their primary diet consisted of un-ripened fruit and vegetables. As a result, diarrhea became a common ailment.

108. Lee strictly prohibited his troops from unauthorized confiscation while in Maryland. He warned his men: [A]ny excesses committed will exasperate the people, lead to disastrous results, and enlist the populace on the side of the Federal forces." The Confederates committed few deprivations. (*OR* 19 (2): 592)

109. Gen. Lee ordered his quartermasters and commissaries to purchase supplies needed by the army. Since acquisitions were made using Confederate script, which was not recognized in Maryland, the payments were in good gesture, but worthless. (*OR* 19 (2): 592)

110. The Confederates discovered 1,500 barrels of flour in Hagerstown, but Gen. Lee feared that in order to supply his army he would "have to haul from the Valley of Virginia." (*OR* 19 (2): 592)

111. At the outset of the campaign, Gen. Lee's greatest concern was the "fear of getting out of ammunition." Lee, aware of previous inadequacies with his munitions—especially his artillery shells—pleaded for President Davis' assistance: "I beg you will instruct the Ordnance Department to spare no pains in manufacturing a sufficient amount of the best kind..." of ammunition. (*OR* 19 (2): 591)

112. Gen. Lee expressed disappointment that the 10,000-12,000 arms captured at Second Manassas "will all be lost, for want of transportation to remove them." Lee reported to Davis on September 8 that the wagons designed for this purpose were diverted "to transport sick and wounded back to Warrenton." (*OR* 19 (2): 601)

113. Straggling—excessive straggling—tested Gen. Lee's patience in the opening days of the advance. "One of the greatest evils," he notified President Davis on September 7, "is the habit of straggling from the ranks. . . . It has become a habit difficult to correct." (*OR* 19 (2): 597)

114. Historians disagree on the number of stragglers and its causes. Some argue the distressed physical condition of the Confederate soldier greatly diminished Lee's strength—the ragged Rebels were simply too worn out to continue. Others maintain a lack of resolve to advance north of the Potomac, claiming limited support for a military offensive that goes beyond defense of home and hearth. Still others suggest Lee lacked the line officers—depleted by death and wounds—necessary to enforce discipline within the ranks.

115. McClellan reported to Halleck on September 11 that the Confederate forces "are numerically superior to ours by at least 25 percent." In the same report, he proclaimed Lee had 120,000 men at Frederick, and that he needed reinforcements sent forward from Washington. (*OR* 19 (2): 254)

116. US Secretary of the Navy Gideon Welles summarized Gen. McClellan: "[He] is an intelligent engineer but not a commander. . . . The study of military operations interests and amuses him. He likes show, parade and power. Wishes to outgeneral the Rebels, but not to kill and destroy them." (Sears, *Landscape Turned Red*, pp. 46-47)

117. Secretary of War Stanton, frustrated by McClellan's incessant call for reinforcements, once remarked during the Peninsula Campaign: "If he had a million men, he would swear the enemy had two million, and then he would sit down in the mud and yell for three." (Murfin, *The Gleam of Bayonets: The Battle of Antietam and the Maryland Campaign*, p. 127)

118. President Lincoln, in response to McClellan's September 11 plea for reinforcements, released the Fifth Corps under Maj. Gen. Fitz John Porter from the Washington defenses. It would reunite with the Army of the Potomac near Frederick.

119. Lee appointed Col. Bradley T. Johnson, a native of Frederick, as provost marshal of that city. Johnson organized the 1st Maryland (CSA) in the spring of 1861. Johnson spent three hours briefing Lee and Jackson on western Maryland's geography and its idiosyncrasies on the night of September 4—the last night in Virginia before the two generals crossed the Potomac and entered the Old Line State.

120. The only recorded act of violence in Frederick during its five-day occupation was the attempted ransacking of two local pro-Union newspapers by secessionist residents. The Confederates thwarted the attack, jailed the perpetrators, and helped the newspaper staffs clean up.

121. While at Frederick, Lee issued a proclamation to the people of Maryland on September 8 explaining why his army was present in the state. After outlining perceived abuses by the Lincoln administration, including suppression of freedom of press and speech, and unlawful imprisonment, Lee concluded: "[T]he South have long wished to aid you in throwing off this foreign yoke." President Davis' proclamation to the people of Maryland did not arrive until after Lee had issued his own. Davis' proclamation was not presented. (*OR* 19 (2): 601-602, 605)

122. Frederick gave Gen. Lee and his army a cool reception and offered indifference to his proclamation. Located in western Maryland—with its Germanic and Scotch-Irish heritage and its limited slave holdings—this region remained loyal to the Union throughout the war.

123. Maj. Gen. Thomas J. "Stonewall" Jackson attended Sunday evening services at the Reformed Church on September 7. Jackson went to sleep at the beginning of the sermon, thus missing a prayer for the President of the United States. (Douglas, *I Rode With Stonewall*, p. 150)

124. President Davis wanted to meet with Gen. Lee shortly after the campaign began. Lee discouraged the venture: "I cannot but feel great uneasiness for your safety should you undertake to reach me," Lee informed the president on September 9. "You will not only encounter the hardships and fatigues of a very disagreeable journey, but also run the risk of capture by the enemy." Lee dispatched Maj. Walter H. Taylor, his aide-de-camp, to Warrenton to meet with President Davis. Taylor arrived on the 10th, carrying dispatches and verbal instructions, but Davis had already returned to Richmond. (*OR* 19 (2): 602-603, 617)

125. Jeb Stuart hosted a ball for invited cavalrymen and local belles at Urbana, a village southeast of Frederick, on the evening of September 11. The social affair within the Landon Female Academy building, with music provided by the 18th Mississippi regimental band, was interrupted by McClellan's advance; but after a brief skirmish, the party continued.

126. The Shenandoah Valley in Virginia would serve as Gen. Lee's supply line. With the mountains of the Blue Ridge towering over the valley's eastern flank, the heights would help protect Confederate wagon trains and depots from Union raiders. (*OR* 19 (2): 593)

127. Federal forces totaling approximately 14,000 men occupied three key positions in the Shenandoah Valley at the outset of Lee's invasion: Harpers Ferry, Martinsburg, and Winchester. Gen. Lee expected the Union to abandon these positions as his army moved north: "I have no doubt that they will leave that section," Lee informed President Davis on September 5, "as soon as they learn of the movement across the Potomac." (*OR* 19 (2): 594)

128. A federal brigade under Brig. Gen. Julius White evacuated Winchester, without a fight, on September 2 after blowing up the magazine and burning large amounts of quartermaster and commissary stores. White retreated north towards Harpers Ferry and Martinsburg. (*OR* 19 (1): 139)

129. Lt. Col. J. H. S. Funk, a native of Winchester and graduate of the Winchester Medical College, was the first Confederate officer to occupy Winchester on September 3. Funk reported the Union abandonment, permitting Gen. Lee to transfer his line of supply into the Shenandoah Valley. (*OR* 19 (1): 139)

130. Winchester, Virginia, in the heart of the northern Shenandoah Valley, became Gen. Lee's base of operations for The Maryland Campaign. No railroads serviced Winchester while Lee utilized the Valley town as his depot. The only railroad in town was the Winchester and Potomac, running northeast to Harpers Ferry, but the line was in poor condition and without rolling stock.

131. Gen. Lee misinformed President Davis on September 7 when he announced; "The Shenandoah Valley has been evacuated." The federals had abandoned Winchester, but remained in position at Harpers Ferry and Martinsburg, despite being isolated from McClellan's army by Lee's interposing force. (*OR* 19 (2): 597)

132. General-in-Chief Halleck made the decision to maintain a strong federal presence in the Shenandoah Valley. "Our army in motion," Halleck wired the commander at Harpers Ferry on September 7. "It is important that Harpers Ferry be held to the latest moment." (*OR* 19 (1): 757)

133. The first unexpected event for Gen. Lee in the invasion occurred when federal forces failed to abandon Harpers Ferry and Martinsburg in the Shenandoah Valley. (*OR* 19 (2): 605)

134. Gen. Lee issued Special Orders 191 at Frederick on September 9 to eliminate the US garrisons at Harpers Ferry and Martinsburg threatening his rear. Their removal would provide the Confederates with an unimpeded line of supply into the Shenandoah Valley. (*OR* 19 (2): 605)

135. Special Orders 191 divided the Confederate infantry into four columns—three marched toward Harpers Ferry to invest that enemy position; the fourth proceeded to Boonsboro to await the outcome of the Harpers Ferry expedition. (*OR* 19 (2): 603-604)

136. The Confederate army began pulling out of Frederick on September 10 to execute Special Orders 191.

137. Stonewall Jackson was designated by Lee to coordinate and command the investment of Harpers Ferry.

138. Jackson rose at 3:00 a.m. on September 10. His column of three divisions began marching west out of Frederick via the National Road shortly after 5:00 a.m.

139. Dr. Lewis H. Steiner, a Frederick native who served as an inspector for the US Sanitary Commission, watched the Confederate army leave Frederick on September 10 with a considerable number of artillery pieces bearing the initials "U.S.". "This rebel army," Steiner wrote in his diary, "seemed to have been largely supplied with transportation by some United States Quartermaster." Dr. Steiner also reported 3,000 black "soldiers"—most likely teamsters—among Lee's army. He described them wearing an assortment of captured blue clothing as well as the gray of the Southern army, and armed with rifles, sabers, and Bowie knives. (Sears, *Landscape Turned Red*, p. 92; Gordon & Gordon, *Frederick County Maryland: A Playground of the Civil War*, p. 79)

140. Stonewall Jackson never passed by the home of Barbara Fritchie, according to his youngest staff officer, Henry Kyd Douglas, who was with Jackson every moment of his time in Frederick.

141. John Greenleaf Whittier's ballad of Barbara Fritchie, first published in the *Atlantic* in October 1863, is fiction. A 96-year-old matron named Barbara Fritchie (also spelled Frietchie) did live in Frederick at the time of the Confederate occupation, and she did wave a US flag, but *not* at Stonewall Jackson.

142. Maj. Gen. Jesse L. Reno, commander of the Union Ninth Corps, visited Barbara Fritchie after learning about her staunch Union sympathies. Fritchie gave Reno a small flag that he placed in his saddlebags.

143. Barbara Fritchie died in December 1862, three months after the Confederates passed by her house. She was buried in Mount Olivet Cemetery in Frederick.

144. Nancy Crouse of Middletown waved the stars and stripes as Confederates passed through on September 10. When the Southerners demanded the flag, Crouse wrapped it around her body, but she handed it over when a pistol met the 17-year-old's temple. The flag was later recovered and returned to Miss Crouse by Union soldiers. An eight-stanza ballad was written in her honor, but not by a poet with Whittier's credentials.

145. After climbing two mountain ranges—Catoctin and South Mountain—and traveling 14 miles west of Frederick, Jackson's force camped on the night of the September 10 near Boonsboro. A field opposite John Murdock's home, located one mile from Boonsboro, was the site of Jackson's headquarters' tents that night.

146. Jackson avoided capture at Boonsboro on September 10 after he was startled by the sudden appearance of Union cavalry operating out of Harpers Ferry.

147. Jackson's instructions in Special Orders 191 directed him toward Sharpsburg and the Potomac. Jackson changed the course of his march at Boonsboro, moving instead northwest toward the river at Williamsport rather than due west toward Sharpsburg. The reason for this diversion was to more directly approach the Union garrison at Martinsburg. (*OR* 19 (2): 603; (1): 953)

148. Light's Ford was the location at Williamsport where Jackson's column crossed the Potomac on September 11 en route to Martinsburg. (*OR* 19 (1): 953)

149. Martinsburg was abandoned by the federals who fled to Harpers Ferry without a fight on the evening of the 11th. Jackson spent the night of the 11th near Martinsburg and the 12th along the banks of the Opequon Creek. He then proceeded toward Harpers Ferry on the morning of the 13th. While at Martinsburg, Jackson was swarmed by well-wishers, several of whom stole his coat buttons as souvenirs of the occasion.

150. The 2nd Virginia Infantry, Stonewall Brigade, remained at Martinsburg as provost guards following Jackson's departure for Harpers Ferry. Many Martinsburg boys in Company D, 2nd Virginia, experienced a homecoming during the second and third week of September. Company D was raised in Martinsburg in April 1861.

151. Seven of the ten companies of the 2nd Virginia Infantry were from Jefferson County and Berkeley County. The regiment did not fight at Sharpsburg or Harpers Ferry, but remained in the Valley after Jackson crossed the river at Williamsport, recruiting and serving on provost duty.

152. Jackson's "foot cavalry" covered 57 miles in three days on its circular trek from Frederick to Harpers Ferry. Jackson's Confederates climbed two mountains and crossed a river during the difficult march.

153. Straggling reduced the effective strength of the Confederate army—by Gen. Lee's own estimate—as much as one-third to one-half. "One great embarrassment is the reduction of our ranks by straggling," Lee informed President Davis on September 13. "Our ranks are very much diminished." *(OR* 19 (2): 606)

154. The effort by the Confederates to destroy the Monocacy Aqueduct on the Chesapeake & Ohio Canal failed. Maj. Gen. John G. Walker, assigned the task by Gen. Lee, arrived at the aqueduct at 11 p.m. on September 9. After several hours of drilling holes to blow up the arches, Walker determined the "insufficiency of our tools and the extraordinary solidity and massiveness of the masonry . . . [required] days instead of hours." Walker abandoned the project and the position by early morning of the 10th. *(OR* 19 (1): 913)

155. Special Orders 191 instructed Maj. Gen. John G. Walker's division to cross the Potomac at Cheek's Ford, near the mouth of the Monocacy River, and then march north to seal in the Union garrison at Harpers Ferry from the south bank of the Shenandoah. The Union advance seized the Monocacy aqueduct and Cheek's Ford on the morning of the 10th, forcing Walker's Confederates to divert their Potomac River crossing northward to Point of Rocks. *(OR* 19 (2): 604; (1): 913)

156. The Confederate army traveled with little or no baggage to expedite its marching and to speed the execution of Special Orders 191. McLaws' command traveled with only one wagon per regiment. (Trimpi, King Diary, p. 31)

157. A fifth separation of the Confederate army—in addition to the four outlined in Special Orders 191—occurred when Gen. Lee learned of a rumor that Pennsylvania militia were advancing upon Hagerstown. Lee dispatched Longstreet's column from Boonsboro to Hagerstown, 13 miles north, on the 10th.

158. Lee accompanied Longstreet on the expedition to Hagerstown where they arrived on the 11th. He discovered no immediate threat from Pennsylvania.

159. Pennsylvania emergency militiamen began arriving at Greencastle on September 15. Eventually 10,000 of these men, who had virtually no military training and were described by one onlooker as "little better than a demoralized mob," moved into the Greencastle area. (Alexander and Conrad, *When War Passed This Way*, pp. 82, 85)

160. The mayor, cashier of the bank, and sheriff of Hagerstown, abandoned their home city in the face of the Confederates and arrived in Greencastle, the first town north of the Mason-Dixon Line, on the afternoon of the 11th. The bank of Chambersburg, Pennsylvania—panicked by the Confederate advance to Hagerstown and Lee's expected move north—sent its money supply to Harrisburg. (*OR* 19 (2): 28)

161. The first Confederates to enter Hagerstown were cavalry who arrived about 9:00 a.m. on the 11th. They were led by Lt. Col. Luke Trunan Brien, a local native who owned a farm near Middleburg, Maryland, just south of the Mason-Dixon Line.

162. The first report revealing a Confederate advance into Pennsylvania occurred about noon on September 11 when Southern cavalry was reported within one-half mile of the Mason-Dixon Line south of Greencastle.

163. Pennsylvania Governor Andrew Curtin sent William W. Wilson, an expert telegrapher, to Greencastle to act as a dispatcher of intelligence reporting to the governor's office in Harrisburg.

164. Two hundred men from the newly organized 15th Pennsylvania Cavalry—so new they have not yet received their horses—were dispatched to Franklin County's southern border to engage in reconnaissance missions.

165. The most successful federal spy in the Hagerstown area was Col. William J. Palmer, commander of the neophyte 15th Pennsylvania Cavalry. Palmer disguised himself as a farmer and traveled to Hagerstown, where he spoke with Southern soldiers and civilians, gathering invaluable intelligence that was passed on to Governor Curtin through telegrapher William Wilson.

166. The northernmost advance of the Confederate army occurred on September 13 at Middleburg, Maryland. According to a message from Governor Curtin to General-in-Chief Halleck, 3,000 Confederates occupied Middleburg, "on the Maryland-Pennsylvania line," at 7:00 p.m. on the 13th. The number may be exaggerated, but the Confederate appearance in Middleburg seemed certain. (*OR* 19 (2): 287)

167. The easternmost advance of the Confederate army occurred on September 11, when Confederate cavalry under Fitzhugh Lee entered Westminster, Maryland, about 7:30 p.m. with 500 cavalry and two pieces of artillery. A report of this raid was filed by the *Associated Press*, dated the next day. McClellan confirmed the Westminster raid when he informed President Lincoln on the 12th that, "Cavalry are in pursuit of the Westminster party, with orders to catch them at all hazards." The Confederate cavalry was not captured. (*OR* 19 (2): 272)

168. McClellan's three wings were arrayed in a 25-mile arc on September 11, ranging northeast from the Potomac to the National Road (the main road between Frederick and Baltimore). The head of the arc cautiously waited about 15 miles from Frederick.

169. McClellan ordered the Union advance to Frederick on September 12—two days after most of the Confederates had evacuated the town.

170. The Army of the Potomac marched an average six miles per day between September 8 and September 14, according to General-in-Chief Henry W. Halleck. (*OR* 19 (1): 787)

171. President Lincoln's shortest—and earliest—message to McClellan during the campaign came at 4:00 a.m. on September 12. The five-word message asked: "How does it look now?" (*OR* 19 (2): 270)

172. The last Confederate force in Frederick was Brig. Gen. Wade Hampton's brigade, serving as the rear guard along the National Road, retiring slowly west to Frederick. Hampton's force abandoned the town on the afternoon of the 12th. (*OR* 19 (1): 815-816)

173. Hampton's cavalrymen attempted to destroy the "Jug Bridge" on the National Road on the 12th. Explosions rocked the 1808 stone structure, but the bridge survived with only its walls blackened.

174. The Monocacy River bridge superstructure of the Baltimore & Ohio Railroad was completely destroyed by the Confederates. Railroad president John W. Garrett predicted he could rebuild the bridge in four days, provided he obtained access to timber and necessary material at Harpers Ferry. (*OR* 19 (2): 269-270)

175. Train service via the B&O line from Washington to Monocacy River took five hours; from Baltimore to Monocacy River, four hours. (*OR* 19 (2): 270)

176. The first Union force to occupy Frederick was the division of Brig. Gen. Jacob D. Cox, Ninth Corps, Burnside's wing, advancing west along the National Road. (*OR* 19 (1): 416)

177. The only skirmish in Frederick during The Maryland Campaign occurred on the afternoon of the 12th when Hampton's rear guard cavalry charged the advance of Cox's Ninth Corps. The Confederates scattered the enemy and captured ten, including Col. Augustus Moor of the 28th Ohio Infantry. (*OR* 19 (1): 822-823)

178. The Confederates left 450 of their own sick behind in Frederick.

179. The Union Army, unlike the Confederates, received an enthusiastic welcome from the citizens of Frederick. McClellan described the reception in a letter to his wife: "I was nearly overwhelmed and pulled to pieces. . . . I was seldom more affected than by the scenes I saw yesterday and the reception I met with. Men, women, children crowded around us, weeping, shouting and praying." (Gordon & Gordon, *Frederick County, Maryland: A Playground of the Civil War*, pp. 84-85)

180. McClellan predicted—through intelligence reports informing him that Jackson was recrossing the Potomac—that the Confederate Army was returning to Virginia via Williamsport. This prediction was made in his first message to President Lincoln from Frederick, dated at 9:00 p.m. on September 12: "My apprehension is that they may make for Williamsport, and get across the river before I can catch them." (*OR* 19 (2): 272)

181. President Lincoln, after discovering Confederates were crossing the Potomac at Williamsport, pleaded with McClellan: "Please do not let him get off without being hurt." (*OR* 19 (2): 270)

182. The exact number of copies of Special Orders 191 remains unknown. Historians speculate from seven to nine were written at Lee's headquarters. Eight were distributed to those with assignments, and one was placed in Gen. Lee's order book.

183. General Jackson, who believed D. H. Hill was under his command, made a copy of Special Orders 191 in his own handwriting and had it sent to Hill. Jackson did not know Lee had also sent a copy of the orders to Hill.

184. Two copies of Special Orders 191 were sent to D. H. Hill's headquarters. Jackson's arrived. General Lee's was lost.

185. The "Lost Order"—the copy of Special Orders 191 from Gen. Lee to D. H. Hill—was discovered in a clover field near the Baltimore & Ohio Railroad's Monocacy Junction by skirmishers in the 27th Indiana Infantry shortly after 9:00 a.m. on September 13.

186. Special Orders 191 is called the "Lost Order" in the North and the "Lost Dispatch" in the South.

187. The "Lost Order," a two-page document, was discovered in a yellowish envelope, out of which dropped three small cigars.

188. Three different soldiers in the 27th Indiana later claimed credit for discovering the "Lost Order"—Sgt. John Bloss, Cpl. Barton Mitchell, and Pvt. David Vance. All were present in the clover field when the order was found.

189. The earliest known written account of the discovery of the "Lost Order" was 22 years after the event in an 1884 article that identified Sgt. Bloss as the finder. Sgt. Bloss was the only college graduate in the 27th Indiana.

190. Cpl. Mitchell, sometimes misidentified as a private, was illiterate (he can only scribble his name). He was credited with the discovery of the "Lost Order" in articles cited in *Century* in 1886. Pvt. Vance stated he was the discoverer in 1904.

191. Sgt. Bloss read the order and realized its importance. He then delivered the document to his company commander, Capt. Peter Kop. Kop seconded its significance and hand carried the order to the colonel of the 27th, Silas Colgrove. Colgrove showed it to brigade commander Nathan Kimball, who recommended it be passed directly to corps headquarters.

192. The "Lost Order" arrived at Twelfth Corps headquarters about 45 minutes after its discovery (9:00 a.m.). By 10:30 a.m., a courier was sent galloping to Gen. McClellan with the precious contraband in hand.

193. The most coincidental episode in the "Lost Order" drama occurred when Capt. Samuel E. Pittman, assistant adjutant general of the Twelfth Corps, identified the signature of Col. R. H. Chilton (Lee's assistant adjutant general) on the order. With nearly 130,000 men involved in The Maryland Campaign, it was extraordinary that two paths crossed, with one man (Pittman) recognizing another man's (Chilton) signature. Pittman and Chilton knew each other from their antebellum association in Detroit. Pittman was a teller with the Michigan State Bank and Chilton was an army paymaster stationed in Detroit. Pittman recognized Chilton's handwriting and thus authenticated the orders.

194. Two days after the "Lost Orders" fell into McClellan's hands, the *Washington Star* reported the discovery on the second page of its September 15th issue. The article mislabeled the order as "Order No. 119." The next day, the *Baltimore Sun* published the same article verbatim.

195. Gen. McClellan wrote a note informing President Lincoln at noon on the 13th that he had received and authenticated the "Lost Orders." *(OR* 19 (2): 281)

196. Nearly 14½ hours apparently lapsed before McClellan's note to Lincoln regarding the discovery of Special Orders 191 was received. Curiously, under McClellan's date line was this message: "Received, 2:35 a.m., September 14." *(OR* 19 (2): 281)

197. One of McClellan's most zealous declarations of the war was written in the general's message to the President regarding his providential discovery of Special Orders 191: "I think Lee has made a gross mistake. . . . I have all the plans of the rebels and will catch them in their own trap. . . Will send you trophies." *(OR* 19 (2): 281)

198. McClellan is so buoyed by his fortunate, almost miraculous discovery of the "Lost Orders," his exuberance gushes in one decidedly non-military statement in his message to the president: "My respects to Mrs. Lincoln." *(OR* 19 (2): 281)

199. McClellan's confidence in military success reaches its optimum moment with the discovery of the "Lost Orders." "Here is the paper with which," he boasted to Brig. Gen. John Gibbon, "if I cannot whip Bobbie Lee, I will be willing to go home." (Gibbon, *Personal Recollections of the Civil War*, p. 73)

200. McClellan did not inform General-in-Chief Halleck of his discovery of the "Lost Orders" until 11 p.m. on the night of the 13th. *(OR* 19 (2): 281)

201. "Little Mac" assured General Halleck that—as a result of the fortunate discovery of Special Orders 191—he was absolutely confident "there is little probability of the enemy being in much force south of the Potomac." McClellan contended that both Washington and Baltimore were safe, for the moment. *(OR* 19 (2): 282)

202. One fact the "Lost Orders" did not reveal to McClellan was the number of men in Lee's army. The locations and assignments of divisions were outlined, but McClellan—in his message to Halleck on the late evening of the 13th—proclaimed he was facing "120,000 men or more." *(OR* 19 (2): 281)

203. The most accurate intelligence reports on numbers in the Confederate army in The Maryland Campaign occurred on two occasions. The first came on September 11, at 8:20 a.m., when Maj. Gen. John E. Wool in Baltimore wired Halleck that "15,000 rebel infantry, cavalry, and artillery passed through Boonsborough last night." (this was Jackson's column). This information was highly accurate, and was reported by Gen. White at Martinsburg to his commander, Gen. Wool. A second intelligence report, written to President Lincoln from Pennsylvania Governor Curtin on September 11 at 3:30 p.m., confirmed the 15,000 in Jackson's column. This source was "a gentlemen who saw Jackson and was in his camp on Monday." *(OR* 19 (2): 266-68)

204. One of the greatest mysteries of The Maryland Campaign—in fact, one of the most significant unsolved mysteries of the war is—who lost Special Order 191?

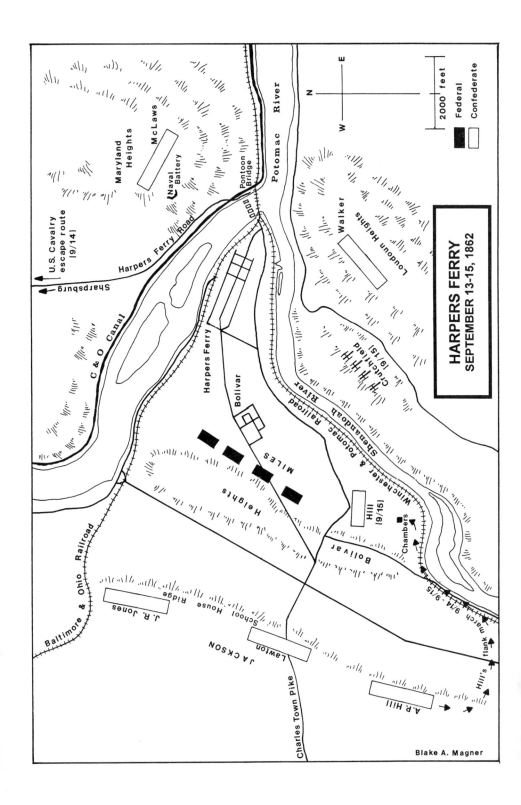

HARPERS FERRY
SEPTEMBER 13-15, 1862

Federal
Confederate

2000 feet

N E
W S

Potomac River

Maryland Heights

McLaws

Naval Battery

Pontoon Bridge

Harpers Ferry Road

U.S. Cavalry escape route (9/14)

Sharpsburg

C & O Canal

Walker

Loudoun Heights

Harpers Ferry

Bolivar

MILES

Crutchfield (9/15)

Shenandoah River

Winchester & Potomac Railroad

Hill (9/15)

Bolivar Heights

Chambers

march 9/14-9/15

Hill's flank

Baltimore & Ohio Railroad

J.R. Jones

School House Ridge

Lawton

JACKSON

A.P. Hill

Charles Town Pike

Blake A. Magner

THE SIEGE OF HARPERS FERRY

205. The largest surrender of US troops during the Civil War occurred at Harpers Ferry on September 15, 1862.

206. The battle of Antietam would not have happened without the preceding Confederate victory at Harpers Ferry.

207. The largest, insofar as numbers, engagement in the Civil War in present-day West Virginia—involving 38,000 combatants—was at Harpers Ferry from September 13 to 15, 1862.

208. Harpers Ferry was one of the few battles of the war where Confederate forces (24,000) outnumber their Union opponents (14,000).

209. Stonewall Jackson, the victor at Harpers Ferry, was a native of Clarksburg, (West) Virginia.

210. Harpers Ferry lay within Virginia at the time of the first Maryland Campaign. Harpers Ferry became part of West Virginia on June 20, 1863—eleven days before Gettysburg—when West Virginia was admitted as the 35th state.

211. Thomas Jonathan Jackson's *first* field command of the Civil War was at Harpers Ferry. Jackson commanded the Southern garrison there, as a colonel, from April 30 to May 23, 1861.

212. Jackson had not yet earned the "nom de guerre" "Stonewall" during his initial assignment at Harpers Ferry in the spring of 1861. That distinction occurred on Henry House Hill during the battle of First Manassas on July 21, 1861. During the first months of the war, upon the gentle plateaus of Bolivar Heights overlooking the Ferry from the west, Jackson organized, trained, and drilled the First Virginia Brigade—immortalized as the Stonewall Brigade due to its determined stand at First Manassas.

213. Company K, 2nd Virginia Infantry, Stonewall Brigade, was the only unit from Harpers Ferry to serve during the war. It was organized as a militia company after John Brown's 1859 raid. Its captain, Mexican War veteran George W. Chambers, was the town's mayor when the war began. The Stonewall Brigade, including Capt. Chambers' Company K, held the extreme Confederate left on School House Ridge during Jackson's 1862 siege of the Ferry.

214. No arsenal existed at the Ferry during Jackson's siege. The United States arsenal had been burned intentionally by federal troops on April 18, 1861, less than 24 hours after Virginia's secession. The first property destruction in Virginia at the outbreak of the Civil War was the burning of the Harpers Ferry arsenal.

215. No armory operated at the Ferry during the 1862 Confederate investment. During the first 60 days of the war, Jackson—under orders from Richmond—dismantled the armory's machinery and shipped it south to Richmond. Armory machinery from the Musket Factory along the Potomac River produced the CS Richmond Rifle during the war. Machinery from the Rifle Factory on the Shenandoah River was shipped to North Carolina where the CS Fayetteville Rifle was manufactured.

View of Harpers Ferry looking east from Magazine Hill. (*HFHA*)

216. The armory buildings were burned during the Confederate evacuation of the Ferry on June 14-15, 1861. The armory was never reestablished as a small arms factory.

217. The US Army re-roofed and re-utilized many of the armory buildings as a quartermaster and commissary depot beginning in late February 1862. Harpers Ferry, located on the main line of the Baltimore & Ohio Railroad, served as the primary staging area for the Shenandoah Valley operations of Maj. Gen. Nathaniel Prentiss Banks.

218. In support of Nathaniel Banks's campaign in the Valley, McClellan established the Railroad Brigade on March 29, 1862, appointing Col. Dixon Stansbury Miles as its commander. Miles placed his headquarters at Harpers Ferry.

219. Dixon Miles was a native of Baltimore County, Maryland, and was born in 1804. He graduated from West Point in 1824, ranking 27th in a class of 29. He was assigned to the infantry, and his regular army career spanned the next 38 years.

220. Miles distinguished himself during the Mexican War, rising from captain to brevet lieutenant colonel in the first four months of the war. His most famous action occurred at Monterey with the capture of the "fortress known as Bishop's Palace" in September 1846.

221. Miles ascended to full colonel of the 2nd US Infantry on January 19, 1859. Only ten infantry regiments were in service prior to the Civil War, making Miles one of only ten infantry regimental commanders.

222. Miles outranked (in the regular army) Robert E. Lee, John Sedgwick, George Thomas, William Emory, William Hardee, and others who later gained distinction as Civil War generals.
223. Nelson A. Miles, George Custer's counterpart at the battle of Little Big Horn in 1876, was no relation to Dixon S. Miles.
224. During the battle of First Manassas, Col. Miles commanded the Union reserve division. As the federals retreated, he was accused of drunkenness by an old army foe, Col. Israel B. Richardson. A court of inquiry determined "evidence cannot be found sufficient to convict Colonel Miles," but the highly public affair damaged Miles's reputation and ruined opportunities for his promotion to general. (Frye, "Stonewall Attacks: The Siege of Harpers Ferry," *Blue & Gray Magazine*, 5, No. 1 (1987), p. 13)
225. The Railroad Brigade that Miles commanded was never a "brigade." It actually equated to a division or a corps, numbering between 6,000 and 15,000 men, or six to ten times the usual strength of a brigade. Although headquartered at Harpers Ferry, Miles's men patrolled 380 miles of railroad, stretching from Washington to Baltimore to the South Branch of the Potomac. Miles understood his mission was to protect the railroad and its bridges from guerrillas. He emphasized his force did not exist "with the intention of fighting an army." (Frye, "Stonewall Attacks," p. 12)
226. The B&O Railroad crossed the Potomac River at Harpers Ferry. The original 900-foot covered wooden bridge was torched by the Confederates on June 14, 1861, severing the railroad's connection between Maryland and Virginia (today's West Virginia) for nearly nine months. A makeshift iron bridge, reaching precariously from stone pier to stone pier, was in operation at the time of Miles's arrival.
227. Three heights surround Harpers Ferry forming a mountain triangle around the town. Maryland Heights (1,463 feet) towers north of the Potomac. Loudoun Heights (1,180 feet) casts its shadow from the south bank of the Shenandoah. Bolivar Heights (650 feet) lies about two miles west of the town.
228. Camp Hill (580 feet), a round knoll separating Lower Town Harpers Ferry and Bolivar Heights, received its name when the 7th and 8th US Infantry regiments camped here in 1798-99. The Potomac guards its northern flank and its southern edge overlooks the Shenandoah.
229. Maryland Heights, the highest of the mountains surrounding the Ferry, was the key to the position. Jackson recognized this in 1861, ordering his troops to occupy and fortify the heights.
230. The first Confederate occupation of Maryland during the Civil War occurred in May 1861, when Jackson ordered the defense of Maryland Heights. Southerners built a wooden stockade on the crest of Maryland Heights, but abandoned this post with their departure from the Ferry the next month. (*OR* 2 (1): 809, 814)
231. Jackson's tenure as garrison, and then brigade commander at the Ferry in the spring of 1861, permitted him to study and memorize the terrain features of the position. Stonewall's familiarity with this terrain—a primary reason Gen. Lee selected him for the

mission against Harpers Ferry—proved invaluable with deployments and tactical decisions during his siege.

232. Stonewall threatened an attack on Harpers Ferry during his famous Valley Campaign. After defeating Banks at First Winchester on May 25, 1862, and forcing a precipitous federal retreat to Maryland, Jackson desired to sweep the Valley of all Union presence. The only Yankees still remaining garrisoned Harpers Ferry. (*OR* 12 (1): 707)

233. Union authorities sent 300 sailors from the Washington Naval Yard to help defend the Ferry during Stonewall's May 1862 demonstration. The sailors erected the "Naval Battery" on May 27 at a point towering 400 feet above the Potomac on the southwest slope of Maryland Heights. (*OR* 12 (1): 627, 636, 640)

234. The Naval Battery, commanded by Lts. Ulric Dahlgren and C. S. Daniels during Jackson's May 1862 advance, fired a 9-inch Dahlgren naval cannon at Confederate infantry on Loudoun Heights and on School House Ridge. Its effectiveness helped thwart the Stonewall Brigade's advance against Bolivar Heights on May 31. Ulric Dahlgren was the son of United States Navy Admiral John Dahlgren, the inventor of the Dahlgren cannon.

235. The Naval Battery was the only *permanent* battery on Maryland Heights prior to Jackson's September siege. It was also known as "Battery Stanton," in honor of Secretary of War Edwin M. Stanton, who dispatched the sailors and naval cannon to Harpers Ferry to aid with the defense against Jackson.

236. Brig. Gen. Rufus B. Saxton rushed from Washington to defend the Ferry during Jackson's May 1862 approach. Dixon Miles served as his aide-de-camp, watching and learning from Saxton's decisions.

237. Saxton's defensive strategy against Stonewall's spring 1862 campaign deployed the bulk of his infantry on Bolivar Heights, with supporting artillery on Camp Hill and from the Naval Battery. Saxton placed no infantry on Loudoun Heights, reasoning Confederate small arms could cause no harm from that distance. The crest of Maryland Heights remained undefended since it was not threatened.

238. Gen. Saxton's defense earned him a commendation from the War Department. "By your gallantry and skill great service was rendered to the country," applauded Secretary of War Edwin M. Stanton. Saxton's success influenced Miles to emulate his defense—with disastrous consequences—when Jackson returned in September 1862. (*OR* 12 (1): 641-642)

239. Jackson retired from Harpers Ferry on May 31, *not* because of Saxton's defense, but to avoid entrapment by two federal armies converging against Stonewall's rear at Strasburg, 50 miles to the south.

240. The 300 sailors manning the Naval Battery returned to Washington on June 8 after the Confederate threat at Harpers Ferry subsided. The heavy guns in the Naval Battery were not removed with the departure of the sailors, but instead remained as part of the Harpers Ferry defenses. The cannon left behind include two 9-inch Dahlgrens and one 50-pounder gun.

Camp Hill looking west and showing the Barbour House in late 1862 (*HFHA*)

241. Miles had ample time to prepare permanent fortifications at the Ferry. His commander, Maj. Gen. John G. Wool, a Mexican War hero, instructed Miles in June 1862, to entrench Camp Hill. In late August, Wool inspected the Ferry and ordered Miles to entrench Bolivar Heights, place abatis on Camp Hill, and construct a blockhouse on Maryland Heights to protect the Naval Battery. With the exception of Camp Hill, Miles failed to follow through with these orders. (*OR* 12 (1): 788)

242. The infantry of Col. Miles was the first to encounter the Confederate invasion force. Col. Henry B. Banning's 87th Ohio, guarding the Potomac near Point of Rocks, 13 miles downstream from Harpers Ferry, reported Rebels crossing the river at Noland's Ferry on September 2. (*OR* 19 (1): 532)

243. Gen. Wool, in Baltimore, orders Miles via telegraph on September 5 to "(b)e energetic and active, and defend all places to the last extremity. There must be no abandoning of post, and shoot the first man that thinks of it." Miles received another telegraph from Wool on September 5 recommending a defensive strategy: "The position on the heights ought to enable you to punish the enemy passing up the road in the direction of Harpers Ferry." Wool did not define which heights, which road, or which direction. (*OR* 19 (1): 790)

244. General-in-Chief Henry W. Halleck suggested to Gen. Wool on September 5 "the propriety of withdrawing all our forces in that vicinity to Maryland Heights." No evidence indicates Miles received this specific recommendation. (*OR* 19 (1): 757)

245. Confederates severed all telegraph lines between Harpers Ferry and Baltimore on September 7. Miles's final message to Wool, dated 2:30 a.m. on the 7th, declared: "I am ready for them." (*OR* 19 (1): 791)

246. Miles deployed his Railroad Brigade infantry as follows: 2,000 on Maryland Heights; 1,000 on Camp Hill; 7,000 on Bolivar Heights; zero on Loudoun Heights. Fourteen pieces of artillery, including four twenty-pounder Parrott rifles, stared through embrasures on Camp Hill toward Bolivar Heights. (*OR* 19 (1): 533-536)

247. The defensive alignment of Miles mirrored Rufus Saxton's May 1862 defense— except for the presence on Maryland Heights. Miles anticipated minimal harm from Confederate small arms from Loudoun Heights. He also expected the primary attack force to advance down the Shenandoah Valley toward Bolivar Heights.

248. Raw recruits comprised one-third of Miles's command. Four New York infantry regiments—the 111th, 115th, 125th, 126th—arrived at Harpers Ferry less than two weeks after mustering into federal service. Miles complained to Wool that his garrison had become nothing more than "a fortified camp of instruction." (Frye, "Stonewall Attacks: The Siege of Harpers Ferry," *Blue & Gray Magazine*, 5, No. 1 (1987), p. 14)

249. The senior regiment at Harpers Ferry was the 39th New York Infantry, mustered into service on May 28, 1861. The newest regiment in Miles's command was the 125th New York Infantry, mustered in on August 29, 1862.

250. Two of Miles's regiments are 3-months militia regiments—the 12th New York State Militia and the 87th Ohio Infantry. The time of service had expired for the 12th New York State Militia, but they were unable to leave Harpers Ferry because of the Confederate invasion of Maryland.

251. McClellan formally requested that Miles's force be withdrawn from the Ferry on September 11. "He can do nothing where he is, and could be of great service if ordered to join me." General-in-Chief Halleck refused McClellan's request for the Harpers Ferry garrison: "There is no way for Colonel Miles to join you at present. His only chance is to defend his works until you can open communication with him." (*OR* 19 (1): 43-44)

252. Facing a Confederate invasion to his east, Brig. Gen. Julius White withdrew his brigade of approximately 3,800 from Winchester north to Harpers Ferry, arriving at the Ferry on September 4. Gen. White's men were veteran troops compared to Col. Miles's men, with most having experienced some action against Jackson in the Valley Campaign.

253. Gen. Wool ordered White to Martinsburg on September 4. When the Confederates approached Martinsburg on September 11, White abandoned his position and retreated to Harpers Ferry, arriving there on the 12th. (*OR* 19 (1): 524)

254. Brig. Gen. Julius White *waived his command* to Col. Miles. Recognizing the 42-year military experience of Miles, White acknowledged that Miles's familiarity with the terrain and troop deployments made him better suited to command with "the enemy in heavy force in the immediate vicinity." (*OR* 19 (1): 525)

255. White was a political general. When Lincoln was inaugurated, he was appointed collector of customs in Chicago, but later resigned this post to organize and command the

37th Illinois Infantry. He led a brigade at the battle of Pea Ridge, Arkansas, on March 6-8, 1862.

256. The first battle in the Confederate siege of Harpers Ferry occurred on Maryland Heights on September 12-13.

257. Special Orders 191 gave Maj. Gen. Lafayette McLaws the responsibility of securing Maryland Heights and blocking any federal escape routes north of Harpers Ferry. (*OR* 19 (2): 603)

258. No record indicates that Col. Miles at Harpers Ferry ever learned of McClellan's fortunate discovery of Special Orders 191. Communications between McClellan's army and Miles were severed by the interposing Confederates.

259. Gen. McLaws was a native of Georgia and a West Point graduate, graduating with James Longstreet in the class of 1842. McLaws was a nephew by marriage of President Zachary Taylor.

260. McLaws moved against Harpers Ferry with his own division and the division of Maj. Gen. Richard H. Anderson—totaling about 8,000 men. The route from Frederick to Harpers Ferry for McLaws' column—a march of approximately 20 miles—was west along the National Road to Middletown, south to Burkittsville, and then west into Pleasant Valley.

261. The first Confederates to arrive in the vicinity of Harpers Ferry belonged to McLaws, who occupied Pleasant Valley on September 11. (*OR* 19 (1): 852)

262. McLaws did not cross South Mountain at Crampton's Gap, but instead one mile south at Brownsville Pass. The Brownsville Pass route from Burkittsville into Pleasant Valley was a more direct route toward Harpers Ferry.

263. The village of Brownsville is located at the mid-point of Pleasant Valley. It was not named after John Brown of Harpers Ferry abolitionist fame, but John Brown who laid out the town in 1824. A welcoming party for Gen. McLaws and staff was held at the home of Dr. Boteler, about three miles south of Brownsville, with the house crowded with over 100 guests. (Trimpi, King Diary, p. 32)

264. Pleasant Valley lies between South Mountain and Elk Ridge. It is about one mile wide at its northern end.

265. Elk Ridge is the northern-most extension of the Blue Ridge, and is the only segment of the Blue Ridge in Maryland. The ridge begins with a 300-foot cliff overlooking the north bank of the Potomac River at Harpers Ferry and extends eight miles north, where it gradually terminates near Rohrersville.

266. The only gap in Elk Ridge is Solomon's Gap, a saddle-shaped depression at the mid-point of the mountain, located four miles north of Harpers Ferry.

267. The southern terminus of Elk Ridge is designated as Maryland Heights.

268. Gen. McLaws recognized Maryland Heights as the highest of the three mountains surrounding Harpers Ferry and thus the key to the position: "So long as Maryland Heights was occupied by the enemy," McLaws wrote in his official report, "Harpers Ferry could never be occupied by us." (*OR* 19 (1): 852)

269. Defending the crest of Maryland Heights were approximately 2,000 men from Miles's Harpers Ferry command.

270. Col. Thomas H. Ford commanded the brigade of federal troops defending Maryland Heights. He was a native Virginian, born in 1814 in the Shenandoah Valley's Rockingham County. He was elected lieutenant governor of Ohio—as a Republican. He served two years under Governor Salmon P. Chase, who later became secretary of the treasury in the Lincoln cabinet.

271. No fortifications existed on the crest of Maryland Heights when Ford took command of the mountain on September 5. (*OR* 19 (1): 542)

272. Col. Ford's request to place artillery at Solomon's Gap and at the "Lookout" on the crest of Maryland Heights was rejected by Col. Miles. Miles did bolster artillery on Maryland Heights, ordering two 12-pounders to the Naval Battery on September 10 and two more 12-pounders on the 11th. No artillery was positioned on the crest of Maryland Heights—either Union or Confederate—during the battle of September 12-13. (*OR* 19 (1): 542, 697)

273. Col. Miles visited Maryland Heights four times between September 7 and 11 to meet with Ford and discuss preparations against attack. (*OR* 19 (1): 535-536)

274. The two 9-inch Dahlgren cannon at the Naval Battery were turned 180 degrees, away from Harpers Ferry to face north toward the crest of Maryland Heights. One hundred yards of woods north of the battery was cut down to permit support fire in the direction of the crest—800 feet higher than the battery. (*OR* 19 (1): 542-543)

275. Capt. Eugene McGrath, Company F, 5th New York Artillery, had commanded the Naval Battery since mid-June 1862. He had perfected his aim south toward Loudoun Heights and west toward Bolivar Heights. Prior to the September investment, McGrath never had any reason to turn his guns north toward Maryland Heights.

276. A 9-inch Dahlgren shell fired from the Naval Battery in the summer of 1862 destroyed an abandoned school house on School House Ridge two miles distant. During the battle for Maryland Heights, many of the 9-inch Dahlgren shells missed their Confederate targets, instead flying harmlessly over the crest and landing on the east side of the mountain in Pleasant Valley. (*OR* 19 (1): 854)

277. The first federal breastworks on the crest of Maryland Heights were constructed by Capt. John Whittier of the 1st Maryland Potomac Home Brigade on September 11—the same day the Confederates arrived in Pleasant Valley.

278. Gen. McLaws ordered the brigades of Joseph Kershaw and William Barksdale to the crest of the Elk Ridge to seize Maryland Heights. Both Kershaw and Barksdale were lawyers during the antebellum period. Kershaw's South Carolina brigade brought 1,041 effectives into the fight for Maryland Heights. The Mississippi brigade of Barksdale numbered 960 men. (*OR* 19 (1): 853, 860-861)

279. The highest elevation at which Kershaw's South Carolinians and Barksdale's Mississippians fought during the war was atop Elk Ridge and Maryland Heights (1,400 feet above sea level).

280. Joseph Kershaw was a native of South Carolina who was twice elected to the Palmetto State legislature and was also elected to the state's 1860 secession convention.

281. William Barksdale was a former US congressman from Mississippi. First elected in 1852 he resigned his seat following Mississippi's secession.

282. The first shots of the siege of Harpers Ferry occurred on September 12 when Kershaw and Barksdale ascended Elk Ridge at Solomon's Gap and encounter Union picket fire from the top of the mountain. (*OR* 19 (1): 862)

283. The road Kershaw and Barksdale used to ascend Solomon's Gap still remains, presently passing through the village of Yarrowsburg. Yarrowsburg did not exist at the time of the war.

284. Elk Ridge was originally owned by the Antietam Iron Works and was used as a source of wood for charcoal. Miles of charcoal roads crisscrossed the mountain and the Confederates used these abandoned roads to help gain access to Maryland Heights.

285. The narrow topography of Elk Ridge—at some points the crest is only 100 feet across, with steep bluffs bordering the mountain top—was unsuitable for maneuver in brigade formation. Confederate success on Maryland Heights was delayed one full day by the rugged, boulder-ridden terrain and tangled undergrowth of Elk Ridge "The natural obstacles were so great," reported a frustrated Kershaw, "that we only reached a position about a mile from the point of the mountain at 6:00 p.m. on the 12th" (*OR* 19 (1): 863)

286. The first federal obstacle Kershaw encountered was abatis extending across the mountain. Sharp skirmishing ensued beginning at 3:00 p.m. and continued until dusk on the 12th, facing the abatis. Kershaw then formed his brigade into two lines, facing south, extending across the crest and flanked on either side by "a ledge of precipitous rocks." Darkness ended the advance, and the Confederates "rested on their arms." (*OR* 19 (1): 863)

287. No water existed on the crest of Maryland Heights. The Confederates were furnished water during the night—but it had to be hauled 2½ miles. (Trumpi, King Diary, p. 32)

288. Only 100 yards separated Union defenders and Confederate attackers atop Elk Ridge on the night of September 12. The two armies were "within speaking distance of each other." (*OR* 19 (1): 543)

289. The battle for Maryland Heights would last nine hours, beginning at 6:30 a.m. on the 13th and concluding at 3:30 p.m.

290. The largest regiment in the Union Army at Harpers Ferry—the 126th New York Infantry, boasting nearly 1,100 men—defended the center of the federal breastworks on Maryland Heights. Eight of the regiment's ten companies were on the crest of the mountain.

291. The 126th New York Infantry had been in the army for 22 days, mustered into service on August 22, 1862.

292. At 100 yards, Kershaw's South Carolinians faced "a most obstinate resistance" and "a fierce fire," from the federals defending the breastworks. With his advance stalled, Kershaw ordered Barksdale's brigade to flank the enemy position. (*OR* 19 (1): 863)

293. The Confederate brigade that suffered the heaviest casualties in Jackson's siege of Harpers Ferry was Kershaw's South Carolina brigade—33 killed and 154 wounded—while under severe fire for four hours during the battle on Maryland Heights. (*OR* 19 (1): 861)

294. One of the most difficult flanking movements of the war—made treacherous by the steep mountain terrain—occurred when Barksdale's men scaled down the precipitous eastern ledge of Elk Ridge and then clawed their way back toward the top into a position to the enemy's right rear. (*OR* 19 (1): 863)

295. Maryland Heights became jeopardized for the federals when the center of the Union line collapsed about 10:30 a.m. Disaster struck when Col. Eliakim Sherrill, commander of the 126th New York, was shot in the jaw. The loss of their commander panicked some in the raw-recruit regiment, and the Union defense at the breastworks crumbled. (*OR* 19 (1): 863)

296. Col. Sherrill was the highest-ranking Union officer wounded during the siege of Harpers Ferry. Sherrill survived his injury only to be killed on July 3, 1863, at the battle of Gettysburg.

297. The precise reason the federals abandoned the breastworks is muddled. Three explanations were given by participants: 1) the 126th New York panicked, compromising the position; 2) mysterious orders arrived demanding the breastworks be abandoned and a new position defended; and 3) Confederate flankers from Barksdale's brigade fired a volley into the Union right and caused a rout. (Frye, "Stonewall Attacks," p. 20)

298. The federals did not abandon Maryland Heights after they lost the breastworks. The remaining regiments on the crest—including companies of the 32nd Ohio, 39th New York, and 1st Maryland Potomac Home Brigade—retired south some 400 yards to a stronger new position. Much of the 126th New York rallied around this position as well.

299. Col. Miles visited Col. Ford during the battle of the 13th about 11:00 a.m., leaving his command post on Bolivar Heights—nearly 2¼ miles distant—in order to encourage Ford and his forces to hold the mountain. Miles and Ford, with "great spirit and energy," attempted to rally troops (primarily remnants of the 126th New York), at Ford's headquarters. After an hour and a half, this resulted in a partial restoration of order and the return of a portion of the troops to the field. (*OR* 19 (1): 537, 543)

300. Miles reinforced Ford early on the morning of the 13th with the 3rd Maryland Potomac Home Brigade and seven companies of the 115th New York Infantry—approximately 1,200 men. (*OR* 19 (1): 537, 543-544)

301. Col. Ford's headquarters was on the southwest slope of Maryland Heights at the Buckles' house. The house was near the Naval Battery, less than halfway up the mountain.

302. Ford never witnessed the battle on the crest of Maryland Heights. He remained near his headquarters throughout the 13th, attempting to direct the fight at an elevation 800 feet below the battlefield. Ford was suffering from a fistula during the battle, and he was in such pain that he could not ride a horse. His mobility was very limited and he remained confined in the vicinity of his headquarters. (A fistula is a painful physical ailment that results from an abnormal duct or passage leading to the body surface from an abscess, cavity, or hollow organ within the body.)

303. The most significant blunder in the battle for Maryland Heights occurred when Col. Ford ordered his forces to retire from the crest of the mountain. The order arrived between 3:00 and 3:30 p.m. It stated: "You are hereby ordered to fall back to Harpers Ferry in good order. *Be careful to do so in good order.*" (*OR* 19 (1): 619)

304. No Confederate attack was underway when the orders from Ford arrived to abandon the crest. The Union defenders of Maryland Heights were not forced off the mountain by the enemy; instead they abandoned it to the Confederates through the preemptory orders of Col. Ford.

305. Ford later claimed Col. Miles ordered the retreat from Maryland Heights. In his official report, filed in late September, Ford wrote: "In obedience to the positive orders of Colonel Miles, I ordered the guns to be spiked and dismounted and the forces withdrawn to the opposite side of the river, all of which was done in good order." Col. Miles's aide-de-camp, Lt. Henry M. Binney, refuted Ford's claim that Miles gave orders permitting the withdrawal from Maryland Heights. In his official report, dated September 18, 1862, Binney summarized the action on the 13th: "Colonel Ford fearful he cannot hold the heights, Colonel Miles tells him; 'You can and you must.'" (*OR* 19 (1): 544, 536)

306. The most controversial order issued during the siege of Harpers Ferry was from Col. Miles to Col. Ford on September 13, shortly after Miles returns to Bolivar Heights following his 11:00 a.m. conference with Ford. "Since I returned to this side, on close inspection I find your position more defensible than it appears when at your station. Covered as it is at all points by the cannon of Camp Hill, you will hold on, and can hold on, until the cows' tails drop off." (*OR* 19 (1): 537)

307. The "cows' tails" order was later proven fraudulent, written by Lt. Binney, after the fact, in an effort to protect Col. Miles's reputation.

308. A woman on Maryland Heights at the time of the battle testified Col. Miles did issue Ford instructions to leave the mountain. Mrs. Elizabeth Brown, wife of an officer in the 1st Maryland Potomac Home Brigade, was on the second floor of Ford's headquarters, listening down a stovepipe hole to a conversation between Miles and Ford about noon on the 13th. "The reason I listened was that I was anxious to hear what was going on. . . . I heard Colonel Miles tell you that your men would have to fall back to the Ferry; they could not hold the heights; the thing was impossible; the rebel force was too strong." (*OR* 19 (1): 719)

309. Col. Miles witnessed the withdrawal from Maryland Heights from his command post on Bolivar Heights. "God Almighty!" screamed the astonished colonel, standing within 30 feet of Chaplain Sylvester Clemans of the 115th New York Infantry. "What does that mean? They are coming down! Hell and damnation!" (*OR* 19 (1): 537, 576)

310. The seven cannon at the Naval Battery were spiked by Capt. McGrath during the evacuation of Maryland Heights in order to prevent their use by the Confederates.

"Spiking" a cannon involves the insertion of a metal rod into the vent hole, then breaking the rod so that it cannot be removed. By jamming the vent hole, the cannon becomes useless since the friction primer cannot be inserted to spark a discharge of the powder.

311. McLaws did not communicate with Gen. Lee from the time he left Frederick on the 10th until late on the 13th. Lee did not know McLaws' progress, and this dearth of communication brought a mild reprimand from Gen. Lee on the 13th: "You are also desired to communicate as frequently as you can with headquarters." *(OR* 19 (1): 606)

312. The first Confederate force to seize a mountain overlooking Harpers Ferry was John G. Walker's division. Walker faced no opposition as his men ascended Loudoun Heights on the 13th—the same day McLaws was battling for position upon Maryland Heights. Walker's division of 2,500 men—by occupying Loudoun Heights and the south bank of the Shenandoah River—sealed off any Union escape routes to the south. *(OR* 19 (1): 913)

313. Stonewall Jackson's column approached Harpers Ferry from the west on the morning of the 13th, with the advance arriving on School House Ridge at 11:00 a.m. *(OR* 19 (1): 953)

314. The first Confederate division to mount School House Ridge was A. P. Hill's "Light Division."

315. Jackson released A. P. Hill from arrest on September 11 while his column was on the march to Harpers Ferry.

316. The largest Confederate column that participated in the investment of Harpers Ferry was Stonewall Jackson's command. It was comprised of three divisions totaling approximately 14,000 men and included A. P. Hill's division; Richard Ewell's division (under the command of A. R. Lawton); and Jackson's division, commanded by John R. Jones.

317. Jackson's force was the last to arrive at Harpers Ferry in execution of Special Orders 191. The Confederate encirclement of Harpers Ferry was completed when Jackson's column arrived near noon on the 13th, cutting off the federal escape routes to the west.

318. Stonewall Jackson's initial challenge at Harpers Ferry was the coordination of, and communications between, his troops. Two rivers and three mountains separated his command from McLaws and Walker, with a federal army positioned in between.

319. Jackson's first order of business when he arrived near Harpers Ferry was to open communications with Walker on Loudoun Heights and McLaws on Maryland Heights. His first attempt was by signal flags, but when that failed, he dispatched couriers. Jackson was frustrated by his difficulty in communications: "Before the necessary orders were thus transmitted, the day [the 13th] was far advanced." *(OR* 19 (1): 953)

320. Gen. Jackson established his signal station on the first hill south of Halltown, about four miles west of Harpers Ferry.

321. Col. Miles sent the bulk of his infantry and artillery onto Bolivar Heights following the loss of Maryland Heights. The Union defensive position on Bolivar Heights was superior to Jackson's position on School House Ridge as Bolivar Heights is more than

Bolivar Heights looking west from Camp Hill in late 1862 (*HFHA*)

200 feet higher in elevation. "The position before me is a strong one," Jackson noted in a message to McLaws and Walker on the 14th. (*OR* 19 (2): 607)

322. A valley, nearly 1,000 yards wide, separates School House Ridge from Bolivar Heights. The valley was open, with almost no forest, presenting clear lines of sight for artillery and infantry fire between the opposing lines.

323. Confederate infantry on Maryland Heights and Loudoun Heights were unable to cause much harm to the Union positions on Bolivar Heights and Camp Hill because the distances for small arms fire surpass accurate rifle range. The accurate range for a rifle musket is 400 to 500 yards.

324. Col. Miles attempted to inform US authorities of his predicament on the night of September 13. He ordered Capt. Charles H. Russell, 1st Maryland Cavalry, to pass through the enemy lines and: "try to reach somebody that had ever heard of the United States Army, or any general of the United States Army, or anybody that knew anything about the United States Army, and report the condition of Harpers Ferry." Miles told Captain Russell to inform General McClellan that "he thought he could hold out for forty-eight hours." (*OR* 19 (1): 720)

325. Russell left Harpers Ferry on the night of the 13th with nine men in search of McClellan. Capt. Russell's messenger party moved north from Harpers Ferry along the west bank of the Potomac to the mouth of the Antietam Creek; then across the river; then via back roads to South Mountain; then across the mountain through the woods to Middletown. (*OR* 19 (1): 721)

326. Russell's detachment of cavalry eluded Confederates on three occasions: between Bolivar Heights and School House Ridge along the Potomac; crossing the river at the mouth of the Antietam; and at South Mountain.

327. Capt. Russell reached Gen. McClellan at 9:00 a.m. on Sunday the 14th. He gave McClellan the message that Miles could hold on for 48 hours. McClellan then dispatched Russell to Gen. William B. Franklin, who was leading the rescue effort for Harpers Ferry with the Sixth Corps. Russell arrived at Franklin's headquarters about 3:00 p.m., as Franklin was fighting the battle of Crampton's Gap.

328. Confederate efforts during the night and early morning of September 13-14 were focused on dragging artillery up to the crests of Maryland and Loudoun Heights. An abandoned charcoal road ascending the east side of Maryland Heights, constructed by the Antietam Iron Works, was utilized by Gen. McLaws as the route for his artillery. McLaws stated in his official report, dated October 18, 1862, that his men cut a road; but, in fact, they cleared an existing road. (*OR* 19 (1): 854)

329. One of the most difficult, if not *most* difficult, artillery assignments of the war in the Eastern Theater was the effort by Confederate gunners to conquer vertical ascents of 1,000 feet on Maryland Heights and 700 feet on Loudoun Heights.

330. Gen. Walker was the first to place his guns in position on Loudoun Heights. By 1:00 p.m. on the 14th, he had three 10-pounder Parrotts and two other rifled pieces in position on the crest overlooking the southern end of Bolivar Heights and Camp Hill. Four cannon had been placed atop Maryland Heights by 2:00 p.m. on the 14th. These included three 10-pounder Parrotts and a 3-inch ordnance rifle. Their effective range would reach the federal positions at the north end of Bolivar Heights. (*OR* 19 (1): 913, 854)

331. No cannon were placed on the vertical cliffs of Maryland Heights overlooking the lower town of Harpers Ferry.

332. McLaws and cavalry commander Jeb Stuart ascended Maryland Heights to direct artillery fire and to watch the bombardment of the hapless Union garrison below. (*OR* 19 (1): 819)

333. Sealing the ring of artillery fire were the Confederate batteries Jackson aligned on School House Ridge, including the guns of Pogue, Brockenbrough, Carpenter, and Courtney.

334. Stonewall Jackson, a former professor of artillery at the Virginia Military Institute, had his cannon in position surrounding Harpers Ferry "to drive the enemy" into extinction. Gen. Jackson desired all batteries to coordinate their fire to effect the greatest damage upon the enemy. He signaled, via flag, a 157-word message to McLaws and Walker: "I do not desire any of the batteries to open until all are ready on both sides of the river," Jackson concluded. "I will let you know when to open all the batteries." (*OR* 19 (1): 958)

335. Jackson instructed both Walker and McLaws to concentrate their fire upon the enemy artillery on Bolivar Heights and near "Barbour's House." "Barbour's House" was a two-story brick house in the center of Camp Hill. Jackson identified it by its last occupant, Alfred M. Barbour, the last superintendent of the Harpers Ferry armory.

336. Jackson informed McLaws and Walker at 7:20 a.m. on the 14th that he intended to "send in a flag of truce, for the purpose of getting out the non-combatants," should Miles refuse to surrender. (*OR* 19 (2): 607)

337. Stonewall Jackson threatened ruthless measures if the Union commander refused to surrender. "Should we have to attack, let the work be done thoroughly," Jackson instructed McLaws and Walker on the morning of the 14th. "[F]ire on the houses when necessary. The citizens can keep out of harm's way from your artillery. Demolish the place if it is occupied by the enemy, and does not surrender." (*OR* 19 (2): 607)

338. The first Confederate cannon to open an artillery barrage at Harpers Ferry were Walker's gunners on Loudoun Heights, who commenced firing between 1:00 and 2:00 p.m. on the 14th. (*OR* 19 (1): 913)

339. Gen. Walker claimed his artillery from Loudoun Heights silenced, in just two hours, an eight-gun federal battery on Camp Hill near the Barbour house. Gen. White, in his official report, admitted the federals had one 20-pounder Parrott and three other guns disabled on Camp Hill, in addition to the blowing up of two caissons. (*OR* 19 (1): 913, 527)

340. The Confederate artillery barrage on September 14 only caused a few casualties for the Union garrison as most of the federals sought shelter in long and narrow ravines cutting diagonally across Bolivar Heights.

341. Exploding shells from the Confederate guns made it impossible for Union regiments to remain in formation. "[W]e were obliged to change our line very frequently," recalled Lt. James H. Clark of the 115th New York, "to save the men from slaughter." Demoralization of the Union garrison, especially the new recruits, was the primary affect of the Confederate artillery barrage. "I tell you it is dreadful to be a mark for artillery," declared Capt. Samuel Chapman Armstrong of the 125th New York. "[B]ad enough for any but especially for raw troops; it demoralizes them . . ." (Frye, "Stonewall Attacks," p. 26)

342. The Union Chief of Artillery at Harpers Ferry, Maj. H. B. McIlvaine, reported only 36 rounds of ammunition left "for the most effective guns" by the evening of the 14th, and "it was equally divided." (*OR* 19 (1): 548)

343. Federal troops encountered no Confederate opposition when four companies of infantry—two from the 39th New York and two from the 65th Illinois—returned to Maryland Heights about noon on Sunday the 14th to retrieve ammunition and the four 12-pounders abandoned at the Naval Battery the previous day. The Union detachment returned with no casualties. (*OR* 19 (1): 596-597, 527)

344. Fifty tailors in the 39th New York Infantry worked all day Saturday the 13th making bags for ammunition, reducing large powder bags into smaller ones that could be inserted and fired from 20-pounder Parrotts. (*OR* 19 (1): 597)

345. The US cavalry force at Harpers Ferry—numbering between 1,300-1,400 horsemen—escaped from Stonewall Jackson's noose on the night of September 14.

346. Col. Benjamin F. "Grimes" Davis, commander of the 8th New York Cavalry, suggested the cavalry escape to Col. Miles about 7:00 p.m. on Sunday the 14th. Davis indicated that the cavalry "was of no use there, and if obliged to surrender . . . would be as great a prize as the enemy could get." (*OR* 19 (1): 583-584)

347. Davis graduated from West Point in 1854 along with Jeb Stuart, John Pegram, and Custis Lee. Col. Davis was a Mississippian—one of only two officers from the deep South who remained with the US Regular Army at the outbreak of the war.

348. The 8th New York Cavalry's tenure at Harpers Ferry began the second week of June 1862, without horses, and their manning of the Naval Battery on the side of Maryland Heights. "I regret to report this regiment is in a disorganized and mutinous condition and cannot be relied upon," wrote Col. Miles on June 8, "being dissatisfied at not being mounted and being armed as infantry." (*OR* 19 (1): 665)

349. Col. Davis and Col. Miles were the only two former Regular Army officers in the Union garrison at Harpers Ferry during the siege.

350. Col. Miles granted Davis and the cavalry permission to leave Harpers Ferry in Special Order No. 120, dated September 14. The order specified the force would leave at 8:00 p.m. "without baggage wagons, ambulances, or led horses" and "without noise or loud command." (Heysinger, "The Cavalry Column From Harpers Ferry in the Antietam Campaign," *The Morningside Notes*, p. 15)

351. Miles agreed to the cavalry breakout but, "he did not wish the infantry to be aware of it until they were gone." According to Miles's aide-de-camp Lt. Henry Binney, Miles was "afraid if the infantry became aware of it, it would cause a stampede among them." (*OR* 19 (1): 584)

352. A debate ensued between Miles and Davis over what route showed the best opportunity for the breakout of the cavalry. Davis suggested following the [West] Virginia shore to Shepherdstown and then crossing the Potomac. Miles recommended following the Maryland roads from Harpers Ferry to Sharpsburg. Another suggestion was to cross the Shenandoah River and head south into Loudoun County and toward Washington. (*OR* 19 (1): 584)

353. The route Miles selected for the cavalry breakout was the Harpers Ferry to Sharpsburg road that begins on the north bank of the Potomac.

354. Special Order 120 specified the order of march for the cavalry breakout. In the lead, as designated by Col. Miles, was the 1st Maryland Potomac Home Brigade Cavalry of Col. Henry Cole—a regiment comprised of many local men. Following Cole's Marylanders were the 12th Illinois, 8th New York, 7th Squadron Rhode Island, and 1st Maryland. The Loudoun Rangers also joined the march, although not specifically designated in Special Order 120. (Heysinger, "The Cavalry Column From Harpers Ferry in the Antietam Campaign," p. 16)

355. Col. Arno Voss, 12th Illinois Cavalry—not Grimes Davis, who suggested the action—commanded the cavalry breakout, as dictated by Special Order 120.

356. Miles provided the cavalry with great discretion in Special Order 120 once he outlined their initial route from Harpers Ferry to Sharpsburg: "No other instructions can be given to the commander than to force his way through the enemy's lines and join our army." (Heysinger, "The Cavalry Column From Harpers Ferry in the Antietam Campaign," p. 16)

357. Local civilian Thomas Noakes of Martinsburg and Lt. Hanson Green of the 1st Maryland Cavalry led the breakout expedition. Noakes had been working as a guide for US forces for about six months, first with Gen. Banks, and then with Gen. White.

358. Noakes had an unscrupulous background. Prior to the war he was convicted of larceny. By February 1864, Brig. Gen. Jeremiah C. Sullivan, the Union general commanding the Harpers Ferry district, complained about Noakes: "a poor man before the war, he is now in comfortable circumstances without any apparent means of livelihood; sells whiskey to soldiers; enters private houses and purloins private property; is a noted horse thief; was arrested, broke jail, was re-arrested and has been sent out of the lines of my division." (Fishel, *The Secret War for the Union*, p. 635)

359. The Confederates were not guarding or blocking the Harpers Ferry-Sharpsburg road on the night of the 14th. The Union cavalry encountered no opposition as it left the Ferry.

360. Jeb Stuart stated—in his official report of The Maryland Campaign, dated February 13, 1864, *17 months after the fact*—that he warned Gen. McLaws to watch the Harpers Ferry-Sharpsburg road. Stuart was familiar with the roads in this vicinity because of his duty here during the John Brown Raid: "[I] repeatedly urged the importance of [McLaws] holding with an infantry picket the road leading from the Ferry by the Kennedy farm [John Brown's headquarters] toward Sharpsburg." (*OR* 19 (1): 818)

361. The explanation for the lack of Confederates on the Harpers Ferry-Sharpsburg road was that McLaws had pulled most of his infantry north into Pleasant Valley to counter the expected attack of the Union Sixth Corps on the morning of September 15.

362. The secret cavalry breakout was nearly exposed when instead of turning left toward Sharpsburg, Company D of the 12th Illinois crossed the Potomac and turned *right*— directly into the Confederate pickets at Sandy Hook. The errant horsemen turned around and were not followed by the Confederates.

363. Accounts vary regarding the route of the cavalry from Sharpsburg to Williamsport. According to Isaac Heysinger, a corporal in the 7th Squadron Rhode Island Cavalry, the route from Sharpsburg went north along the Hagerstown Pike to Tilghmanton, then cut cross-country to the west and north before intersecting with the Boonsboro-Williamsport Pike near the College of St. James.

364. The first Confederates that the cavalry encounter are at Sharpsburg—the advance of Gen. Lee's retreating army from South Mountain. The encounter occurs near the junction of the Hagerstown Pike and the Boonsboro Pike near the old Lutheran Church cemetery.

365. The first Confederate general to encounter the Harpers Ferry cavalry was Brig. Gen. William Nelson Pendleton, Lee's chief of artillery. Pendleton reported "a large cavalry force of the enemy not far ahead of us" at Jones' crossroads early on the morning of the 15th. (*OR* 19 (1): 830)

366. Longstreet's reserve ammunition train was attacked and captured by the Harpers Ferry cavalry about 5:00 a.m. near Williamsport, Maryland. The captured booty was escorted across the Mason-Dixon Line to Greencastle, Pennsylvania.

367. Gen. Pendleton studiously avoided any mention of the embarrassing capture of Longstreet's reserve ammunition train in his September 24, 1862, report to Gen. Lee.

368. The Harpers Ferry cavalry expedition lasted 12½ hours, from its departure from the Ferry about 8:30 p.m. on the 14th through its arrival in Greencastle, Pennsylvania, at 9:00 a.m. on the 15th.

369. The first official report of the success of the Harpers Ferry cavalry breakout came in a message from Pennsylvania Governor A. G. Curtin to Secretary of War Edwin M. Stanton shortly after 9:00 a.m. on September 15. (*OR* 19 (2): 305)

370. No official report of the cavalry breakout has been discovered. The first detailed unofficial report appeared 21 years later (1883) in Col. Arno Voss's account published as part of Sgt. Samuel Pettengill's *The College Cavaliers*, a history of the 7th Squadron Rhode Island Cavalry.

371. The number of wagons captured by the Harpers Ferry cavalry varied from a low of 40 to a high of 91. Governor Curtin reported on the morning of September 15 that there were 40 captured wagons at Greencastle. Col. Voss, in writing to Sgt. Pettengill, stated that 85 wagons were captured. Isaac Heysinger, in his 1914 article, remembered bringing 75 wagons into Greencastle after blowing up 16 that broke down along the way. (*OR* 19 (2): 305)

372. Col. Benjamin F. Davis was recommended by Gen. McClellan for promotion to "brevet of major" in the regular army for his "conspicuous conduct . . . in the management of the withdrawal of the cavalry from Harpers Ferry." (*OR* 19 (1): 802)

373. Many of the teamsters in the captured Confederate wagon train were slaves. They were offered freedom upon reaching Greencastle.

374. Clagget Fitzhugh, a slave catcher from Franklin County, was serving as a guide for Longstreet's reserve ammunition train when it was captured near Williamsport. When he was returned to Greencastle as a captive of the federals, local citizens shouted "Hang him!" and "Down with the Traitor!" thus threatening to kill him. Fitzhugh was placed under the protective custody of the federals. (Alexander & Conrad, *When War Passed This Way*, pp. 80-81)

375. Stonewall Jackson became convinced by the evening of September 14 that artillery alone would not reduce the Harpers Ferry garrison, nor force its surrender. "[N]ot much could be expected from [our] artillery so long as the enemy retained his advanced position on Bolivar Heights." (*OR* 19 (1): 953)

376. Jackson devised three tactical initiatives on Sunday the 14th to break the Union resistance: 1) flank the Union left on Bolivar Heights; 2) feint an assault against the Union right to deceive the enemy and draw attention away from his flanking column; and 3) transfer artillery from School House Ridge to Loudoun Heights to enfilade at close range all Union positions on Bolivar Heights. (*OR* 19 (1): 954)

377. A. P. Hill's "Light Division" was selected for the flanking movement. Late on the afternoon of the 14th, Hill began marching his six brigades obliquely from School House Ridge south toward the Shenandoah River. During the night he followed the river and ascended steep ravines to deploy his division on an open eminence on the southwest end of Bolivar Heights—behind the Union lines. (*OR* 19 (1): 954)

378. The Chambers farm (today known as the Murphy farm) was where Gen. Hill deployed his 3,000 men and 20 pieces of artillery. Hill placed his infantry within 150 yards of the enemy's left on Bolivar Heights during the night of the 14th and 15th. His artillery was 1,000 yards from the federal line and in a position to enfilade their left and center. (*OR* 19 (1): 980)

379. The "Stonewall Division," commanded by Brig. Gen. John R. Jones, made a feint demonstration against the enemy's right on the 14th, while Ewell's division under A. R. Lawton advanced to School House Ridge to menace the federal center. (*OR* 19 (1): 954)

380. Maj. Thomas B. Massie, 12th Virginia Cavalry, commanded the cavalry guarding Jackson's extreme left flank. The unit watched the routes along the Potomac to ensure no federal escape via the river bank on the [West] Virginia shore. The 12th Virginia Cavalry included local companies raised in Jefferson County, including two companies from Charles Town and a company from Shepherdstown.

381. One of the most difficult and extraordinary flank marches of the war was executed by Col. Stapleton Crutchfield, Jackson's chief of artillery, on the night of the 14th-15th. Crutchfield moved 10 cannon from School House Ridge, across the Shenandoah River at Key's Ford, over imperfect mountain roads, and then onto a plateau at the base of Loudoun Heights. Most of this was accomplished in darkness. (*OR* 19 (1): 954, 962)

382. Jackson's men repositioned 30 pieces of artillery during the night of the 14th-15th, using the cover of darkness to disguise their movements from the federals. (*OR* 19 (1): 954)

383. Gen. Jackson received a dispatch from Gen. Lee on the 14th warning of a federal advance and the need to concentrate his forces. (*OR* 19 (1): 951)

384. Stonewall Jackson's first message predicting positive results for the Confederates at Harpers Ferry was dispatched to Gen. Lee at 8:15 p.m. on the 14th. "Through God's blessing," Jackson began, "the advance, which commenced this evening, has been successful thus far, and I look to Him for complete success tomorrow." (*OR* 19 (1): 951)

385. A thick fog blanketed Harpers Ferry at dawn on the 15th, but as the fog rose Miles discovered the new Confederate positions taken up during the night—Hill with his 3,000 men and 20 guns on his left flank and Crutchfield's 10 guns on Loudoun Heights. Miles was surrounded and nearly helpless.

386. The federals survived the Confederate barrage on the 15th for about an hour. "We are as helpless as rats in a cage," recalled Capt. Edward Ripley of the 9th Vermont Infantry. (*OR* 19 (1): 980)

387. One Medal of Honor was awarded for courage at Harpers Ferry on September 15. Lt. Frederick W. Fout, of the 15th Battery, Indiana Light Artillery, received the prestigious award for remanning guns that had been abandoned.

388. Surrender was decided upon by Gen. White and Col. Miles during a consultation "in the midst of shell and round shot" on Bolivar Heights with two of Miles's brigade commanders—Col. Trimble and Col. D'Utassy. The surrender decision was unanimous. (*OR* 19 (1): 539)

389. White flags, in the form of waving white handkerchiefs, were first hoisted about 8:00 a.m. on the 15th. Col. Miles rode to his various batteries ordering them to cease fire.

390. Miles commented to his aide-de-camp shortly after the surrender decision: "Well, Mr. Binney, we have done our duty, but where can McClellan be?" (*OR* 19 (1): 539)

391. Artillery firing ceased for about 15 minutes after the white handkerchiefs were waved; however, the Confederates opened up again "with a terrific cannonade." (*OR* 19 (1): 539)

392. Col. Miles was mortally wounded—after the white flags were flying—by a Confederate shell that exploded behind him on Bolivar Heights, tearing the flesh entirely from his left calf and cutting his right calf. This occurred after a Confederate battery on Loudoun Heights reopened fire after the initial cessation. (*OR* 19 (1): 539)

393. Dixon Miles died the next day, September 16, at 4:30 p.m. in his headquarters in the Master Armsrer's House. He commented on his death bed that: "He had done his duty; he was an old soldier and willing to die." Miles's remains were taken to Frederick, then to Baltimore, and finally to Sweet Air in Baltimore County, where he was buried on September 19. (*OR* 19 (1): 540)

394. Six reasons were listed for the surrender by Gen. White in an appendix report issued by him on September 25. The reasons: 1) loss of Maryland Heights; 2) long range ammunition expended; 3) no hope of reinforcement; 4) an enemy double the federal strength; 5) prevent sacrifice of life "without a reasonable hope of success"; and 6) a unanimous decision by a council of war "that further resistance was useless." (*OR* 19 (1): 531)

395. Lt. Henry M. Binney, Miles's aide-de-camp, was asked by Miles (while on his death-bed) to write his official report of the action at Harpers Ferry. Binney completed the report on September 18, 1862.

396. Lt. John H. Chamberlayne, the adjutant of A. P. Hill's artillery commander, was the first Confederate sent into the Union lines to determine if the federals had surrendered. (*OR* 19 (1): 980)

397. The first Confederate general that Union Gen. White met was A. P. Hill.

398. Gen. Jackson appointed A. P. Hill as his commissioner to negotiate the terms of surrender with the federals.

399. The terms of the Harpers Ferry surrender were as follows: all US troops would surrender and be paroled, not to fight again until exchanged; all munitions and public property of the US would be relinquished to the Confederates; US officers would be allowed to retain their side arms and personal property. (*OR* 19 (1): 529,539)

400. A second clause in the terms of surrender required that any Confederate deserter now serving in the US Army must be handed over. No one was delivered to the Confederates who met this stipulation.

401. Two days of full rations, captured at Harpers Ferry, were issued to the captured federals by the Confederates. (*OR* 19 (1): 961)

402. Jackson's victory at Harpers Ferry captured 73 pieces of artillery, 13,000 small arms, 200 wagons, and 12,737 prisoners (including wounded). (*OR* 19 (1): 955, 549)

403. The federals reported only 47 guns "used in the defense of Harpers Ferry, and turned over to the enemy." (*OR* 19 (1): 548)

404. The Confederate commissary reported seizing 155,954 pounds of hard bread, as well as 19,267 pounds of bacon and 4,930 pounds of coffee. (*OR* 19 (1): 961)

405. Quartermaster John Harman of Jackson's command reported, following the surrender of Harpers Ferry, that "many worn-out wagons were exchanged for good Yankee ones, the useless ones being left behind." (*OR* 19 (1): 961)

406. Stonewall earned his victory at Harpers Ferry with minimal loss. His casualties were 39 killed and 247 wounded. Nearly 75% of the Confederate casualties occurred in the battle for Maryland Heights.

407. Federal casualties (excluding prisoners) during the investment are 44 killed and 173 wounded.

408. Col. F. G. D'Utassy, commander of the 39th New York Infantry, had his regimental flag stashed among his private baggage. The terms of surrender allowed officers to retain their personal property.

409. The flag of the 32nd Ohio Infantry was saved from capture by the color bearer, Omar S. Lee. Lee wrapped the flag around his body and covered it with clothes to hide it from the Confederates. The 125th New York Infantry shredded its flag and distributed the pieces throughout the regiment.

410. No federal prisoners captured at Harpers Ferry were sent to Confederate prisoner-of-war camps.

411. A. P. Hill paroled all the federal prisoners. A parole is a promise not to serve against the enemy until exchanged for an equal number of the enemy's parolees. Union and Confederate authorities had a parole/exchange agreement in place, known as the Dix-Hill cartel, at the time of the Harpers Ferry surrender.

412. The paroled federal command marched out of Harpers Ferry, without Confederate escort, on September 16. It proceeded to Frederick, Maryland, and then to Annapolis, where it arrived on the 21st. (*OR* 19 (1): 528)

413. The Harpers Ferry parolees were sent from Annapolis to Chicago and assigned to Camp Douglas for training and refitting for other military duty—some for fighting the Sioux Indians. The Confederates complained that this action violated the terms of parole, and US authorities stopped the Indian project.

414. Camp Douglas was named after and situated on a portion of the estate of Senator Stephen A. Douglas, the "Little Giant," who helped bring notoriety to Abraham Lincoln in the Lincoln/Douglas debates of 1858. Confederate prisoners taken at Fort Donelson had occupied Camp Douglas until exchanged in August 1862.

415. Not all of the Harpers Ferry parolees were sent to Camp Douglas. The three-month term of service for the 12th New York State Militia and the 87th Ohio Infantry had expired and men in these regiments were mustered out. The 1st and 3rd Maryland Potomac Home Brigade regiments remained in Annapolis' Camp Parole until exchanged.

416. The captured Harpers Ferry federals felt humiliated by their confinement in a US prison camp under the guard of US soldiers. With many of their officers absent in Washington testifying about the siege and surrender, parolee discipline was lax. This lack of discipline and the feeling of humiliation led to outrage, and the angry troops at times became mobs that burned barracks and destroyed the perimeter fence of the prison.

417. The paroled New York regiments at Camp Douglas were exchanged on November 19, 1862. All the other Harpers Ferry parolees were declared exchanged on January 10, 1863.

418. Gen. White, in his official report dated September 20, stated that he expected to assume his share of the disgrace for the surrender. "[I] scorn to shelter myself behind the funeral pall of an officer who, whatever his military errors, died in defense of our country." (*OR* 19 (1): 529)

419. General-in-Chief Henry W. Halleck ordered the arrest of Gen. White and the brigade commanders—colonels D'Utassy, Trimble, Ford, and Ward, on September 22. (*OR* 19 (1): 801)

420. Eight days after the Harpers Ferry surrender, the War Department ordered that a special commission be assembled to investigate the evacuation of Maryland Heights and the subsequent surrender, and to "report all the facts bearing, in their judgment, upon the conduct of commanding officers, or their subordinates, in making said evacuation and surrender." (*OR* 19 (1): 549)

421. Maj. Gen. David Hunter was appointed president of the Harpers Ferry commission. General Hunter was a staunch Republican who presided over three well-known special investigations: Harpers Ferry; the controversial court-martial of Union Gen. Fitz John Porter; and the military court which tried the Lincoln conspirators.

422. Testimony before the Harpers Ferry commission began on October 4 and ended on October 23. Fifteen full days of testimony occurred between these dates.

423. The commission asked nearly 1,800 questions, ranging from such complex issues as "What necessity existed for the surrender of Harpers Ferry?" to the easily answered, "How long have you been in the service?" (*OR* 19 (1): 556-794)

424. Specific and probing questions about Col. Dixon Miles, who was not there to defend himself, were also asked: "From what you know of Colonel Miles as a military man, do you think he was morally, mentally, and physically competent to command?" A more troubling question also arose: "Did you ever see anything in [Miles's] conduct that would lead you to question his loyalty?" (*OR* 19 (1): 662, 751)

425. Not one witness charged Col. Miles with treason. Only one witness, Capt. Samuel Means, testified Miles had been drinking. All other witnesses refuted this assertion. Means was commander of the Loudoun Rangers—a federal cavalry battalion from north-western Loudoun County, Virginia.

426. Forty-four witnesses appeared before the Harpers Ferry military commission, ranging in rank from a lieutenant to Maj. Gen. Henry W. Halleck.

427. Nine hundred pages of evidence—written in long hand—were produced by the witnesses. When printed in the *Official Records*, the number of pages totaled 251.

428. The Harpers Ferry military commission issued its findings on November 3, 1862. The tribunal applauded Gen. White for acting "with decided capability and courage." No brigade officer, with the exception of Col. Ford, was censored or reprimanded. (*OR* 19 (1): 794, 798)

429. Col. Thomas H. Ford, the commission determined, should be dismissed from the service. The commission declared Ford: "should not have been placed in command on Maryland Heights; that he conducted the defense without ability, and has shown throughout such a lack of military capacity as to disqualify him . . . for a command in the service." (*OR* 19 (1): 799)

430. The Harpers Ferry commission carefully considered the case of Col. Miles, approaching any decision about him with reluctance: "An officer who cannot appear before any earthly tribunal to answer or explain charges gravely affecting his character . . . is entitled to the tenderest care and most careful investigation." (*OR* 19 (1): 799)

431. The commission concluded: "Colonel Miles' [sic] incapacity, amounting to almost imbecility, led to the shameful surrender of this important post." (*OR* 19 (1): 799)

432. Two men were dismissed from the service for their actions at Harpers Ferry—Col. Thomas H. Ford and Maj. William H. Baird. Baird was released for "his bad conduct" in the "disgraceful" behavior of the 126th New York Infantry on Maryland Heights. (*OR* 19 (1): 800)

433. Maj. Gen. John G. Wool was "guilty to this extent of a grave disaster," according to the commission, for placing an "incapable" in command at Harpers Ferry. Gen. McClellan actually assigned Miles the Harpers Ferry post. (*OR* 19 (1): 800)

434. The commission censored Gen. McClellan for failing to relieve Harpers Ferry in a timely matter. (*OR* 19 (1): 800)

435. Jackson's official report concerning the siege of Harpers Ferry was not completed until April 23, 1863—just nine days before his mortal wounding in the battle of Chancellorsville. (*OR* 19 (1): 952)

436. Gen. Jackson announced his Harpers Ferry victory to Gen. Lee in a dispatch dated "near 8:00 a.m." on the 15th. Its opening sentence read: "Through God's blessing, Harpers Ferry and its garrison are to be surrendered." A courier was sent soon afterward to deliver the good news to Lee near Sharpsburg. (*OR* 19 (1): 951)

437. A. P. Hill and his division, who had "borne the heaviest part of the engagement," were left behind at Harpers Ferry by Jackson to dispose of prisoners and captured property while the rest of Stonewall's command marched north toward Sharpsburg. (*OR* 19 (1): 951)

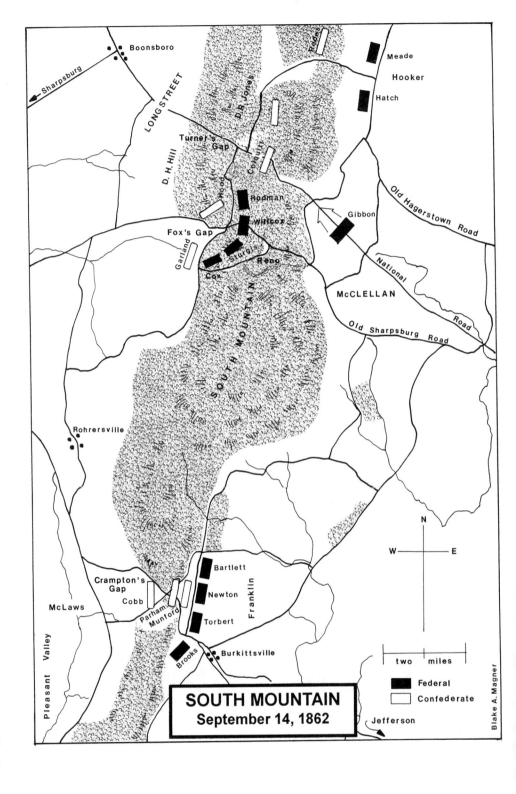

Boonsboro

← Sharpsburg

LONGSTREET

D. H. Hill

Turner's Gap

D. R. Jones

Reade

Meade
Hooker
Hatch

Colquitt

Hood

Rodman
Whitcox

Gibbon

Old Hagerstown Road

Fox's Gap

Garland

Sturgis

Reno

Cox

National

SOUTH MOUNTAIN

McCLELLAN

Old Sharpsburg Road

Road

Rohrersville

N
W —— E
S

Crampton's Gap

Bartlett

Newton

Franklin

McLaws

Cobb

Parham
Munford

Torbert

Pleasant Valley

Brooks

Burkittsville

two   miles

■ Federal
□ Confederate

Blake A. Magner

**SOUTH MOUNTAIN
September 14, 1862**

Jefferson

The Battle(s) For South Mountain

438. Robert E. Lee did not plan for, nor did he expect to wage, a battle atop South Mountain.

439. South Mountain is a ridge that begins at the Potomac River and continues north into Pennsylvania, terminating near Carlisle. South Mountain is east of—and *not* part of—the Blue Ridge.

440. Through the execution of Special Orders 191, Gen. Lee adopted the Cumberland Valley as his new theater of operations, and South Mountain—which defined the eastern edge of the Valley—became a barrier between Lee and the federals.

441. Gen. McClellan, as a result of his fortunate discovery of Special Orders 191, planed his offensive strategy. "My general idea is to cut the enemy in two and beat him in detail," he explained to Sixth Corps commander William B. Franklin. (*OR* 19 (1): 46)

442. McClellan's strategy dissected the Confederate army into three parts. Two of the three parts could be trapped in Maryland by slicing through South Mountain. A bold move against Crampton's Gap would seal 8,000 Confederates in Pleasant Valley. A drive against Turner's Gap toward Boonsboro could potentially cut off Lee's routes of retreat back into Virginia. The third part of the Confederate army—Jackson's and Walker's columns operating south of the Potomac against Harpers Ferry—was beyond McClellan's immediate reach. (*OR* 19 (1): 45-46)

443. Four engagement areas constitute the South Mountain battlefield. The southern most action was waged at Crampton's Gap and Burkittsville. Six miles north, the armies collided at Fox's Gap. One mile north of Fox's Gap, the struggle was for control of Turner's Gap. The northern most sector of the battlefield was slightly north of Turner's Gap.

444. The most protracted battle of South Mountain occurred at Fox's Gap. The fighting began here at 9:00 a.m. and firing did not cease until 9:00 p.m.

445. The bloodiest battle of South Mountain was at Fox's Gap. Confederate casualties totaled 899. Union casualties were only ten less at 889.

446. The battle(s) of South Mountain were the direct result of George McClellan's discovery of Special Orders 191. McClellan was on the offensive, attempting to destroy Lee's army before it could reunite. Lee was on the defensive, responding to McClellan's sudden and unexpected aggressiveness.

447. South Mountain represented Robert E. Lee's first defensive battle since he assumed command of the Army of Northern Virginia in June 1862.

448. Virtually all the fighting in each of the battles of South Mountain was on the eastern side of the ridge. The Confederates—who approached the mountain from the west—defended the crest and eastern slopes against Union attackers arriving from the east.

449. McClellan's first official action following his discovery of Special Orders 191 on the 13th was a 3:00 p.m. request to his cavalry commander, Alfred Pleasanton, to verify the positions of Lee's army. McClellan warned Pleasanton to approach South Mountain "with great caution" because the passes might be disputed. (*OR* 19 (1): 820)

450. By the provisions of Special Orders 191, McClellan believed the first concentration of Confederates he would encounter was near Boonsboro. The captured orders instructed Longstreet's command to "halt [here], with reserve, supply, and baggage trains of the army." Lee modified this plan when he instructed Longstreet to proceed to Hagerstown. (*OR* 19 (2): 604)

451. Lee determined on the night of the 13th that he would withdraw Longstreet's command from Hagerstown and return it south—back toward Boonsboro, but not to South Mountain. (*OR* 19 (2): 604)

452. Beaver Creek would be Longstreet's position on the 14th, according to a judgment Lee made at 10:00 p.m. on the 13th. Beaver Creek is located about midway between Boonsboro and Hagerstown, and its north bank presents a strong defensive position. (*OR* 19 (2): 607)

453. Only one Confederate division—Maj. Gen. Daniel Harvey Hill's five brigades that totaled approximately 5,000 men—was positioned to defend South Mountain on the morning of September 14. Hill commanded the rear guard of the army, stationed near Boonsboro.

454. Gen. D. H. Hill, in his colorful article published more than 20 years after the fight at South Mountain in *Battles and Leaders of the Civil War*, claimed the battle was "one of extraordinary illusions and delusions." Hill explained the federals were under "the self-imposed illusion that there was a very large force opposed to them," when, in fact, his division stood alone until late in the afternoon of the 14th. The delusions resulted from moving the Confederate forces from point to point and meeting the Union attacks wherever they occurred. Hill concluded the Confederates "deluded the Federals into the belief that the whole mountain was swarming with rebels." (D. H. Hill, "The Battle of South Mountain, or Boonsboro: Fighting for Time at Turner's and Fox's Gaps," *Battles and Leaders of the Civil War*, Vol. 2, p. 559)

455. The first indication that Gen. Lee suspected a forward movement of the Union army from Frederick is found in a 10:00 p.m. message to Lafayette McLaws on September 13. "General Lee directs me to say," wrote his aide-de-camp, "that from reports reaching him, he believes the enemy is moving toward Harpers Ferry to relieve the force they have there." (*OR* 19 (2): 607)

456. Gen. Lee considered the force of Lafayette McLaws most endangered by a Union advance. Fearing McLaws may become trapped in Pleasant Valley—with federals to his front at Harpers Ferry and federals to his rear at South Mountain—Lee warned McLaws to hurry his effort to bring about the Harpers Ferry capitulation. "You will see, therefore, the necessity of expediting your operations as much as possible." (*OR* 19 (2): 607)

457. Gen. Lee instructed McLaws to move to Sharpsburg as soon as his Harpers Ferry mission was complete. Positioning McLaws at Sharpsburg provided insight into Gen. Lee's strategic thinking on the night of the 13th. Moving McLaws to Sharpsburg provided three advantages: 1) it protected Lee's right flank with Longstreet posted on Beaver Creek; 2) it protected Boteler's Ford, providing McLaws with a means of escape, if necessary; and 3) it provided access, via Boteler's Ford, for Jackson's and Walker's commands to march from Harpers Ferry and reunite with Lee in Maryland. *(OR* 19 (2): 607)

458. Gen. Lee changed his strategic thinking on the 14th. He decided to move Longstreet into the Boonsboro Valley—which is south of Beaver Creek—"so as to protect [McLaws'] flank from forces coming from Frederick, until the operations at Harpers Ferry are finished." *(OR* 19 (2): 608)

459. Gen. Lee gave McLaws two options on the morning of the 14th. Should Harpers Ferry not capitulate, Lee instructed McLaws to bring his forces up the Boonsboro Valley to cooperate with Longstreet and D. H. Hill. McLaws position on the 14th was in Pleasant Valley—the Boonsboro Valley is north of Pleasant Valley. The second option, should Harpers Ferry fall, was to move McLaws to Sharpsburg. *(OR* 19 (2): 608)

460. The first directive Gen. McClellan sent to a corps commander after his discovery of Special Orders 191 was to Maj. Gen. William B. Franklin, commander of the Sixth Corps. The directive was dated from McClellan's camp near Frederick at 6:20 p.m. on September 13—fully six hours after McClellan first saw the "Lost Order." *(OR* 19 (1): 45)

461. McClellan's instructions to Franklin were direct and specific. He was to move at daybreak on the morning of the 14th, taking the road from Jefferson to Burkittsville. He then must seize Crampton's Gap "as soon as practicable," if not held by the enemy, and if opposition occurred, to attack "about half an hour after you hear severe firing at the pass on the Hagerstown pike" (Turner's Gap). Once Crampton's Gap was seized, McClellan stated: "[Y]our duty will be first to cut off, destroy, or capture McLaws' command and relieve Colonel Miles" at Harpers Ferry. *(OR* 19 (1): 45)

462. Franklin's Sixth Corps left its bivouac three miles east of Jefferson at 6:00 a.m. on the 14th. The lead brigade arrived east of Burkittsville six hours later. Three more hours pass, when finally, at 3:00 p.m., Franklin began movements to seize Crampton's Gap. *(OR* 19 (1): 374)

463. William Buel Franklin finished first in his class at West Point in 1843—the same class in which U. S. Grant finished 21st. At the outset of the war, Franklin was in Washington directing the construction of the new Capitol dome.

464. Lafayette McLaws had not prepared for the approach of the Union army against his rear. On the east side of Crampton's Gap near Burkittsville on the morning of the 14th there was only one regiment of infantry—the 16th Virginia; two diminutive cavalry regiments—the 2nd and 12th Virginia; and two pieces of artillery positioned one mile south at Brownsville Pass and supported by the 10th Georgia and the 41st Virginia. Approaching this rearguard was the 13,000 federals of the Sixth Corps.

465. Franklin held a 13 to1 advantage when his corps first arrived at Burkittsville, yet at 12:30 p.m., he sent a message to McClellan that revealed an extraordinary delusion: "I think from appearances that we may have a heavy fight to get the pass." (Timothy Reese, *Sealed with Their Lives: The Battle for Crampton's Gap*, p. 59)

466. Three Cramptons—Thomas, Eli, and John—lived within one mile of the gap that bore their name, all within Pleasant Valley on the west side of the mountain.

467. The Confederates initially defending Crampton's Gap held a stone wall and road at the eastern base of South Mountain that ran parallel to the mountain's crest. During the three hour lull between Franklin's arrival at Burkittsville and the commencement of the Union advance, the Confederates attempted to reinforce this position with the arrival of the 12th and 6th Virginia infantry regiments from Col. William Parham's brigade and the 10th Georgia from Brig. Gen. Paul Semmes's brigade. The horse artillery of R. Preston Chew and a section of the Portsmouth Battery was placed in position about half way down the mountain to support the infantry position.

468. About 800 Confederates defended a 1,000 yard position extending along the eastern base of Crampton's Gap. These troops, both infantry and cavalry, were commanded by Thomas T. Munford, colonel of the 2nd Virginia Cavalry, fighting dismounted. On Munford's extreme right were 200 men from the 2nd and 12th Virginia Cavalry. Holding the road from Burkittsville to Crampton's Gap was the 16th Virginia Infantry. On the right center was the 12th Virginia Infantry. In the left center was the 6th Virginia Infantry and anchoring the left flank was the 10th Georgia.

469. At 3:00 p.m., the federal column of attack was formed. Col. Joseph P. Bartlett's brigade of Henry Slocum's division formed the van. Leading Bartlett's brigade was the 27th New York Infantry, deployed as skirmishers. Following Barlett was Brig. Gen. John Newton's brigade, and in the rear of Slocum's advance was the New Jersey Brigade of Col. A. T. A. Torbert. Each brigade was formed in two lines. (*OR* 19 (1): 380, 388)

470. Bartlett's brigade focused its drive against the Confederate left. It drove to within 300 yards of the stonewall defended by the 10th Georgia and 6th Virginia where it stopped near the crest of a knoll and began a one-hour fight that featured heavy infantry fire. Meanwhile, Newton arrived to extend Bartlett's right and left flanks, and the New Jersey Brigade began pressing the Confederate left center. The 96th Pennsylvania formed on the extreme right of the Union line. The extreme left was held by the Vermont Brigade of Brig. Gen. William T. H. Brooks.

471. At 5:30 p.m. the entire federal line charged at the double quick and pushed the Confederates from behind the stone wall, sending them flying up the mountain toward Crampton's Gap. The federals pursued them "up an almost perpendicular steep, over rocks and ledges, through the underbrush and timber," toward the gap. (*OR* 19 (1): 389)

472. Howell Cobb received an urgent message from Lafayette McLaws at 1:00 p.m. on the 14th ordering him north to Brownsville to reinforce Paul Semmes' brigade holding Brownsville Pass. Cobbs's men left their post in southern Pleasant Valley and arrived at the village of Brownsville three hours later.

473. At 5:00 p.m., Cobb received a message from the beleaguered Thomas Munford at Crampton's Gap, requesting immediate assistance. Cobb subsequently divided his brigade, sending the 24th Georgia and the 15th North Carolina to support Munford. The remainder of Cobb's brigade was held at Brownsville in support of Semmes.

474. With the situation deteriorating at Crampton's, McLaws ordered Cobb to send his remaining force from Brownsville to Crampton's Gap. Cobb arrived atop the mountain about 5:30 p.m. Completely unaware of the situation and the terrain, Cobb deferred to

Munford's judgement, who recommended sending half the brigade to strengthen the Rebel left and the other half to the right. This maneuver proved disastrous, as Cobb's Confederates were rapidly surrounded and overrun by Franklin's federals scaling the mountain.

475. Brig. Gen. Howell Cobb, a native of Georgia, had turned 47 one week before the battle of Crampton's Gap.

476. Cobb served as Speaker of the US House of Representatives from 1849-1851, during the time of the excruciating Compromise of 1850. He was elected governor of Georgia in 1851.

477. President James Buchanan appointed Cobb as his Secretary of Treasury in 1857. As a Southern moderate, Cobb did not advocate secession until after Lincoln's election. He resigned from the Buchanan administration in December 1860.

478. At the secession convention in Montgomery in February 1861—to form the provisional government of the Confederacy—Cobb was unanimously elected president *pro tem* by acclamation.

479. Cobb received serious consideration for the position of president of the Confederate government, but he deferred to the selection of Jefferson Davis. At the inauguration, Cobb swore in Davis as President of the Confederate States.

480. Shortly after Cobb's arrival at Crampton's Gap, Munford relinquished command to the Georgian. Although Munford oversaw the gap's defense from dawn of the 14th until one hour before dusk, history blamed the disaster at Crampton's Gap on Howell Cobb.

481. Cobb faced three-to-one odds when he came to Munford's rescue, bringing with him approximately 1,340 men. He arrived too late to assist the broken Confederate line at the eastern base of the mountain, and was too late to shore up the Confederate position at the gap itself.

482. Cobb's Georgia Legion, advancing to the right toward Burkittsville, was cut off and virtually surrounded about half way down the mountain's eastern slope by the 3rd and 4th New Jersey Infantry.

483. Cobb's brigade suffered the highest casualties of any brigade of either army at Crampton's Gap—153 killed; 255 wounded; 252 prisoners—a total of 660 of 1341 engaged, or 49 percent. The original statistics compiled after the battle showed Cobb's Legion suffering the heaviest percentage of casualties of either army at Crampton's—190 of 248 engaged, or 77 percent. (Reese, *Sealed with Their Lives*, p. 302)

484. Sixty-three percent of Cobb's Legion, or 156 of 248 engaged, were captured at Crampton's Gap, according to official reports. Timothy Reese, in his 1998 examination of Confederate records, adjusted this number downward to 44 POWs. Reese's compilation increased the number of killed or mortally wounded from 11 to 57, and he also increased the number of wounded from 23 to 78. Hence, Reese's total of 179 casualties in Cobb's Legion differs only by 11 from the original count of 190. (Reese, *Sealed with Their Lives*, p. 302)

485. More recent statistical analysis, compiled by Timothy Reese in 1998 after a review of Confederate records, reveals the 16th Georgia Infantry with higher casualties (192) than Cobb's Legion (179). The original enumeration for the 16th Georgia was 187. (Reese, *Sealed with Their Lives*, p. 302)

486. Crampton's Gap was particularly devastating to the Ragsdale family of Company C, Cobb's Legion. Privates Marshall and Warner Ragsdale were killed. Sgt. Elijah Ragsdale died of wounds four months later while Pvt. William Ragsdale survived but as a wounded prisoner. (Reese, *Sealed with Their Lives*, p. 300)

487. Lt. George Hooker of the 4th Vermont Infantry received the Medal of Honor for capturing 116 Confederates of the 16th Virginia Infantry just south of Crampton's Gap. (Reese, *Sealed with Their Lives*, p. 151-152)

488. Darkness ended the federal pursuit of the Confederates into Pleasant Valley, but not before Franklin's men had captured 400 prisoners from 17 different organizations, as well as 700 stand of arms, one piece of artillery, and three enemy colors. (*OR* 19 (1): 375, 383)

489. Gen. Franklin did obtain success at Crampton's Gap, but his victory was only partial. His seizure of the mountain gap *does not* complete McClellan's September 13 assignment. Franklin made no mention in his official report of South Mountain (dated September 30, 1862) of his *failure* to relieve Harpers Ferry. Franklin's South Mountain report also ignored any references to his face-off with McLaws in Pleasant Valley on the 15th, where he *failed* to cut off or destroy McLaws. (*OR* 19 (1): 374-376)

490. The second part of McClellan's plan to "cut the enemy in two and beat him in detail" required the crossing of South Mountain at the gaps near Boonsboro. To accomplish this, McClellan ordered the Ninth Corps and First Corps to drive forward on the 14th. (*OR* 19 (1): 46-47)

491. Maj. Gen. Daniel Harvey Hill—stationed near Boonsboro and assigned to guard the rear of the army by Special Orders 191—first learned of the federal movement toward South Mountain on the 13th, when Pleasonton's cavalry pushed west through the Middletown Valley. Hill positioned two of his five brigades on the mountain near Turner's Gap to counter Pleasonton's threat. (*OR* 19 (1): 1019)

492. D. H. Hill established his command post at the Mountain House, a stone dwelling at Turner's Gap located along the south side of the National Road.

493. Three roads intersect near the Mountain House. The National Road runs perpendicular to South Mountain, crossing the range at Turner's Gap. A mountain road runs along the crest, one mile south toward Fox's Gap, providing a critical communications and travel link between the two gaps. A third mountain road runs north from Turner's, leading into in a deep gorge on the east side of the mountain at the hamlet of Frostown.

494. The lead division of the Ninth Corps—the Ohio troops of Brig. Gen. Jacob D. Cox's Kanawha Division—departed from its bivouac west of Middletown at 6:00 a.m. on the 14th. It was traveling west on the National Road, in support of Alfred Pleasonton's cavalry, which was operating in front of Turner's Gap. (*OR* 19 (1): 458)

495. Cox's route was diverted from Turner's Gap to Fox's Gap (one-mile south) as a result of a chance meeting. When Cox arrived at Catoctin Creek he encountered Col.

Augustus Moor, who had been captured the day before in Frederick, returning to the Union lines as a paroled prisoner. "Where are you going?" inquired Moor. Cox responded that he was moving toward Turner's Gap. "My God! be careful," exclaimed Moor. Then, checking himself, Moor stated, "But I am paroled!" and he turned away, giving Cox no more information. (Jacob D. Cox, "Forcing Fox's Gap and Turner's Gap," *Battles and Leaders of the Civil War*, Vol.2, pp. 585-586)

496. Col. Moor's inadvertent warning deflected Cox's advance south toward Fox's Gap. Cox reasoned that a push there will turn the Confederate right upon South Mountain.

497. The first Confederate brigade to arrive at Fox's Gap was Brig. Gen. Samuel Garland's brigade of five North Carolina regiments. D. H. Hill ordered Garland to leave Turner's Gap at sunrise on the 14th, and to follow the mountain road south to Fox's Gap. (*OR* 19 (1): 1039-1040)

498. Three roads intersect at Fox's Gap. The Old Sharpsburg Road, also known as the Braddock Road, runs perpendicular to the mountain, but generally parallel to the National Road. A narrow mountain road stretches north and joins with the Pike near the Mountain House in Turner's Gap. A third mountain road follows the crest south for about one mile, then abruptly turns down the east side of the mountain toward the Peter Beachley farmstead.

499. The mountain cabin of Daniel Wise stood near the intersection of the three roads at Fox's Gap. Just east and northeast of the cabin were open fields. The western edge of the crest and the west slope of the mountain was wooded.

500. The first Union brigade to attack Fox's Gap was Col. Eliakim P. Scammon's brigade of 1,455 Buckeyes. Scammon arrived on the scene at 9:00 a.m., and promptly struck Garland's right flank. He soon received support from the brigade of Col. George Crook. (*OR* 19 (1): 458, 461-462)

501. The 23rd Ohio Infantry led the Union assault at Fox's Gap. The regiment smashed into the 5th North Carolina and 23rd North Carolina, defending Garland's right.

502. The 23rd Ohio Infantry had within its ranks two future US presidents. Lieut. Col. Rutherford B. Hayes—who led the regiment at Fox's Gap and was badly wounded in the left arm—became the 19th president in 1877. Commissary Sgt. William McKinley was elected president in 1896 and 1900.

503. Brig. Gen. Samuel Garland, Jr., a collateral descendant of James Madison, was mortally wounded on the Fox's Gap battlefield. Garland was the first of eight generals who would be killed or mortally wounded during The Maryland Campaign. Garland, at age 31, was also the youngest of the eight generals to die. General Garland's remains were first moved to the Mountain House, and then to Boonsboro for embalming in the cabinet shop of John C. Brining, the local undertaker.

504. Cox outnumbered Garland by nearly three to one, and the federals eventually pushed Garland's troops over the western crest of the mountain or north toward the Old Sharpsburg Road. Between noon and 2:00 p.m., a lull occurred in the fighting as both sides rushed reinforcements to the Fox's Gap battlefield. (*OR* 19 (1): 459, 1041)

505. Brig. Gen. George B. Anderson's North Carolina brigade was the first to arrive and assist Garland's hard-pressed and demoralized troops. D. H. Hill also directed Roswell Ripley's brigade to Fox's Gap, but it was misplaced by Ripley and "did not draw trigger." (*OR* 19 (1): 1020-1021)

506. Gen. Hill watched the approach of Union reinforcements across the Middletown Valley from his Mountain House headquarters with admiration and trepidation. "The marching column extended back as far as eye could see," he remembered. "It was a grand and glorious spectacle, and it was impossible to look at it without admiration. I had never seen so tremendous an army before, and I did not see one like it afterward." (Hill, "The Battle of South Mountain, or Boonsboro," *Battles and Leaders of the Civil War*, Vol. 2, p. 559)

507. Longstreet arrived, marching from Hagerstown, with the head of his column reaching Turner's Gap about 3:00 p.m. Hill directed the first two brigades—the 1,900 men of Thomas Drayton and George T. Anderson—south to Fox's Gap. Hill was anxious to "beat the force on my right before the Yankees [made] their grand assault," which Hill determined will come north of Turner's Gap. (*OR* 19 (1): 1020)

508. Support arrived for Cox's division beginning about 2:00 p.m. The first division to march up the mountain in the afternoon was Orlando B. Willcox's two brigades. Samuel Sturgis then pushed forward with his division and aligned in support of Willcox. The final Union division to reach Fox's Gap was Isaac P. Rodman's division. Rodman separated his force sending Harrison Fairchild's brigade to the extreme left and placing Edward Harland's brigade on the extreme right. (*OR* 19 (1): 459-460)

509. The final Confederate brigades that arrived at Fox's Gap belonged to John Bell Hood's division. Hood learned that Drayton's brigade, defending the Old Sharpsburg Road, had broken on the left. To seal this dangerous breach, Hood approached the battlefield from the western slope, fixed bayonets and charged, "regaining all of our lost ground" on the Confederate left. (*OR* 19 (1): 922)

510. Despite a Union advance along the entire front of the Ninth Corps beginning at 4:00 p.m., the Confederates were not pushed off the mountain and they retained control of the Old Sharpsburg Road.

511. Maj. Gen. Jesse L. Reno, commander of the Ninth Corps, was mortally wounded near Wise's field while reconnoitering in front of his line at dusk on the 14th. Reno was the second and final general to die during the action at Fox's Gap.

512. Jesse Lee Reno was a native of Wheeling, [West] Virginia. In a comment in his official battle report, Gen. D. H. Hill scorned Reno's allegiance to the North: "The Yankees on their side lost General Reno, a renegade Virginian, who was killed by a happy shot from the Twenty-third North Carolina." (*OR* 19 (1): 1020)

513. The body of Gen. Reno was taken to Baltimore and embalmed by the inventor of the embalming process, William E. Chenowith.

514. Maj. Gen. Ambrose Burnside, commander of McClellan's right wing (the Ninth and First Corps), ordered the First Corps, which arrived at the battlefield about 3:00 p.m., to the right of the National Road. Its assignment was to assault the Confederate left flank holding the Old Hagerstown Road, about 1½ miles north of Turner's Gap.

515. The First Corps, under the command of Maj. Gen. Joseph Hooker, departed its encampment near the Monocacy River at 6:00 a.m. on the 14th and commenced a 12-mile march toward South Mountain via the National Road.

516. Joseph Hooker was a 47-year-old native of Hadley, Massachusetts, and the grandson of a Revolutionary War captain. He graduated from West Point in 1837 and during the Mexican War he received more brevets than any other first lieutenant in the US Army.

517. "Fighting Joe Hooker" was the *nom de guerre* Hooker received while commanding a division during the Peninsula Campaign. The title was awarded as a result of a press wire that originally read "Fighting—Joe Hooker." The dash was dropped when it appeared in newspapers throughout the North.

518. Hooker arrived in Middletown at 1:00 p.m. with his lead division commanded by Brig. Gen. George G. Meade. He then rode to the front at the eastern base of South Mountain to confer with McClellan and to examine the country. (*OR* 19 (1): 214)

519. Hooker's corps was the last Union force to arrive at, and participate in, the battle of South Mountain. Hooker's men began arriving at the front more than six hours after the Ninth Corps began its battle for Fox's Gap (9:00 a.m.).

520. Gen. Hooker established his headquarters at a stone church known as Mount Tabor, located about one mile north of the National Road. The church no longer stands, but its location is identified by the adjacent graveyard. (*OR* 19 (1): 221)

521. George Gordon Meade, pegged with the unflattering nickname of "old snapping turtle," was 47-years-old and an 1835 graduate of West Point. Prior to the war he served as an engineer in the Army building lighthouses and breakwaters, and conducting coastal and geodetic surveys.

522. At Glendale, on June 30, 1862, General Meade had, as senior brigade commander, assumed command of the Pennsylvania Reserve Division with the capture of Brig. Gen. George McCall.

523. Hooker called Meade's division forward from Middletown at 2:00 p.m. As it approached Turner's Gap via the National Road, Hooker directed Meade to turn north on a road running perpendicular to the National Road—"to make a diversion in favor of Reno"—and to strike the enemy's extreme left. Meade advanced along this road for nearly 1½ miles before he deployed into a line of battle. (*OR* 19 (1): 214, 267)

524. The second division of Hooker's First Corps to reach South Mountain was commanded by Brig. Gen. John P. Hatch. Hatch's division departed its Monocacy River bivouac at 6:00 a.m. and arrived at Catoctin Mountain at 12:30 p.m. After a two hour delay, the division was ordered forward, following the route of Meade's division, and arrived at Hooker's headquarters at Mount Tabor Church about 3:30 p.m. (*OR* 19 (1): 214, 221, 241)

525. Gen. Hatch replaced Brig. Gen. Rufus King as division commander while on the march from Frederick to South Mountain. Hatch received division command while at Catoctin Mountain. (*OR* 19 (1): 221)

526. John Porter Hatch commanded his division for only about six hours. He was badly wounded during the attack of his division at South Mountain. Hatch would never recover enough to assume field command again, but he would perform various administrative functions, such as commander of the District of Charleston, South Carolina, at the end of the war.

527. Three different commanders led the First Division of the First Corps on September 14. Rufus King was relieved by noon. He was replaced by John Hatch, who was wounded about dusk. Abner Doubleday then assumed command on the evening of the 14th.

528. The final First Corps' division to arrive at South Mountain was Brig. Gen. James B. Ricketts' division. Ricketts approached the east side of the mountain about 5:00 p.m. and took position about one mile north of the National Road, near the location of Meade's and Hatch's divisions. (*OR* 19 (1): 214)

529. Gen. Hooker had massed before the Confederate left three divisions numbering over 12,000 men. He outnumbered the enemy in this sector by more than three to one.

530. A deep gorge, dividing two summits of South Mountain, faced Hooker. This divided terrain subsequently directed Hooker's deployment and his battle plan. Meade would advance on the right or north side of the of gorge—his assignment was the extreme Confederate left. Hatch would drive on the left or south side of the gorge—with his objective the enemy's left center. Ricketts would follow behind, offering close support. (*OR* 19 (1): 214)

531. Brig. Gen. Robert Rodes' brigade of 1,200 men held the extreme Confederate left. Four of Rodes' five Alabama regiments defended the mountain summit north of the deep gorge. The 12th Alabama was sent to the summit south of the gorge to protect a Confederate battery. Rodes was unsupported in his position. (*OR* 19 (1): 1034)

532. Robert Emmett Rodes was a 33-year-old native of Lynchburg, Virginia. He graduated from the Virginia Military Institute in 1848 and continued as an assistant professor at the school until 1851. Rodes was engaged in the profession of civil engineering when the war began. His first command was as colonel of the 5th Alabama Infantry, and his distinguished conduct at First Manassas earned him a brigadier's star in October 1861.

533. Rodes' brigade was not ordered to South Mountain until noon on the 14th. Rodes remained one half mile west of Boonsboro until Gen. Hill called for his advance at midday. Rodes then ascended the west side of South Mountain via the National Road, and when he arrived at Turner's Gap, Hill sent him north to defend the approaches north of Turner's Gap. (*OR* 19 (1): 1034)

534. Rodes discovered a good road running by his extreme left, nearly two miles north of Turner's Gap. This road climbed the east face of the mountain and after surmounting the crest turned south, intersecting with the National Road on the mountain's western slope, about one half mile west of Turner's Gap. Once over the crest, the road ran parallel to and to the rear of Rodes' position. Rodes determined he must hold this road at all hazards to prevent the enemy from "marching entirely in our rear without difficulty." (*OR* 19 (1): 1034)

535. Rodes assigned the 6th Alabama under Col. John Brown Gordon the mission of defending the mountain road on the extreme Confederate left." (*OR* 19 (1): 1034)

536. John Brown Gordon was a 30-year-old native of Upson County, Georgia. He had no military training or experience before the Civil War and began his wartime career as the captain of a Georgia mountaineer company known as the "Raccoon Roughs." No slot was available in a Georgia regiment so the "Raccoon Roughs" traveled to Alabama and were mustered in as the 12th company, 6th Alabama Infantry.

537. Brig. Gen. Truman Seymour's brigade was the first of Meade's divisions to advance against the Confederate left. It followed a narrow road that ascended South Mountain about two miles north of the National Road. This road passed the extreme Confederate left, defended by the 6th Alabama of Rodes' brigade. (*OR* 19 (1): 267, 272, 1034)

538. Gen. Meade deployed his remaining two brigades in support of Seymour's advance. Col. Thomas F. Gallagher's brigade was the second to push forward, in a parallel line behind Seymour. Col. Albert L. Magilton's brigade brought up the rear of Meade's division. (*OR* 19 (1): 267)

539. Meade outnumbered Rodes by more than three to one and the federal advance extended beyond both of Rodes' flanks. Rodes decided to sacrifice his right, and to concentrate his Alabama regiments on his left to stave off the federal advance on the critical road north of the gorge. (*OR* 19 (1): 1035)

540. Rodes' redeployment—much of it made in full view of the federals—threatened Meade's right, and he called for reinforcements. Duryea's brigade of Ricketts's division was sent up the mountain to support Meade, but due to the "distance to be traveled to reach the scene of the action," Duryea did not arrive until the close of the engagement, but did extend Seymour's left. (*OR* 19 (1): 267)

541. Seymour's men carried the summit and the road defended by Rodes, but darkness intervened and prevented a continued advance by Meade's men. Rodes abandoned his forward position and retired south toward Turner's Gap, keeping skirmishers out in case the federals decided upon a night pursuit. (*OR* 19 (1): 267, 1036)

542. Rodes' brigade suffered the second highest brigade casualties at South Mountain— 61 killed; 157 wounded; and 204 missing—total 422. Only the 686 casualties in Cobb's brigade at Crampton's Gap surpassed Rodes' losses. (Michael Priest, *Before Antietam: The Battle For South Mountain*, p. 324)

543. Accolades for Rodes appear in the report of his division commander, D. H. Hill. "Affairs were now very serious on our left," Hill began. "Rodes handled his little brigade in a most admirable and gallant manner, fighting, for hours, vastly superior odds, and maintaining the key points of the position until darkness rendered a further advance of the Yankees impossible." Hill concluded with this sage observation: "Had [Rodes] fought with less obstinacy, a practicable artillery road to the rear would have been gained on our left and the line of retreat cut off." (*OR* 19 (1): 1021)

544. Gen. Rodes had particular praise for John B. Gordon in his official report. Rodes claimed Gordon handled his 6th Alabama "in a manner I have never heard or seen equaled during this war." In addition, he praised his brigade's performance. "We did not drive the enemy back or whip him, but with 1,200 men we held his whole division at bay without assistance . . . losing in that time not over half a mile of ground." (*OR* 19 (1): 1035-1036)

545. Hatch's Union division advanced south of the gorge, simultaneous with Meade's drive on the north side of the gorge. A narrow road ascends the eastern face of the mountain south of the gorge. The road turns south about half way up the summit, and after nearly one-half mile, intersects with the National Road just east of Turner's Gap. (*OR* 19 (1): 212, 220)

546. Hatch moved up the mountain with three brigades, totaling 3,500 men deployed in a line of battle. Leading the advance was Brig. Gen. Marsena Patrick's brigade. Two hundred paces to the rear followed the brigade of Col. Walter Phelps, Jr. After another 200 pace interval was the final brigade of Brig. Gen. Abner Doubleday.

547. Hatch's men discovered the Confederates about three quarters of the way up the mountain, defending a fence running parallel to the summit, fronted by woods and backed by a cornfield full of rocky ledges.

548. Confederates returning from Hagerstown in Longstreet's command were the enemy Hatch encountered, arriving north of Turner's Gap about 5:00 p.m. Three brigades from Maj. Gen. David R. Jones's division began taking a defensive position near the Rent house along the dirt road running from Turner's Gap north into the gorge. (*OR* 19 (1): 885)

549. Jones's brigades were fatigued and straggling. Not only had they marched from Hagerstown to Boonsboro, but upon arrival at Boonsboro, they were directed south to Fox's Gap, only to be counter-marched north to Turner's Gap, and then directed still further north, during which they pass through a galling enemy artillery fire. (*OR* 19 (1): 885-886, 894-895)

550. The first Confederate brigade to arrive in position to contest Hatch was Brig. Gen. James L. Kemper's brigade of five Virginia regiments, numbering about 400 men. Second to arrive was Brig. Gen. Richard B. Garnett's brigade of five more Virginia regiments, numbering 407. Last on the scene was Micah Jenkins' South Carolina brigade, commanded by Col. Joseph Walker and totaling 562 men. (*OR* 19 (1): 885-886, 894-895)

551. Walter Phelps' brigade was the first to strike D. R. Jones's Confederates. At 80 paces from the fence defended by Garnett and Kemper, Phelps drove forward in line of battle. He seized the fence, forcing the Confederates to retire about 30-40 paces toward the summit and in the direction of Turner's Gap. Firing at this range continued for the next hour and a half. (*OR* 19 (1): 221-222, 231, 238)

552. Gen. Hatch was wounded near the fence, with the advance of Phelps' brigade. Gen. Doubleday assumed command of the division.

553. Marsena Patrick's brigade approached the Confederate position on the right of Phelps' brigade. The 80th New York and 21st New York hit the rebel right, driving away

Kemper's Virginians (defending the Confederate left). These regiments then silenced a Confederate battery operating in the near vicinity. (*OR* 19 (1): 242)

554. Doubleday's brigade arrived to relive Phelps about dusk. The Confederates attempted a counterattack, and reached to within 15 paces before Doubleday ordered his men to spring to their feet and deliver a deadly volley. Confederate dead were discovered the next morning within 30 feet of Doubleday's line. (*OR* 19 (1): 222. 235)

555. Firing continued along Doubleday's front well into dark, with both sides aiming at the flashes of the enemy's guns. William A. Christian's brigade of Ricketts' division relieved Doubleday and the federals rested on their arms throughout the night. The Confederates abandoned the position about 11:00 a.m. and began their retreat toward Sharpsburg.

556. Only one federal brigade advanced against Turner's Gap. Gen. Burnside detached John Gibbon's brigade from Hatch's division to make a demonstration against the gap through which the National Road passes. (*OR* 19 (1): 220)

557. Gibbon's brigade, with about 1,340 men, was the largest in Hatch's division. It commenced its advance west along the National Road about 5:00 p.m.

558. The National Road split Gibbon's brigade. On the north side of the Road was the 7th Wisconsin Infantry followed by the 6th Wisconsin. The lead regiment on the south side of the road was the 19th Indiana followed by the 2nd Wisconsin. About 200 yards separate the front regiments from the rear. The brigade formed in lines of battle at 3:00 p.m., but nearly two hours passed before it advanced. (*OR* 19 (1): 247, 249, 252)

559. The Confederate brigade opposing Gibbon's advance on the National Road was Col. Alfred H. Colquitt's four regiments of Georgians and the 13th Alabama—totaling 1,429 men. Colquitt had the largest brigade in D. H. Hill's division. (*OR* 19 (1): 1052)

560. Colquitt's brigade was the first Confederate infantry to arrive in defense of South Mountain. Gen. Hill positioned it at Turner's Gap on September 13 to support Jeb Stuart's rear guard cavalry actions. (*OR* 19 (1): 1052)

561. Colquitt adopted a defensive position on September 14 about half way down the eastern slope of the mountain. Three of his regiments aligned south of the National Road and two others move behind a stone wall on the north side of the road. The 13th Alabama was on Colquitt's extreme right. The 27th Georgia held the right center and the 6th Georgia anchored its left flank on the south side of the National Road. Adjoining the north side of the road was the 23rd Georgia and holding Colquitt's extreme left was the 28th Georgia. (*OR* 19 (1): 1053)

562. Gibbon's brigade was exposed to both artillery and small arms fire as it advanced the one half mile through a cornfield and into an open field fronting the woods at the base of South Mountain.

563. The first attack of Gibbon's brigade was launched against the extreme Confederate right. Four companies of Colquitt's skirmishers, concealed in a thick woods, open on the Union left. Conflicting claims confuse the story in this sector. Colquitt claimed the "sudden and unexpected fire . . . cause[d] the troops on this part of his line to give back in confusion." The regimental commanders of the 19th Indiana and the 2nd Wisconsin state that they opened a flanking fire on Colquitt's right that caused the Confederates "to retreat precipitately," bringing a cessation to fire on the front of the Hoosiers and the 2nd Wisconsin. (*OR* 19 (1): 249-250, 1053)

564. The 2nd Wisconsin and 19th Indiana, following the initial encounter on their front, turned to the right and attempted to enfilade Colquitt's two Georgia regiments holding the stone wall on the north side of the National Road. Despite the concentrated fire of four Union regiments against the 23rd and 28th Georgia—and a Union charge at only 40 paces from the wall—the Georgians held the wall into the night. "The fight continued with fury until after dark," Colquitt recorded. "Not an inch of ground was yielded." (*OR* 19 (1): 250 1053)

565. Colquitt inflicted nearly three times more casualties on Gibbon than he suffered in his brigade—318 federal casualties versus 109 Confederate casualties. Gibbon's brigade suffered the heaviest losses in the First Corps. (Priest, *Before Antietam: The Battle For South Mountain*, pp. 324-325)

566. Hooker's First Corps failed to seize Turner's Gap, but it did rupture the Confederate left north of the gap. Hooker's official account about his battle was boastful and misrepresentative. The first false conclusion—"When the advantages of the enemy's position are considered, and his preponderating numbers"—Hooker actually outnumbered the enemy he faced by nearly three to one. The second false conclusion—"the forcing of the passage of South Mountain"—Hooker failed to capture Turner's Gap and his attack on the left came too late to cut off Lee's retreat. Hooker concluded by claiming South Mountain would be "classed among the most brilliant and satisfactory achievements of this army, and its principal glory will be awarded to the First Corps." (*OR* 19 (1): 215)

567. Gen. Burnside, Hooker's immediate commander at South Mountain, discovered two additional errors in Hooker's official report. Hooker claimed Cox's division was retiring from Fox's Gap when he arrived. "This is untrue," stated Burnside. Hooker also claimed he attacked because he anticipated "no important sequence from the attack to the south of the turnpike," i.e.—Reno's attack at Fox's Gap. Burnside set the record straight, indicating that he ordered Hooker to advance four separate times. (*OR* 19 (1): 422)

568. D. H. Hill summarized the strategic implications of South Mountain. "If the battle . . was fought to prevent the advance of McClellan, it was a failure on the part of the Confederates. If it was fought to save Lee's trains and artillery, and to reunite his scattered forces, it was a Confederate success." (Hill, "The Battle of South Mountain, or Boonsboro," *Battles and Leaders of the Civil War*, p. 580)

569. George McClellan declared victory at South Mountain in a 9:40 p.m. message to General-in-Chief Halleck on the 14th: "The action continued until after dark, and terminated leaving us in possession of the entire crest." McClellan was incorrect in this assessment. His forces did not seize Turner's Gap, nor did they hold Fox's Gap. The only gap the federals controlled was Crampton's. Nevertheless, McClellan praised his men: "The troops behaved magnificently. They never fought better. . . . It has been a glorious victory." (*OR* 19 (1): 289)

The Eve of Battle

570. Robert E. Lee's first retreat, as a field commander, from a Civil War battlefield occurred when he abandoned South Mountain on the night of September 14, 1862.

571. Lee canceled the campaign in Maryland and decided to return to Virginia. This decision was made by 8:00 p.m. on Sunday the 14th.

572. Gen. Lee announced his retreat intention in a message to Lafayette McLaws. "The day has gone against us," Lee stated matter-of-factly in his opening sentence. "[T]his army will go by way of Sharpsburg and *cross the river.*" The emphasis was added—Lee was leaving Maryland. (*OR* 51 (2): 618)

573. The "day" Lee referred to in his message to McLaws had a double meaning. The "day," September 14, referred to the actions at South Mountain, where the Confederates had been attacked, losing Crampton's Gap, and barely holding on to Fox's and Turner's gaps. A second meaning for "day" expressed frustration and disappointment at the turn of events in the campaign. The unexpected advance of the Union army, while Lee's forces were divided, made it imperative that the Confederate commander consolidate his scattered army as soon as possible.

574. A second indicator showing Lee had canceled the campaign appeared when he ordered McLaws to evacuate Maryland Heights and Pleasant Valley as soon as possible. "It is necessary for you to abandon your position tonight," Lee instructed, in the second sentence of his 8:00 p.m. message to McLaws. (*OR* 51 (2): 618)

575. A third indicator of Lee's determination to retire into Virginia occurred when Lee asked McLaws to cross the river between Harpers Ferry and Shepherdstown, but "leave Shepherdstown [Boteler's] Ford for this command." This made it certain that Lee intended to move his column from South Mountain back into the Old Dominion. (*OR* 51 (2): 619)

576. The slow pace of communications—including the dependence upon couriers when no telegraphic links existed—was illustrated by Jackson's message to Lee announcing his expectation of Harpers Ferry's surrender. Jackson's message on the 14th was dated 8:15 p.m.—15 minutes *after* Lee's message to McLaws announcing the retreat back to Virginia. Both messages would be delivered by courier, but would not arrive until hours after they were written. (*OR* 19 (1): 951)

577. The first indication that Lee decided to halt the retreat came at 11:15 p.m. in a message to Lafayette McLaws. Lee notified his beleaguered subordinate that the column from South Mountain would "take position at Centreville . . . with a view of preventing the enemy . . . from cutting you off and enabling you to make a junction with [me]." (*OR* 19 (2): 608)

578. Centreville was also known as Keedysville. The village was on the Boonsboro-Sharpsburg Pike about midway between the two towns.

579. Gen. Lee provided McLaws with two options to escape his predicament in Pleasant Valley. In a message dated 11:15 p.m. on the 14th, Lee suggested passing through the

South Mountain river gap at Weverton, then heading south along the Potomac in search of a ford at Point of Rocks or Berlin (modern-day Brunswick). The second option—move to Sharpsburg via the river road beside Harpers Ferry or across Elk Ridge at Solomon's Gap.

580. Had McLaws abandoned Pleasant Valley on the night of the 14th, via the river road at Harpers Ferry, he would have encountered—head on—the escaping federal cavalry.

581. Lee gave McLaws preemptory orders to abandon Maryland Heights and Pleasant Valley early on the morning of the 15th: "You are desired to withdraw immediately from your position . . . and join us here [near Keedysville]. . . . The utmost dispatch is required." (*OR* 19 (2): 610)

582. McLaws did not follow Lee's orders to abandon his position. He acknowledged receiving several communications from Lee, but he acted, "in departing from them, as I believed the commanding general would have ordered had he known the circumstances." (*OR* 19 (1): 856)

583. McLaws listed six reasons in his official report, dated October 18, 1862, as to why he did not abandon his position: 1) the enemy occupied Crampton's Gap and northern Pleasant Valley, cutting off any hope of joining Lee near Boonsboro; 2) the Solomon's Gap escape route was too near the enemy's position in Pleasant Valley; 3) the Weverton Pass escape route depended upon a "doubtful ford" and his unlikely ability to outrun an enemy that would chase him east of South Mountain; 4) the force at Harpers Ferry could cut off his escape route "under the bluffs along the river"; 5) he could not pass over the mountain "except in a scattered and disorganized condition; and 6) "In no contingency could I have saved the trains and artillery." (*OR* 19 (1): 856)

584. Gen. McLaws did not completely evacuate his command from Pleasant Valley until the early morning of September 16. His withdrawal from in front of the Sixth Corps came nearly 24 hours after Harpers Ferry's surrender.

585. Jeb Stuart left Pleasant Valley on the morning of the 15th, later crossing the pontoon bridge at Harpers Ferry. He met with Gen. Jackson and then rode north to Gen. Lee at Sharpsburg "to communicate to him General Jackson's news and information." (*OR* 19 (1): 819)

586. George McClellan's first order on September 15 was directed to Gen. Franklin near Crampton's Gap at 1:00 a.m. It was McClellan's most ambitious order of The Maryland Campaign requiring Franklin to fight potentially on two battlefields—separated by ten miles—and to remove public property and guns to safety, as well as marching at least eight miles to cut off the enemy's escape. (*OR* 19 (1): 47)

587. "Little Mac" outlined his offensive strategy for Franklin: 1) attack and destroy the enemy in Pleasant Valley; 2) open communications with Colonel Miles at Harpers Ferry and have him join Franklin's command; 3) carry all guns and public property from Harpers Ferry, and destroy any property and spike any guns left behind; 4) proceed to Boonsboro and join in the attack against the enemy at that position; or) if the enemy has retired from Boonsboro, chase him toward Sharpsburg and cut off his line of retreat. (*OR* 19 (1): 47)

588. McClellan added a defensive component to Franklin's 1:00 a.m. instructions—occupy Pleasant Valley and place a force at Rohrersville to defend against a possible attack coming south from Boonsboro.

589. The only part of McClellan's 1:00 a.m. order that Franklin vigorously pursued was the detachment of one brigade and one battery to Rohrersville, these from the recently arrived division of Darius Couch. (*OR* 19 (1): 47)

590. Franklin began his advance from Crampton's Gap into Pleasant Valley at daylight on the 15th. Nearly three hours later, at 8:50 a.m., he reported to McClellan that "I am waiting to have [my command] closed up." He saw one brigade of Confederates in line of battle, but said he would not move forward until "I am sure Rohrersville is occupied," which may be two hours distant. Franklin feared Harpers Ferry may have surrendered due to a cessation of firing, and if so, he suggested to McClellan, "it is my opinion that I should be strongly re-enforced." (*OR* 19 (1): 47)

591. Franklin threatened no attack against McLaws on the morning of the 15th. He certainly made no aggressive effort to relieve the besieged garrison at Harpers Ferry.

592. Gen. Franklin saw McLaws' Confederates in a line of battle two miles to his front. The enemy was in a two-parallel line formation, stretching entirely across Pleasant Valley, with a large column of infantry and artillery posted on McLaws' left.

593. McLaws repositioned his 7,000 effectives in Pleasant Valley 1½ miles south of Crampton's Gap—on a high ridge running perpendicular to the valley, this following his disaster at the gap on the evening of the 14th. In one of the greatest understatements of The Maryland Campaign, "Fortunately, night came on," observed the weary McLaws, "allow[ing] a new arrangement of the troops to be made to meet the changed aspect of affairs." (*OR* 19 (1): 855)

594. Maryland Heights was abandoned by all of Kershaw's and Barksdale's infantry, with the exception of one regiment and two cannon. Anderson spread his infantry across the valley, with the remnants of Semmes', Mahone's, and Cobb's brigades in the front line and the brigades of Kershaw, Barksdale, and Wilcox anchoring the second. Maj. Gen. Richard H. Anderson commanded the parallel lines facing Crampton's Gap.

595. Four of McLaws' brigades remained in the southern end of Pleasant Valley, even after the redeployment. McLaws had to guard the gaps to his east and west. Thus, two brigades of Confederate infantry continued to guard the South Mountain gap at Weverton and two brigades watched the gap at Harpers Ferry.

596. McLaws was faced with three strategic challenges during the night of the 14th and 15th: 1) present a strong front in Pleasant Valley, facing the enemy to the north, who had cut off McLaws from any reinforcements or opportunity to escape toward Boonsboro; 2) guard the Weverton Gap to ensure no back door federal approach from the east; and 3) to hold the Harpers Ferry gap to ensure no opportunity for escape of the Union garrison. (*OR* 19 (1): 855)

597. Couriers went in search of Gen. Lee to inform the commander of McLaws' predicament. One was killed, but McLaws' aide-de-camp, Lt. Tucker, escaped. Jeb Stuart also started couriers at various times throughout the night to apprise Lee of the situation. (*OR* 19 (1): 855)

598. At 11:00 a.m. on the 15th, Gen. Franklin informed Gen. McClellan, after accessing the situation in Pleasant Valley: "The enemy outnumber me two to one. It will, of course, not answer to pursue the enemy under these circumstances . . . . I shall wait here until I learn what is the prospect of re-enforcement." Franklin outnumbered McLaws closer to two-to-one: 12,000 to 7,000. (*OR* 19 (1): 47)

599. McLaws was relieved of his predicament by Franklin's inaction. "The enemy did not advance," he marveled in his official report, "nor did they offer any opposition to the troops taking position across the valley." (*OR* 19 (1): 855)

600. McLaws learned officially of the surrender of Harpers Ferry at 10:00 a.m., when it was signaled to him from Maryland Heights. (*OR* 19 (1): 855)

601. Franklin suspected a surrender in his 8:50 note to Gen. McClellan: "If Harpers Ferry has fallen—and the cessation of firing makes me fear that it has—it is my opinion that I should be strongly re-enforced." Franklin feared the Southerners would move north from the Ferry to further strengthen Gen. McLaws. Apparently he did not consider the prospect that McLaws would retire south and join his fellow Confederates back in [West] Virginia. (*OR* 19 (1): 47)

602. The only offensive action taken by the Sixth Corps on the 15th and 16th occurred atop South Mountain at Brownsville Pass. The 6th Maine and 4th Vermont infantry seized the pass and posted two cannon there. This force could enfilade McLaws' position north of Brownsville, so about 2:00 p.m., McLaws moved to another perpendicular ridge south of the town. (*OR* 19 (1): 406, 855)

603. Gen. McClellan assigned Franklin a new responsibility at 4:30 p.m. on the 15th: [K]eep the enemy in your front without anything decisive until the Sharpsburg affair is settled." McClellan's strategy was sound—McLaws could not reinforce Lee if the federals maintained a threat in Pleasant Valley. (*OR* 51 (1): 836)

604. Only one federal brigade pursued—probably too strong a word—the retreating Confederates in Pleasant Valley on the late afternoon of the 15th. Brig. Gen. Winfield Scott Hancock's brigade and his accompanying guns "fires a few shots from the artillery into the retreating cavalry." (*OR* 19 (1): 406)

605. The cavalry brigade of Brig. Gen. Wade Hampton served as the rear guard of McLaws' force as it vacated Pleasant Valley. (*OR* 19 (1): 819)

606. Wade Hampton was a native of Charleston, South Carolina. The 44-year-old general served in both houses of the Palmetto State legislature before the war, and was reputed to be the largest landowner in the South.

607. An aide-de-camp of Jeb Stuart was captured near Rohrersville on the afternoon of the 15th bearing a message from Jackson to Gen. Lee. Franklin sent the prisoner, under guard, to Gen. McClellan at 3:15 p.m.

608. Confederates abandoned their positions at Fox's and Turner's gaps between 10:00 and 11:00 p.m. on September 14, retiring from Turner's via the National Road to

Boonsboro, and then via the Sharpsburg Pike toward Keedysville. Confederates left Fox's Gap via the Old Sharpsburg Road, but then rejoined the main column near Boonsboro.

609. The first Confederate infantry to arrive at Sharpsburg was the 5th and 6th Alabama regiments of Rodes' brigade. They were dispatched from Keedysville, about midnight, "to drive out a Federal cavalry force reported to be [at Sharpsburg]." The cavalry was Davis' column escaping from Harpers Ferry. (*OR* 19 (1): 1036)

610. Rodes initially received orders to rush both his brigade and Colquitt's to Sharpsburg. This indicated the severity of the alarm caused by the presence of the escaping Harpers Ferry cavalry along Lee's line of retreat. Gen. Lee, under no circumstances, could permit enemy forces to block the Sharpsburg-Shepherdstown Pike.

611. McClellan's first message to General Halleck announcing the Confederate retreat was fanciful. "[T]he enemy is making for Shepherdstown in a perfect panic," McClellan exaggerated at 8:00 a.m. on the 15th. "General Lee last night stated publicly that he must admit they had been shockingly whipped." (*OR* 19 (1): 294)

612. "General Lee is reported wounded," McClellan proclaimed in his second message to Halleck, dated 10:00 a.m. on the 15th. "Little Mac's" fantasy continued: "Information this moment received completely confirms the rout and demoralization of the rebel army." (*OR* 19 (1): 295)

613. Fitzhugh Lee's cavalry served as the rear guard of the Confederate army during its retreat from South Mountain to Sharpsburg. It began a running fight with the Union cavalry east of Boonsboro and through the town that continued two miles west of the village.

614. Brig. Gen. Alfred Pleasonton, McClellan's chief of cavalry, led the pursuit of the federals on the morning of the 15th.

615. The primary rear guard action occurred east of Boonsboro, then through the town's streets to the western edge of the village, as Fitzhugh Lee deployed the 9th Virginia Cavalry, under Col. W. H. F. "Rooney" Lee, to stave off repeated attacks of the 8th Illinois Cavalry.

616. "Rooney" Lee was Gen. Robert E. Lee's second eldest son. He was unhorsed and badly bruised, but after hours of close contact with the enemy, he managed to make his way west and into Confederate lines.

617. September 15, 1862, was one of the hardest days of the war for the 9th Virginia Cavalry. The regiment suffered 18 killed or mortally wounded and 10 captured during its rearguard action.

618. Confederates maintained a "bold front" in the Hagerstown area until 8:30 p.m. on September 14, according to an observation filed by Maj. Gen. John Reynolds on the evening of the 14th. Reynolds was arriving at Chambersburg and Greencastle to command the Pennsylvania emergency militia. (*OR* 19 (2): 293)

619. Federal forces coming from Pennsylvania occupied Hagerstown at 4:00 p.m. on the 15th. Both the telegraph and railroad to Hagerstown were operating. (*OR* 19 (2): 306)

620. Six roads intersect at Sharpsburg, coming from each direction of the compass. Three of the six roads are turnpikes—the Hagerstown Pike running north, the Boonsboro

Pike stretching east, and the Shepherdstown Pike traveling west toward the Potomac. Another road leading south connects Sharpsburg with Harpers Ferry.

621. Three stone bridges spanned Antietam Creek in the vicinity of Sharpsburg. Each played a role in the campaign. The Middle Bridge lies between the other two and carries the primary east-west road, the Boonsboro-Sharpsburg Turnpike. The Upper Bridge, approximately 2½ miles upstream from the Middle Bridge, carried the road running from Keedysville north and west toward Williamsport. The Lower Bridge, about one mile downstream from the Middle Bridge, was the avenue for the road leading south and east toward Rohrersville.

622. Gen. Lee learned of the surrender of Harpers Ferry about noon on the 15th, when a courier arrived from Jackson delivering the welcome news.

623. Lee's line of defense stretched, from north to south, nearly four miles—equal to the length of his line at Gettysburg. From Lee's left, posted on the Potomac, the position arced southeast toward Antietam Creek, then ran south paralleling the creek. The Confederate right overlooked Antietam Creek below the Lower Bridge.

624. Lee defended two of the three Antietam bridge crossings—the Middle Bridge was covered with artillery and the Lower Bridge by infantry. The Upper Bridge, located too far east of the Confederates' left anchor on the Potomac, remained uncontested.

625. When Lee determined to make his stand along the west bank of Antietam Creek, 26 of his 40 infantry brigades—or nearly two-thirds of his army—were at Harpers Ferry.

626. Stonewall Jackson rode ahead of his column marching north from Harpers Ferry, arriving at Sharpsburg at noon on the 16th.

627. No Confederates marched through Maryland from Harpers Ferry to Antietam. All the Southerners racing from Harpers Ferry toward Sharpsburg traveled north through Jefferson County, [West] Virginia. The Confederates crossed the river at Boteler's Ford, about 1½ miles south of Shepherdstown, [West] Virginia.

628. Boteler's Ford was three miles east of Lee's position at Sharpsburg. It represented the Confederates' link back into [West] Virginia, and the only practicable ford across the Potomac in that region.

629. Boteler's Ford was identified by four different names: (1) Boteler's on the [West] Virginia bank; 2) Blackford's on the Maryland shore; 3) Packhorse Ford, a colonial label that referred to the river crossing during the migrations from Pennsylvania south into the Shenandoah Valley; and 4) Confederates referred to it as Shepherdstown Ford during The Maryland Campaign

630. Half of Lee's Harpers Ferry detachment—comprising the divisions of Jackson, Ewell, and Walker—arrived on the 16th, bolstering Lee's ranks from 15,000 to 26,000 defenders.

631. The Stonewall Division, under J. R. Jones, completed cooking its two-days' rations at midnight and began marching toward Sharpsburg at 1:00 a.m. on the 16th. (*OR* 19 (1): 1007)

632. Jackson's chief of artillery, Col. Stapleton Crutchfield, returned to Harpers Ferry on the 16th at the request of Gen. Lee's artillery chief Brig. Gen. William Nelson Pendleton.

Pendleton wanted Crutchfield to "get together batteries of the captured guns and such ammunition as I could" and send it to Shepherdstown or Sharpsburg. (*OR* 19 (1): 962-963)

633. No batteries from the captured booty at Harpers Ferry joined Gen. Lee at Sharpsburg. The reason: "I found the quartermaster in charge of the captured guns," Crutchfield reported, "and found he had been busy removing them, and in so doing had mismatched the caissons, limbers, and guns to such an extent that after vainly spending half the day at it, I gave up the task of getting together any batteries." (*OR* 19 (1): 963)

634. Three Confederate batteries—Brown's, Dement's, and Latimer's—were left behind at Harpers Ferry "on account of the condition of their horses." Col. Crutchfield supplied these batteries with fresh horses, and they later proceeded to Sharpsburg. (*OR* 19 (1): 963)

635. Two 3-inch ordnance rifles captured at Harpers Ferry were sent to Sharpsburg in Latimer's battery. Col. Crutchfield exchanged the two 3-inch rifles for two 10-pounder Parrotts "whose vent-pieces had burned out in the action" at Harpers Ferry. (*OR* 19 (1): 963)

636. The most difficult march from Harpers Ferry to Sharpsburg was endured by McLaws' command. It had to pass from Pleasant Valley in Maryland, crossing over the river at Harpers Ferry, then re-crossing the Potomac again at Boteler's Ford. (*OR* 19 (1): 857-858)

637. McLaws crossed the Potomac at Harpers Ferry over a federal pontoon bridge that was not destroyed during the siege. McLaws' trek from Pleasant Valley across the Potomac was impeded by "paroled prisoners passing over the bridge," and "any accident to the bridge," causing "temporary halts in the trains or batteries." (*OR* 19 (1): 857)

638. McLaws' command crossed the Potomac at Boteler's Ford beginning about 2:30 a.m. on the 17th.

639. McClellan's effective strength along Antietam Creek on September 16 was 71,500 men. He outnumbered Lee nearly three to one.

640. McClellan believed—and the emphasis must be placed upon *believed*—the Confederate army opposing him on the west bank of Antietam Creek numbered in excess of 100,000 men. Hence, by McClellan's accounting, it was he and his army that were deficient in troop strength.

641. With the arrival of Jackson and a portion of his forces from Harpers Ferry, Lee divided his line of defense into two wings. Jackson commanded the left from the Dunker Church north and west to the Potomac. Longstreet directed the army from its center at the Sunken Road south to the Lower Bridge.

642. One third of Lee's army—the divisions of McLaws, R. H. Anderson, and A. P. Hill—were not present on the battlefield when action began at dawn on the 17th.

643. The first report informing McClellan that Lee was forming a battle line on the west bank of Antietam Creek arrived at 12:40 p.m. on the 15th from a signal station established at the ruins of the old Washington Monument just north of Turner's Gap.

The Middle Bridge Across Antietam Creek *(USAMHI)*

644. The first Union division to arrive on the west bank of Antietam Creek, on the early-afternoon of the 15th, was Maj. Gen. Israel B. Richardson's division of the Second Corps. Richardson deployed in line of battle on both sides of the Boonsboro-Sharpsburg Pike overlooking the Middle Bridge. (*OR* 19 (1): 54, 293)

645. The Irish Brigade of the Second Corps led the Union pursuit of Lee's army toward Sharpsburg. (*OR* 19 (1): 293)

646. Brig. Gen. Thomas Francis Meagher deployed his Irish Brigade as follows: the 88th and 63rd New York infantry on the north side of the Boonsboro Pike; the 69th New York and the 29th Massachusetts holding the south side.

647. The first Union force to come under artillery fire at Antietam was the Irish Brigade, commencing on the afternoon of the 15th. The 88th and 63rd New York were "constantly annoyed." (*OR* 19 (1): 293)

648. The second Union division to arrive at the banks of Antietam Creek was George Sykes's division of the Fifth Corps. Sykes extended Richardson's Irish Brigade line south of the Boonsboro-Sharpsburg Pike. (*OR* 19 (1): 54)

649. Sykes deployed skirmishers in direct view of the Middle Bridge to thwart any attempt to destroy the structure. Throughout the 15th and 16th, the "only annoyances" were the fire of the enemy's sharpshooters and "his scattering shot and shell." (*OR* 19 (1): 350)

650. The first corps commander to arrive at Antietam Creek was Maj. Gen. Joseph Hooker.

651. Hooker estimated the Confederate strength arrayed before him at 30,000 men. "All of his troops appeared exposed to view," Hooker noted in his official report dated November 8, 1862. The Confederates appeared to be "ostentatiously deployed in two lines" perpendicular to the Boonsboro Pike, with batteries in support. (*OR* 19 (1): 217)

652. Hooker excused any attempted attack by his force on the 15th. "Fully conscious of my weakness in number and *morale*, I did not feel strong enough to attack him in front, even after the arrival of the First Corps." (*OR* 19 (1): 217)

653. A peculiar movement was observed by Hooker on the late afternoon of the 15th. The left of the Confederate line, deployed about one mile north of Sharpsburg, " break[s] into column and march[s] to the rear, behind a forest." This forest soon became famous as the "West Woods." By 5:00 p.m., Hooker determined "one-half of the enemy's infantry force had passed to the rear." (*OR* 19 (1): 217)

654. Hooker considered moving north to parallel the Confederate movement, but abandoned the idea because it would require a night march "through a country of which we were profoundly ignorant." (*OR* 19 (1): 217)

655. The first federal engineers to arrive at Antietam Creek were dispatched by Hooker north from the Boonsboro Pike to find practicable fords for a potential move in that direction. The engineers discovered two fords and the Upper Bridge. (*OR* 19 (1): 217)

656. McClellan began a "rapid examination" of the Antietam Creek position at 3:00 p.m. on the 15th. The concentration of staff, generals, and horses on the ridge east of the creek attracted Confederate artillery fire, forcing McClellan to disperse the party. McClellan and Gen. Porter continued the reconnaissance alone. (*OR* 19 (1): 54)

657. McClellan established his headquarters at the Philip Pry house. The headquarters sat atop a commanding knoll, approximately 400 yards from the Boonsboro Pike, on the eastern side of Antietam Creek. The building was centrally located opposite the middle of the Confederate line.

658. George Armstrong Custer—who later gained fame at the Little Big Horn—was the Union staff officer who announced to the Pry's on the afternoon of the 15th: "General McClellan, the commander-in-chief of the Army of the Potomac, desires to make his headquarters here." (John Schildt, *Roads to Antietam*, p. 101)

659. The Pry House, built in 1844, was an upper-middle class Federal style brick house with an imposing Greek Revival portico. The two-story building had a "hatch" in the northwest corner of the roof that provided access to chimneys and gutters. McClellan's staff utilized the roof portal as an observation post.

660. From the Pry House, looking west, McClellan could see the center, left center, and right center of Lee's line. Key landmarks on the battlefield, however, were not visible to the Union commander. Views of the enemy's left—including the North Woods and The Cornfield—were blocked by the intervening East Woods. The Dunker Church and much of the Hagerstown Pike could not be seen because they were hidden behind a ridge. The Lower Bridge on the Confederate right could not be seen by McClellan because it was depressed into Antietam Creek's drainage.

McCLELLAN'S HEADQUARTERS, ANTIETAM
PUBLISHED BY M. L. BURGAN

The Pry House [McClellan's Headquarters]
M. L. Burgan Postcard (*ANB*)

661. Battlefield surveillance for the federals was improved somewhat with the establishment of a signal station on nearby Red Hill. Although at a greater elevation, terrain changes remained difficult to distinguish, in part due to the greater distance from the Confederate line.

662. None of the town of Sharpsburg, with the exception of the Lutheran Church steeple, was visible from Union headquarters at the Pry House.

663. All of the town of Sharpsburg was behind Confederate lines.

664. Since the battle of South Mountain had separated the First Corps from the Ninth Corps, the wing Burnside had command of was split. McClellan thus "temporarily" suspended Burnside as commander of the right wing on the 15th and directed Hooker to report directly to his headquarters. (*OR* 19 (2): 290, 297)

665. Some unknown problem delayed the advance of the Ninth Corps from Fox's Gap on the morning of the 15th. (*OR* 19 (2): 296)

666. Fifth Corps commander Fitz John Porter discovered, three hours after the designated time, that Burnside had not moved. Porter complained that Burnside was obstructing his advance. McClellan ordered the lead division of the Fifth Corps, under George Sykes, to push by Burnside's men atop South Mountain. (*OR* 19 (2): 296)

667. Burnside received a stiff censure from McClellan on the 16th—for his apparent delay of four hours—before advancing from South Mountain. He was also censored for his late arrival on the east bank of Antietam Creek. McClellan demanded "explanations of these failures."   The commanding general exploded in his last sentence: "[I] cannot lightly regard such marked departure from the tenor of [my] instructions." *(OR* 19 (2): 308)

668. McClellan discovered only one of Burnside's divisions and four batteries in position along the Antietam by sunset of the 16th. "Little Mac" reminded Burnside in his September 16 missive that his corps was supposed to be in place on the Union left by noon on the 16th. *(OR* 19 (2): 308)

669. A heavy fog shrouded the Antietam Valley at dawn on the 16th. McClellan wired Halleck in Washington at 7:00 a.m. that the fog "has thus far prevented us doing more than to ascertain that some of the enemy are still there." In the same message, McClellan promised to attack "as soon as the situation of the enemy is developed." *(OR* 19 (2): 307-308)

670. McClellan squandered the 16th, delivering no major assault. Instead, as he rationalized in his official report, he was busy "examining the ground, finding fords, clearing the approaches, and hurrying up the ammunition and supply trains. . . ." *(OR* 19 (1): 55)

671. As late as the 16th, General-in-Chief Halleck believed the Confederate presence in western Maryland was a ruse. The real target, he argued, was Washington. "I think . . . you will find that the whole force of the enemy in your front has crossed the river," Halleck wired McClellan. "I fear now more than ever that they will recross the river at Harpers Ferry, or below, and turn your left, thus cutting you off from Washington." *(OR* 19 (1): 41)

672. Between noon and 2 p.m. on the 16th, McClellan made the decision that he would fight the next day. He informed his staff: "[T]omorrow we fight the battle that will decide the fate of the republic." (Sears, *Landscape Turned Red*, p. 174)

673. No written orders for September 16 outlining McClellan's battle plan have been discovered. Neither did McClellan call a conference of his commanders to outline his design.

674. McClellan's plan of attack was clear in one respect—he intended to crush Lee's left or northern flank. Beyond this certainty, McClellan's plan was muddled by conflicting accounts in his *own* post-battle reports and reflections.

675. A strategy of attacking and destroying the Confederate left could produce this happy outcome for McClellan—a portion of his army would be wedged between Lee and the Potomac, potentially trapping Lee in Maryland. Success on the left and a subsequent position behind Lee's rear would also cut off Confederate reinforcements attempting to arrive from Harpers Ferry.

676. The Union First Corps, under Maj. Gen. Joseph Hooker, was selected by McClellan to lead the attack against the Confederate left flank. Hooker received his instructions between 1:00 and 2:00 p.m. on the 16th.

677. The flank march designed to turn Lee's left commenced at 4:00 p.m. on the 16th. Hooker's First Corps left the vicinity of Keedysville and marched north and west on the old Williamsport Road. The movement was initially screened from the Confederates by a steep linear north-south ridge that paralleled Little Antietam Creek.

678. Leading the infantry in the flanking column was George Meade's division of Pennsylvania Reserves. Following Meade was James Ricketts. This column crossed Antietam Creek at the Upper Bridge. Abner Doubleday's division crossed the creek at an unnamed ford below the bridge.

679. Scouting and screening for the flanking column were three companies of the 3rd Pennsylvania Cavalry.

680. Hooker's flanking column crossed Antietam Creek at the Upper Bridge unopposed. The only other point on the battlefield where the federals met no resistance crossing the creek was at Pry's Ford, about one mile downstream from the Upper Bridge.

681. At the hamlet of Smoketown, which no longer exists, Hooker shifted the direction of his flank march from west to south. The First Corps left the old Williamsport Road and began marching south on the Smoketown Road. It remains a mystery why Hooker decided to use the Smoketown Road—and not the Hagerstown Pike, only one mile further west—as his primary route of access to the Confederate left.

682. McClellan and his staff joined Hooker on the early evening of the 16th as the flank march was concluding. Hooker complained that his isolated corps was too small "to attack the whole rebel army." He asked for reinforcements, punctuating his message with a warning: "[T]he rebels will eat me up." (*OR* 19 (1): 217)

683. McClellan bolstered Hooker's flanking column with the addition of the Twelfth Corps of Maj. Gen. Joseph K. F. Mansfield—nearly 7,200 strong.

684. The only night march involving a Union force at Antietam occurred during the night of the 16th and 17th when the Twelfth Corps marched across the Upper Bridge and followed Hooker's route to the Confederate left. (*OR* 19 (1): 484)

685. Brig. Gen. Samuel Crawford's brigade led the Twelfth Corps on its nighttime flank march. The corps bivouacked for the night astride the Smoketown Road and on the George Line farm, about one-mile north of Hooker's front line. The Twelfth Corps went into bivouac between 2:00 and 3:00 a.m.

686. The combined force in McClellan's flanking column was just under 16,700 infantrymen—about 23% of the Union army's effective strength when the battle began.

687. The opening skirmish of the battle of Antietam occurred about 6:00 p.m. on the 16th when two companies of the 3rd Pennsylvania Cavalry encountered Evander Laws' brigade of John Bell Hood's division in the East Woods.

688. The first Union officer killed at Antietam was Col. Hugh McNeil, commander of the Pennsylvania Bucktails (13th Pennsylvania Reserves). McNeil was shot through the heart when his regiment encountered Confederate outposts at the George Line farm, near the junction of the old Williamsport Road and the Smoketown Road. (*OR* 19 (1): 270)

689. The first Confederate colonel mortally wounded at Antietam was Col. Philip Frank Liddell, commander of the 11th Mississippi Infantry. Liddell fell during the fighting of the 16th in the East Woods. (*OR* 19 (1): 923)

690. The extent of McClellan's flank march was badly compromised on the evening of the 16th when Hooker "telegraphed his punch" to Gen. Lee. Hooker pressed forward Truman Seymour's *entire brigade* from George Meade's Pennsylvania Reserves to determine the position and strength of the Confederate left. This reconnaissance in force alerted Lee to the federal presence *en masse*. The Pennsylvanians suffered 95 casualties in heavy skirmishing in the vicinity of the East Woods. (*OR* 19 (1): 269, 277)

691. Gen. Lee correctly anticipated his left was McClellan's primary target. Throughout the night of the 16th and 17th, Lee bolstered his left by re-deploying his force, moving troops from south to north.

692. The new defensive line established on the Confederate left, shifted from an eastward orientation to one facing due north. The new position was one-half mile south of Hooker's September 16 bivouac. The right anchor was the East Woods and the left protected approaches along the Hagerstown Pike. Hooker thus faced the heart of a repositioned and reinforced Confederate left rather than the enemy's extreme left flank.

693. The Hagerstown Pike, a north-south axis running the length of Lee's line from his center to his left, provided the Confederates with a strategic advantage as an "interior line." Throughout the 16th and 17th, Lee would utilize the Hagerstown Pike to rapidly move infantry and artillery to pressure points.

694. McClellan could not see Confederate movements along much of the Hagerstown Pike because it sat astride a paralleling north-south ridge that blocked McClellan's view of the road in most areas.

695. Gen. Lee constructed no earthworks at Antietam, even though he was in a defensive posture for four days, beginning on the 15th and remaining on the defensive into the night of the 18th. Gen. McClellan would construct no entrenchments either, even after seizing positions during his attacks of the 17th.

696. Gen. Lee concentrated his artillery on three different ridges: 1) Nicodemous Heights on the Confederate left, one mile northwest of the Dunker Church; 2) a ridge east of the Dunker Church, near the middle of his line; and 3) a ridge east of Sharpsburg, today the location of the Antietam National Cemetery.

697. Following the heavy skirmishing on the evening of the 16th, Hood convinced both Lee and Jackson to allow his division to retire from the front, but only with the guarantee that if called upon, he would respond at once with his 2,400 men. Hood pulled back from the East Woods to the vicinity of the Dunker Church about 10:00 p.m., where his men rested for the night.

698. Hood's men had been without food for three days, with the exception of a half ration of beef and some green corn. (*OR* 19 (1): 923)

699. Hooker's First Corps camped on the north end of the Joseph Poffenberger farm on the night of the 16th. The bivouac was sandwiched between the Smoketown Road to the east and the Hagerstown Pike to the west.

700. The average Union regiment at Antietam numbered 350 men. The average Confederate regiment equaled about 200 soldiers.

701. Supporting McClellan's infantry at Antietam were 293 cannon. Gen. Lee's Army of Northern Virginia had 246 guns. The Union army had 3.5 cannon per 1,000 men—Lee's army had six pieces per 1,000 men.

Knap's Independent Battery E (Pennsylvania Light Artillery) participated in the fighting between the East and West Woods. (*USAMHI*)

702. The Union Sixth Corps was not present on the Antietam Battlefield when the battle began at dawn on the 17th. The Sixth Corps received orders on the night of the 16th to move from Pleasant Valley and Rohrersville toward Keedysville. (*OR* 19 (1): 376)

703. Gen. Franklin commenced the march of the Sixth Corps at 5:30 a.m. on the 17th—about 15 minutes before the battle began. His lead division would arrive near McClellan's headquarters at 10:00 a.m.

704. The first federals across the Middle Bridge were US Regulars in the 4th Infantry. This regiment was in possession of the bridge shortly after 7:00 a.m. on the 16th. It was relieved at sundown by the 1st Battalion of the 12th Infantry. (*OR* 19 (1): 356-357)

705. The Union army never lost possession of the Middle Bridge—nor was the bridge ever attacked during the battle.

706. Clara Barton arrived just behind Union lines about 1:00 p.m. on the 16th. She was traveling with a wagon-full of medical supplies.

707. A dog traveling with the 103rd New York Infantry nearly created a panic on McClellan's left (Burnside's sector) on the night of the 16th. A member of the 103rd stumbled over the regimental canine and then staggered against a stack of muskets, knocking them over. Two regiments believed they were under attack before order was restored. (David Thompson, "With Burnside at Antietam," *Battles and Leaders of the Civil War*, p. 660)

708. On the night of the 16th, McClellan ordered no fires in the bivouacs of the First and Twelfth Corps, apparently in an attempt to disguise the Union position on Lee's left. As a result, dried coffee beans became dinner and breakfast for thousands of Northern soldiers. For many, it was their last meal.

709. A light rain began falling about 9:00 p.m. on the 16th. The miserable and steady drizzle continued throughout the long night.

Middle Bridge across Antietam Creek (*USAMHI*)

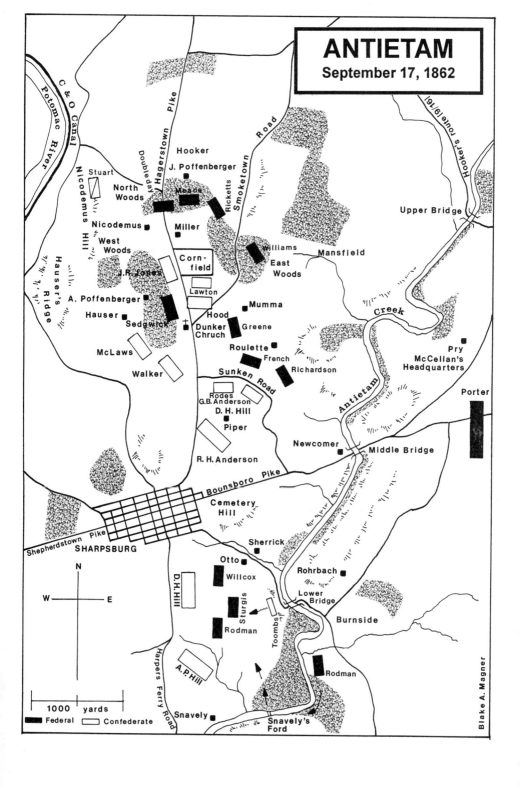

ANTIETAM
September 17, 1862

C & O Canal
Potomac River
Nicodemus Hill
Hauser's Ridge

Doubleday
Hagerstown Pike
Hooker
J. Poffenberger
Smoketown Road
Hooker's route 9/16/62

Stuart
North Woods
Meade
Ricketts
Upper Bridge

Nicodemus
Miller
Williams
Mansfield

West Woods
Corn-field
East Woods

J.R. Jones
Lawton

A. Poffenberger
Mumma
Creek

Hauser
Hood
Dunker Chruch
Greene
Sedgwick

McLaws
Roulette
French
Pry McClellan's Headquarters

Walker
Sunken Road
Richardson

Rodes
G.B. Anderson
Porter

D. H. Hill
Piper

R. H. Anderson
Newcomer
Middle Bridge

Boonsboro Pike

Antietam

Cemetery Hill

Shepherdstown Pike
SHARPSBURG
Sherrick

N
Otto
Rohrbach
W — E
Willcox
Lower Bridge
S
D.H.Hill
Sturgis
Toombs
Burnside
Rodman

Harpers Ferry Road
A.P.Hill
Rodman

1000 yards
Snavely
Snavely's Ford
Federal   Confederate

Blake A. Magner

Early Morning:
The Cornfield, East Woods, and West Woods

710. Sunrise on Wednesday, September 17, was at 5:43 a.m.

711. Gen. Lee arose about 4 a.m. on the 17th.

712. At 4:30 a.m., Gen. Lee ordered his chief of artillery, Brig. Gen. William Nelson Pendleton—who was located on the Virginia side of the Potomac River—to keep artillery in position to guard each of the fords at Williamsport, Falling Waters, and Shepherdstown. (*OR* 19 (2): 610)

713. The temperature at daybreak on the 17th was a comfortable 65 degrees. The high temperature reached 75 degrees by mid-afternoon. Relative humidity measured a nearly intolerable 71 per cent, and the winds were calm, barely moving at two miles per hour from the west. Clouds were high and scattered.

714. The first phase of the battle lasted just over 3½ hours. It can be divided into two sub phases, based upon geography and time. The first phase opened at dawn, just before 6:00 a.m., when the federals attacked in the East Woods, The Cornfield and adjoining pastures. The opening phase concluded just before 9:00 a.m. The second phase began about 9:00 a.m. and closed 30 minutes later with a Union assault into—followed by a precipitous retreat out of—the West Woods.

715. In the battle's first three hours, there were nearly 8,000 Union and Confederate casualties within a 700-yard radius of the center of The Cornfield.

716. The Cornfield is a 30-acre plot owned by farmer D. R. Miller. By mid-19th-century farming practices corn kernels were planted by hand in small dirt "hills," usually about three feet apart. "Rows" were irregular, subject to the guidance of the horse and plow. Full-grown native corn—not yet subject to genetic improvements—typically grew no higher than 6½ feet. Visibility within such a cornfield, with normal stalk height and average spacing between hills, was good.

717. Confederates skirmishers occupied The Cornfield at the outset of the battle—not because they were "hiding in the corn"—but because the terrain provided an east-west ridge ideal for tactical defense, especially in blocking federal attacks from the north.

718. Although The Cornfield was only 30 acres, "The Battle of The Cornfield" refers to combat areas encompassing approximately 150 acres, including attacks and counterattacks in *open pastures bordering* The Cornfield on its north, west, and southern boundaries.

719. The famous woods of Antietam—North Woods, East Woods, and West Woods— were military designations assigned after the battle by US Army engineers who later mapped the battlefield.

720. Three different Poffenberger families farmed property in the area encompassing the battle's first phase: Joseph Poffenberger (North Woods); Samuel Poffenberger (East Woods); and Alfred Poffenberger (West Woods).

D. R. Miller House [circa 1885] (*ANB*)

721. Very little undergrowth cluttered or tangled the wood lots at Antietam. The trees were mature old hardwoods, and visibility within the woods was excellent. Dr. William Child, an assistant surgeon of the 5th New Hampshire Infantry recalled: "You might drive a wagon through the trees anywhere." (Paul Chiles, "Artillery Hell! The Guns of Antietam," *Blue and Gray Magazine*, No.2 (1998), p. 16.)

722. The objective of Gen. Hooker's attack was an elevated plateau opposite the Dunker Church. From Hooker's opening position in the North Woods, the Church was one mile south, and clearly visible—its whitewashed brick exterior stood out like a full moon against the dark background of the West Woods. The federal ranks were told to aim for the church.

723. Maj. Gen. Joseph Hooker, commander of the Union advance against the enemy left, was a Massachusetts native and grandson of a Revolutionary War veteran.

724. Hooker's infantry totals about 8,600 men. Opposing him are 7,700 Confederates under Stonewall Jackson.

725. Hooker did not wait for the arrival of the Twelfth Corps, bivouacked one-mile to his rear, before he attacked. As a result—instead of boasting a more than two to one numerical advantage over the Confederates—Hooker's numbers are nearly the same as the enemy's.

726. The First Corps was comprised of three divisions. Hooker aligned James Ricketts' division on his left, facing the East Woods. In the middle was the Pennsylvania Reserve division of George G. Meade, facing the North Woods and The Cornfield. Positioned on the right was Abner Doubleday's division astride the Hagerstown Pike.

727. Brig. Gen. Abner Doubleday had commanded his division for only two days. He replaced Brig. Gen. John Hatch, who was wounded at South Mountain on the 14th.

728. Abner Doubleday *did not invent* baseball. Doubleday, who has a stadium named in his honor at Cooperstown's Baseball Hall of Fame, helped popularize the sport during the last decades of the 19th-century.

729. Gen. Ricketts' was the only division commander in Hooker's First Corps who did not serve with McClellan during the Peninsula Campaign.

730. Every division commander in Hooker's First Corps was serving in the Regular Army at the outbreak of the war.

731. Two lieutenant colonels commanded Union brigades in The Cornfield/East Woods sector. Robert Anderson, lieutenant colonel of the 9th Pennsylvania Reserves, led the Third brigade of Meade's First Corps division into action north of The Cornfield. Lieut. Col. Hector Tyndale helped drive the Confederates out of the East Woods while commanding the First brigade of Greene's division in the Twelfth Corps.

732. A peculiar and abrupt north-south ridge that begins near the North Woods and continues 800 yards south to The Cornfield—running perpendicular to Hooker's line of attack—made it nearly impossible for Doubleday's federals (operating along the Hagerstown Turnpike), to see the movements of Meade and Ricketts in the center and left of the Union advance.

733. Men from Richard S. "Old Baldy" Ewell's division were the Confederates holding The Cornfield/East Woods sector at dawn on the 17th. Ewell was not present at Antietam, having suffered a severe leg wound at Second Manassas that required amputation of the limb.

734. Supporting the Confederate infantry in The Cornfield/East Woods area was Col. Stephen D. Lee's artillery battalion of four batteries. Lee established his position on a plateau opposite the Dunker Church—the same plateau Hooker had targeted as his objective. (*OR* 19 (1): 845)

735. Holding the extreme Confederate left, on a north-south ridge named Nicodemus Heights, were the 15 guns of Jeb Stuart's horse artillery, commanded by John Pelham. From this position, the gunners had an unobstructed line of fire into the right flank of the federal advance down the Hagerstown Pike.

736. Nicodemus Heights, strategically speaking, was the "Little Round Top of Antietam." If the Confederates lost this ground dominating their extreme left flank, Lee's entire line of defense north of Sharpsburg would become untenable. The line was, however, temporarily abandoned around 6:30 a.m.

737. Hooker never ordered an infantry attack against Nicodemus Heights—the key strategic position to the opening phase of the battle. No explanation exists as to why.

738. Stuart's Horse Artillery suffered no casualties at Antietam, even though it was in action much of the day.

Confederate Dead near the Dunker Church (*USAMHI*)

739. Supporting Hooker's advance were thirty 20-pounder Parrott rifles on the heights overlooking the east bank of Antietam Creek. Firing at a range of 3,000-3,500 yards, these guns caused great consternation, misery, and death for Confederate infantry and artillery operating in the Dunker Church/East Woods area. The Confederates did not have the long-range cannon to respond.

740. The Confederate artillery battalion of Stephen Dill Lee suffered ten times the normal rate of casualties at its position on the ridge opposite the Dunker Church—an easy target of the federal 20-pounder Parrotts on the east side of Antietam Creek.

741. Col. S. D. Lee declared Sharpsburg "artillery hell" two months after the battle in a conversation with fellow gunner E. P. Alexander.

742. The Cornfield was *not* the battlefront position of the Confederates at the opening of the fray. Instead, the Southern line was 150 yards south of The Cornfield in a rolling pasture of clover. The Confederate line, on the left, faced due north toward the D. R. Miller house and barn. The Confederate line then angled southeast toward the Samuel Mumma farm, following a ridgeline that was ideal for tactical defense.

743. The earliest report of firing on the 17th was at 3:00 a.m. This was the time when "firing commences along the line," according to Gen. Hood in his after-action report. (*OR* 19 (1): 923)

744. The first federal advance occurred at dawn on the 17th, when Truman Seymour's brigade of Pennsylvania Reserves moved to the southern edge of the East Woods to establish Hooker's extreme left. (*OR* 19 (1): 272)

745. The Pennsylvania "Bucktails" (13th Pennsylvania Infantry Reserves) led Seymour's assault. The "Bucktails" were armed with Sharps single-shot breechloading rifles, similar to those used by John Brown in his 1859 raid on Harpers Ferry. (*OR* 19 (1): 272)

746. The Confederate brigade of Isaac Trimble, comprised of the 21st Georgia, 21st North Carolina, and the 15th Alabama, defended the Confederate right, holding a ridge line and plowed field on the Mumma farm. Seymour's Pennsylvanians stalled before this resistance and the federals retired into the East Woods, ending the first attack by about 6:20 a.m.

747. The second federal assault, led by Abram Duryea's 1,100-man brigade of Ricketts' division, advanced against the Confederate center shortly after 6:00 a.m.—directly into the heart of The Cornfield. Duryea's movement outdistanced his support on both flanks. The attack failed when A. R. Lawton's brigade of Confederates, with support from Trimble's brigade, turned Duryea's exposed left flank, forcing him to retire about 6:30 a.m.

748. General Ricketts failed to provide support for Duryea, but not intentionally. His remaining two brigades suffered from command breakdowns. Brig. Gen. George Hartsuff was wounded by a shell fragment while reconnoitering, subsequently resulting in confusion and a late start for his brigade. Col. William Christian became frightened—cowardly fleeing to the rear—leaving his alarmed brigade temporarily without leadership.

749. Duryea's brigade suffered nearly 33 percent casualties in just 30 minutes of fighting. His brigade did not return to action that day.

750. The 12th Georgia, which came into the battle with only 100 men, helped hold against Duryea's advance, and lost 40 killed or wounded in the opening half-hour of action.

751. For his cowardice at Antietam, Col. William Christain resigned his commission two days after the battle.

752. Gen. Ricketts commanded a Union battery in the battle of First Manassas. He pressed his cannon forward and fought in close order battle on Henry House Hill with Stonewall Jackson's brigade.

753. At First Manassas, Ricketts was shot four times and captured by the Confederates. He was not exchanged until six months later.

754. The third federal assault—unlike the first two that bore down on the Confederate right and center—struck Stonewall's Jackson's left. Using the Hagerstown Pike as its guide, John Gibbon's brigade formed the advance of Gen. Doubleday's division, and began pressing south about 6:00 a.m.

755. Gen. Doubleday's father was a two-term congressman from New York State.

756. Gibbon's "Black Hat Brigade" was comprised of three Wisconsin regiments and the 19th Indiana. It straddled the Hagerstown Pike, posting two regiments on each side of the road. The 6th and 2nd Wisconsin drove into the western edge of The Cornfield, while the

7th Wisconsin and 19th Indiana approached the north side of the West Woods. (*OR* (1): 248-249)

757. Three of Gen. Gibbon's brothers served in the Confederate army. His wife hailed from Baltimore, Maryland—a hotbed secession city at the war's outset.

758. The Stonewall Brigade, with the support of Jones's brigade of Virginians, charged north out of the West Woods at about 6:20 a.m., halting Gibbon with a furious hail of fire. Gibbon secured his right flank with the arrival of Marsena Patrick's New York brigade, and the Virginians were forced to retire back into the cover of the West Woods.

759. The contest between the Stonewall Brigade and Gibbon's brigade was the second deadly face off in exactly three weeks between the two proud units. Both had inflicted heavy casualties on each other in a close-order, stand-up infantry brawl near the Brawner Farm on August 28, in the opening phase of the battle of Second Manassas.

760. Brig. Gen. John R. Jones, commanding Stonewall Jackson's former division, was apparently incapacitated by a shell burst in the West Woods as his division charged into battle, sending him to the rear. At Chancellorsville in May 1863, Jones left the field due to "the ulcerated condition of one of his legs." He was suspected of cowardice and discharged from division command. (Warner, *Generals in Gray*, p. 165)

761. Capt. R. P. Jennings, wounded in the hip by a case shot, was the only survivor in his company of the 23rd Virginia Infantry following the attack of the Stonewall Division.

762. Gen. Gibbon graduated from West Point in 1847. Two of his classmates were Ambrose Burnside and A. P. Hill.

763. Gibbon halted at the southern edge of The Cornfield following his fight with the Stonewall Division to await additional support from Walter Phelps's brigade of New Yorkers before venturing forward again.

764. A gap on Gibbon's left developed in The Cornfield caused by the rapid retreat of Duryea's brigade. Seeing this opportunity, Lawton's Georgians and the Louisianans of Harry Hays's brigade moved forward into The Cornfield. The Confederate counterattack failed to dislodge Gibbon due to the timely arrival of Phelps, who shored up Gibbon's left.

765. Brig. Gen. Alexander Robert Lawton graduated from Harvard Law School and practiced as a lawyer in Savannah, Georgia. He was president of the Augusta and Savannah Railroad and served in both houses of the Georgia legislature.

766. Lawton delivered the first military blow for Georgia's independence from the United States when he seized Fort Pulaski in January 1861.

767. The fourth Union advance pushed Hartsuff's brigade of Ricketts' division from the North Woods into The Cornfield. Hartsuff's objective was to fill the gap between Gibbon's left and the federal line holding the East Woods. Hartsuff's timely arrival halted the Confederate attack against Gibbon, and his brigade began to press Lawton and Hays south, out of The Cornfield.

768. One out of every two Confederates in Lawton's division, fighting in The Cornfield sector, became a casualty.

769. Eleven of the 15 regimental commanders in Lawton's division who witnessed combat in The Cornfield sector were casualties.

770. The federal infantry regiment with the highest casualty rate at Antietam was the 12th Massachusetts of Hartsuff's brigade—224 casualties out of the 334 men who go into battle (67 %). The casualties occurred in a murderous fight with Hays's Louisiana brigade in the southeast quadrant of The Cornfield and the bloody clover field pasture just to the south. (Sears, *Landscape Turned Red*, p. 190)

771. The 12th Massachusetts was the originator of the popular wartime ballad "John Brown's Body lies a mouldering in the grave," sung to the tune later made famous as Julia Ward Howe's *Battle Hymn of the Republic.*

772. The fifth federal assault tested the Confederate right once again. Christian's brigade of Ricketts' division had recovered from Christian's cowardly defection and was now commanded by Col. Peter Lyle. Lyle drove his New Yorkers and Pennsylvanians south through the East Woods and toward the Samuel Mumma farm and graveyard.

773. Roswell Ripley's brigade of Georgians and North Carolinians—a part of D. H. Hill's division—drove Christian's brigade back into the East Woods, temporarily securing the Confederate right on the Mumma farm.

774. Christian's men did not remain idle after their fight with Ripley, but instead turned their attention west to link with Hartsuff's brigade in The Cornfield. This sealed the gap on the federal left, and the resulting action pinned the attacking Louisianans of Hays in a deadly crossfire from the north and east.

775. The Louisiana "Tigers" were a colorful regiment in Hay's brigade raised in New Orleans. They suffered 61% casualties in the fighting in and around The Cornfield. Every one of the regimental commanders was killed or wounded. (Sears, *Landscape Turned Red*, p. 190)

776. The sixth Union assault bounced back to the Confederate left in the West Woods. With Doubleday's own left now connected to Ricketts' division, Doubleday attempted to clear the West Woods of Southern defenders. His offensive ended with a furious counterattack by two more Confederate brigades that rushed out of the West Woods—Taliaferro's Virginians and William Starke's Louisianans—totaling 1,150 fresh reserves.

777. The name "Taliaferro" is pronounced (TAHL-I-vur). (Robert Quigley, *Civil War Spoken Here*, p. 153)

778. Brig. Gen. William Edwin Starke lived in New Orleans at the outbreak of the war where he was a very successful cotton broker.

779. A post-and-rail fence along the Hagerstown Pike broke the momentum of Starke's counterattack, but even worse, it concentrated his formations into a huddled mass. The result was deadly as converging fire from the pastures north and east of the West Woods, as well as from The Cornfield, butchered the trapped Confederates.

780. The first general mortally wounded at Antietam was Confederate Brig. Gen. William E. Starke. Starke was struck by three bullets while leading a charge through the West Woods against Doubleday's right flank. He died within an hour of his wounding.

781. One third of the Stonewall Division that attacked Doubleday's federals north of the West Woods and west of The Cornfield became casualties.

Confederate Dead along the Hagerstown Pike (*USAMHI*)

782. Gen. Doubleday was stationed at Fort Sumter, South Carolina, in April 1861, when the South opened the war. Tradition holds that Doubleday—who served in the Regular Army as an artillerist—aimed the first shot fired in reply to the Confederate batteries in Charleston.

783. The most successful Confederate counterattack in The Cornfield/East Woods sector began about 7:00 a.m. John Bell Hood's division of 2,300 troops—previously held in reserve near the Dunker Church—swept into The Cornfield, shattering Phelps's and half of Gibbon's brigades and driving Hartsuff to the north as well.

784. Hood referred to the Dunker Church as "Saint Mumma church." Samuel Mumma donated the land where the church sits. (*OR* 19 (1): 923)

785. Hood's counterattack was the only Confederate assault that completely cleared The Cornfield of federal opposition.

786. Hood's men were preparing breakfast—baking hoecakes on their ramrods—when orders arrived to advance. Breakfast was not completed.

787. Hood's line of attack was nearly a half mile wide, stretching from the Hagerstown Pike to the East Woods. The brigade of Col. William T. Wofford constituted Hood's left while Evander Law's brigade swept forward on the right.

788. Law's brigade forced the last Union opposition—Christian's brigade of Ricketts' division—out of the East Woods. As a result, the East Woods was occupied by the

Confederates for the first time since the battle opened. The Confederate right was free from the enemy.

789. Gen. Ricketts had two horses shot out from under him and was badly injured when the second one fell on top of him.

790. The northern-most advance of any Confederate brigade on September 17 occurred when three of Evander Law's regiments—the 2nd Mississippi, 11th Mississippi, and the 6th North Carolina—punched their way into the north end of The Cornfield and into the pasture beyond.

791. The highest number of killed in a Union brigade in the fighting for The Cornfield—82 killed-in-action—struck Hartsuff's men while defending the northeast quadrant of the field against the successive attacks of Lawton's, Hays's, and Law's brigades.

792. Law's infantry encountered Union artillery firing double canister at them from 200 yards north of The Cornfield. The concentrated fire of Law's men forced the abandonment of one federal battery, the silencing of a second, and the driving off of a third.

793. General Hooker countered Law's advance and the drive of the 1st Texas by pushing forward his last uncommitted troops—two brigades from Meade's Pennsylvania Reserves, located in the North Woods.

794. Gen. Meade was born in Cadiz, Spain, on New Year's Eve 1815.

795. Col. Albert McGilton's brigade of Pennsylvanians came within 30 feet of Law's brigade, when suddenly, the Confederates holding the north end of The Cornfield, sprang from the earth and delivered a volley that smashed and routed the 4th and 8th Pennsylvania Reserves and stampeded the 3rd Reserves trailing behind them. The Confederates, without support on their left or right, did not pursue.

796. Hood's spearhead on his right was not matched by equal success on his left. Wofford's assault in the western sector of The Cornfield was hampered by federal flanking fire from the west side of the Hagerstown Pike by Patrick's brigade and the half of Gibbon's brigade not in The Cornfield—the 7th Wisconsin and the 19th Indiana.

797. Three regiments from Wofford's command—the 4th Texas, 18th Georgia, and Hampton's Legion—changed their attack from north to west in order to confront the flanking fire from the remnants of Gibbon's and Patrick's brigades and a section of Battery B, 4th US Artillery, on the west side of the Hagerstown Pike. Wofford formed a line perpendicular to the Confederate advance in the eastern sector of The Cornfield.

798. Only 50 yards separated Wofford—in position in the southwest quadrant of The Cornfield and parallel to the Hagerstown Pike—from the advance section of Battery B.

799. Fourteen artillerymen in Lt. James Stewart's section of two 12-pounder Napoleons (Battery B, 4th US Artillery) were gunned down within minutes during Wofford's counterattack into The Cornfield.

800. Wofford's men were not able to capture Stewart's section because their momentum was stopped by a five-foot high post-and-rail fence paralleling the Hagerstown Pike. The fence, in fact, completely stalled Wofford's movement.

801. The 1st Texas Infantry became separated from Wofford's brigade, racing 150 yards north of Wofford's position into the northwestern edge of The Cornfield. There it encountered Col. Robert Anderson's brigade of Pennsylvanians, pressed forward by Meade to stabilize Hooker's front. When the Texans came within 30 yards, the Pennsylvanians opened a murderous fire from behind a split-rail fence.

802. Gen. Gibbon called upon the four remaining Napoleons of Battery B to help save his precarious line. The guns were moved into a field just south of the D. R. Miller barn along the west side of the Hagerstown Pike.

803. John Gibbon taught at West Point prior to the war, serving as an artillery instructor for five years.

804. Gen. Gibbon—a former artillery commander—noticed the canister and double canister of his artillery (Battery B, 4th US) flying harmlessly over Wofford's Confederates in The Cornfield. Gibbon himself then raised an elevating screw to lower a muzzle, and that blast and the others that followed slaughtered Hood's Confederates crammed against the fence bordering the Hagerstown Pike. "Whole ranks went down," Gibbon later recorded, "and after we got possession of the field, dead men were found piled on top of each other." (Gibbon, *Personal Recollections of the Civil War*, pp. 83-84)

805. Capt. Joseph Campbell, commander of Battery B, had a 15-year-old bugler by his side named Johnny Cook. When Campbell was wounded, Cook delivered the captain's verbal instructions to the other officers in the battery.

806. Johnny Cook received the Medal of Honor for assisting in loading and firing cannon at the Confederates in The Cornfield. Cook may be the youngest recipient of the nation's highest military honor.

807. Two other Medal of Honor recipients were serving with Battery B, 4th US Artillery, at Antietam. William P. Hogarty was recognized for firing a cannon unaided. John Johnson filled several different positions on a crew after so many men went down with wounds, including the gunner.

808. Battery B fought closer to the Confederate infantry—within 90 feet—than any other federal battery at Antietam. No guns from the battery were captured.

809. Battery B was the only Union battery at Antietam that stopped a close-order Confederate infantry brigade attack.

810. The federal battery that suffered the highest number of casualties at Antietam was Battery B—9 killed, 31 wounded—more than double the casualties in any other Union battery.

811. The 1st Texas Infantry lost 186 killed, wounded, and missing of its 226 engaged, in less than 30 minutes of action in The Cornfield.

812. Eight color-bearers were shot down in the 1st Texas and the regiment had its flag captured during its retreat from The Cornfield.

813. The 1st Texas Infantry suffered 82.3% casualties—a casualty rate surpassed only by the 6th Georgia, which suffered 90% losses.

814. The number of killed in the 1st Texas was more than all of the other regiments in the Texas Brigade combined.

815. At roll call for the 1st Texas following the battle, no one answered in Company F; one man reported from Company A; and two soldiers responded in Company C.

816. The 1st Texas lost its colors during the retreat from The Cornfield. The flag was found on the ground with 13 dead men lying on and around it.

817. Hood's brigade suffered 64.1% casualties in the seven regiments that fought in The Cornfield or along the Hagerstown Pike—the third highest loss for any Confederate brigade during the war.

818. Hood's division lost 940 men or 44% of those engaged.

819. Reflecting upon his own strength versus the strength of his enemy, Hood declared in his official report: "The two little giant brigades of this division wrestled with this mighty force, losing hundreds. . . but driving the enemy from his position." (*OR* 19 (1): 923)

820. In his official report, written only 10 days after the battle, Gen. Hood commented he had "witnessed the most terrible clash of arms, by far, that has occurred during the war." (*OR* 19 (1): 923)

821. Gen. Hood later reported that the dead and wounded of both sides so thickly covered The Cornfield and the pasture to its south that he gingerly guided every step of his horse to ensure he did not trample any of the casualties.

822. Three members of Hood's staff had their horses shot from under them during the battle—chief of staff Maj. W. H. Sellers; and aides Maj. B. H. Blanton and Lieut. James Hamilton. (*OR* 19 (1): 924)

823. Gen. Hood specifically acknowledged in his official report the "valuable services rendered" by ten couriers who transmitted his orders. Each individual was named in Hood's report. (*OR* 19 (1): 924)

824. No Confederate reinforcements were available on Lee's left to sustain Hood's momentum. As a result, Hood's attack collapsed, but it succeeded in driving the federal First Corps off the field.

825. The remnants of Hood's division, which abandoned The Cornfield and later evacuated the East Woods, withdrew to the rear where its ammunition was replenished. It then moved forward again about noon to take a defensive position in the West Woods just behind the Dunker Church.

826. The federal First Corps, following the devastating attack of Hood's division, withdrew to the safety of the North Woods. With its battle-torn and weary-worn brigades and regiments fragmented and scattered, it ceased to be an effective offensive force, and would not attack again at Antietam.

827. Total casualties in Hooker's First Corps equaled almost 2,600—about one third of those engaged.

828. Gen. Ricketts' division suffered the heaviest casualties of the five federal divisions fighting in The Cornfield/East Woods sector—1,204 men. Ricketts also had the highest number of killed—172. In addition, his division claimed the highest number of wounded—946.

829. During The Cornfield/East Woods fight, Gen. Lee threw every brigade into battle that was stationed in his northern sector with the exception of Jubal Early's brigade of

Virginians. Early's brigade remained to the rear on Hauser's Ridge and Nicodemus Heights to protect Confederate artillery positions.

830. The collapse of the First Corps in the face of Hood's vicious attack forced Gen. Hooker to call for support from Mansfield's Twelfth Corps that had been held in reserve approximately one mile north of the fighting.

831. The smallest federal corps in the Army of the Potomac at Antietam was the Twelfth Corps. It consisted of only two divisions, totaling five brigades. The Twelfth Corps brought 7,200 effectives into battle.

832. Antietam was the first battle in which the Twelfth Corps fought as a corps with the Army of the Potomac. Previously, the majority of its regiments had served with Nathaniel Banks in the 1862 Shenandoah Valley Campaign, and with Banks at Cedar Mountain and Second Manassas.

833. Prior to Antietam, most of the men of the Twelfth Corps had fought in no battle that ended in a Union victory.

834. The Twelfth Corps approached the battlefield heading south via the Smoketown Road. It was closed en masse, deployed in column of divisions—translation: two company front, fifteen ranks deep. This compact formation made the Twelfth Corps very susceptible to Confederate artillery fire.

835. Maj. Gen. Joseph King Fenno Mansfield, leader of the Twelfth Corps, was the second oldest Union corps commander at Antietam. At age 59, he was six years younger than Second Corps commander Edwin V. Sumner.

836. Mansfield entered West Point at the age of 13 and graduated five years later, second in his class.

837. Mansfield had been in the army since 1817, when he entered West Point. His 45 years of continuous service in the military was the longest for any Union general officer, including Edwin Sumner. Sumner began his career in the army in 1819.

838. Mansfield had commanded the Twelfth Corps for exactly two days. He joined the corps on September 15.

839. Mansfield's first infantry command in the Civil War began with his appointment as the commander of the Twelfth Corps. Prior to this field command, he had been serving as an engineer for the defenses of Washington.

840. The first division of the Twelfth Corps to go into action was Brig. Gen. Alpheus Starkey Williams' division.

841. The only lawyer to command a Union division at Antietam was Gen. Alpheus S. Williams. Gen. Williams graduated from Yale University in 1831.

842. Gen. Williams served as postmaster of Detroit prior to the outbreak of the Civil War.

843. Williams separated his two brigades. He posted George Gordon's brigade in the North Woods and in the pasture north of The Cornfield to mend the hole in Hooker's First Corps line. Samuel Crawford's brigade was sent to the East Woods to shore up the Union left.

844. Gen. Williams was the only division commander in The Cornfield/East Woods sector who was not serving in the Regular Army at the outbreak of the Civil War.

845. Gen. Lee—in one of his riskiest decisions of the war—moved troops out of the center of his line and north toward The Cornfield and East Woods to blunt the offensive of the Twelfth Corps. Lee's weakened center was now vulnerable, but not yet under pressure.

846. The Confederates that Gen. Lee pulled away from his center were three brigades from D. H. Hill's division.

847. Brig. Gen. Roswell Sabine Ripley commanded the first brigade that arrived from Lee's center. Ripley had been posted along a ridge on the Mumma farm (Lee's left center) and had previously stalled federal sorties pushing south from the East Woods.

848. Gen. Ripley was a native of Ohio who married into the Middleton family of Charleston, South Carolina.

849. Ripley occupied and commanded Fort Sumter after its fall in April 1861, serving as a lieutenant colonel of state forces. By August 1861, he was a brigadier general commanding all of South Carolina.

850. Ripley's men charged to the north end of The Cornfield, relieving Hood's battered regiments, and ensuring no follow-up pursuit by Meade's brigades. Then federal reinforcements arrived, with Gordon's brigade of the Twelfth Corps smashing into Ripley's advance.

851. Brig. Gen. George Henry Gordon attended Harvard law school in 1854 and was a practicing lawyer in Massachusetts at the outbreak of the war.

852. Ripley's attack caught the 21st New York of Patrick's brigade and Gibbon's 19th Indiana in the flank in The Cornfield. The regiments were thwarted in their escape by the stout post-and-rail fence bordering the Hagerstown Pike. The confused concentration that resulted made the federals easy targets.

853. In only 15 minutes, the 21st New York—trapped by the fence and under severe fire from Ripley—lost 40% of its men as casualties.

854. Antiquated smooth-bore muskets firing "buck and ball"—a cartridge containing three buckshot and a round bullet, giving the effect of a shotgun—were in the hands of many of Ripley's soldiers.

855. The buck and ball volleys from the 3rd North Carolina Infantry—one of the largest Confederate regiments on the field, numbering 520 men—caused heavy casualties in the 27th Indiana opposing it—11 wounded for every one man killed.

856. Col. Silas Colgrove, commander of the 27th Indiana Infantry, was one of 18 children.

857. The tallest regiment in the Union army at Antietam was the 27th Indiana Infantry. Fifty men towering six-feet or taller were killed or wounded on the 17th.

858. The discoverers of Special Order 191—Sgt. John Bloss, Corp. Barton Mitchell, and Pvt. David Vance of the 27th Indiana—were wounded in the pasture north of The Cornfield. All would survive. Capt. Peter Kop, the company commander who decided to send the "Lost Orders" up the chain of command, was killed.

859. Gordon's brigade earned the distinction for the Union brigade with the highest casualty toll in The Cornfield/East Woods sector—646 (71 killed, 548 wounded, and 27 missing).

860. The Confederate regiment with the highest number of casualties in The Cornfield was the 3rd North Carolina—320 killed, wounded, and missing—of the 520 who go into action (62%).

861. The 3rd North Carolina suffered horrendous losses in its officer corps—23 of 27 line officers were shot down.

862. Capt. Robert Gould Shaw, who later became colonel of the 54th Massachusetts Infantry—the black regiment made famous in the movie *Glory*—commanded a company in the 2nd Massachusetts (Gordon's brigade) that fought north of The Cornfield.

863. Gen. Mansfield—satisfied with Gordon's resolute stand against Ripley—personally led his second brigade (Crawford's) onto the field and moved them into the East Woods to secure the Union left flank.

864. Brig. Gen. Samuel Wylie Crawford graduated from the University of Pennsylvania's medical school in 1850. He then entered the Regular Army as a surgeon.

865. Crawford was the only surgeon serving as a Union infantry general at Antietam.

866. Gen. Mansfield rode to the front in the East Woods to deploy Crawford's brigade. He mistook remnants of Hood's men as federals and was subsequently shot down with a bullet in his chest.

867. Members of the 10th Maine attempted to warn Gen. Mansfield of the enemy's presence, but their warning came too late to protect the Union commander from the deadly volley of the 4th Alabama and 21st Georgia.

868. Mansfield was taken to the rear after his wounding where he died the next day at a field hospital at the George Line farm.

869. Mansfield was the highest ranking general—and the only corps commander—mortally wounded at Antietam.

870. Gen. Williams assumed command of the Twelfth Corps following Mansfield's mortal wound. Williams had been in charge of the corps prior to Mansfield's arrival on September 15.

871. The smallest Union regiment engaged at Antietam was the 28th New York Infantry (Crawford's brigade). It went into action in The Cornfield with only 60 soldiers present.

872. Three of Crawford's regiments—the 124th, 125th, and 128th Pennsylvania—had been mustered into service just three weeks prior to the battle and had very little training. Antietam was their baptism of fire.

873. Crawford's "raw recruit" Pennsylvania regiments were "Nine-Month" regiments. These soldiers had voluntarily enlisted in response to President Lincoln's July 1862 plea for 300,000 more Union men to squash the South's rebellion. The time of service was only nine months.

874. The 128th Pennsylvania was positioned north of and within the East Woods by Gen. Mansfield. Confusion struck when Mansfield was mortally wounded. Shortly thereafter, the regiment's colonel was killed and the lieutenant colonel wounded. With its leadership decimated, the regiment did not panic but instead charged the Confederates in the northeast quadrant of The Cornfield. Ripley's Confederates ripped into the rookie regiment, killing or wounding 118 in only minutes.

875. Ripley's shot-up brigade was relieved in The Cornfield by the timely arrival of Alfred Colquitt's 1,000 Georgians—the second of the brigades sent from Gen. Lee's center.

876. Brig. Gen. Alfred Holt Colquitt, a native of Georgia, was a lawyer who graduated from Princeton and who served one term (1853-1854) as a congressman in the US House of Representatives.

877. The second division of the Twelfth Corps, under Gen. Greene, arrived in time to blunt Colquitt's attack and to secure the federal left.

878. Brig. Gen. George Sears Greene graduated second in his 1823 West Point class. Greene was an engineering instructor at West Point for 13 years during the ante-bellum period.

879. Gen. Greene was building the Croton Reservoir in Central Park, New York City, in January 1862, when he reentered the army as colonel of the 60th New York Infantry.

880. Greene positioned his lead brigade under Col. Tyndale in a pasture just north of The Cornfield and in the northwestern end of the East Woods. Tyndale filled a gap in the federal left center, linking with Gordon on the right and Crawford's remnants on the left.

881. Lieut. Col. Hector Tyndale was in Paris on business when the Civil War erupted. He was a large importer of glass and ceramics.

882. Tyndale escorted Mrs. John Brown (Mary Brown) to Charles Town, [West] Virginia, in November-December 1859, for her last visit with the condemned abolitionist. Tyndale then escorted Brown's body north following his execution.

883. Tyndale had three horses shot from under him at Antietam and he was wounded twice.

884. The three Ohio regiments in Tyndale's brigade—5th, 7th, and 66th—were so depleted that they could muster only 415 men for action. (A *new* Union regiment at full strength in the late summer of 1862 typically numbered 750-800 men.)

885. Tyndale positioned the 28th Pennsylvania—nearly 800 strong—in the East Woods, perpendicular to his main line of Ohio regiments facing The Cornfield. The maneuver boxed in the 6th Georgia on Colquitt's right, and began to break the Confederates' defense in The Cornfield.

886. Colquitt's 6th Georgia, that he organized and originally commanded, lost 90% of its ranks in The Cornfield—81 killed, 115 wounded, 30 missing—226 of the 250 men it carried into action.

887. The third and final Confederate brigade—shifting from Lee's center to his left—was Garland's brigade of North Carolinians. Without the leadership of its general (Garland was killed at South Mountain), and fresh off a tough fight at Fox's Gap in which they were outnumbered, outmaneuvered, and flanked, these Tar Heels lacked their customary resolve.

888. As Garland's brigade approached the East Woods, it mistook a large Union regiment (28th Pennsylvania) for an enemy brigade turning the Confederate right. Weary from its

South Mountain experience, the 5th North Carolina panicked, sending the brigade to the rear: "The most unutterable stampede occurred," according to temporary commander D. K. McRae. "It was one of those marvelous flights that beggar explanation or description." (Sears, *Landscape Turned Red*, p. 209)

889. The flight of Garland's brigade exposed the Confederate right, permitting Gen. Greene to march Stainrook's brigade, with support from Tyndale, through the East Woods and The Cornfield to take possession of the plateau overlooking the Dunker Church.

890. The smallest brigade in the Army of the Potomac at Antietam belonged to Col. Henry J. Stainrook. The entire brigade, with its three diminutive regiments—3rd Maryland (148 men); 102nd New York (145 men); and 111th Pennsylvania (230 men)—sent only 523 soldiers into action.

891. Hooker achieved only one objective in his sector—the high ground east of the Dunker Church came into Union possession when a portion of Greene's division seized the position.

892. Gen. Greene was the father of Lt. Dana Greene, who served as the executive officer of the USS *Monitor* during the historic ironclad's fight with the CSS *Virginia* (*Merrimack*) at Hampton Roads, Virginia.

893. Gen. Hooker looked for any *organized* large body of federal troops to support Greene's new position and saw the 125th Pennsylvania—one of the raw-recruit regiments in the Twelfth Corps—crouched along the Smoketown Road in a field just north of Greene.

894. Hooker, riding his white charger, was shot in the left instep between 8:40 a.m. and 8:50 a.m. by Confederate snipers. At the time, he was ordering Col. Jacob Higgins of the 125th Pennsylvania to move forward and clear the West Woods. The wound proved to be too painful for him to continue in command, so he left the field in an ambulance.

895. George Meade assumed command of the shattered First Corps following the wounding of Hooker.

896. George Smalley, a special correspondent for the New York *Tribune*, served as a courier for General Hooker on the 17th. Two horses were shot from under Smalley as he performed his temporary duties.

897. The 125th Pennsylvania was the first Union regiment to enter the West Woods.

898. Company C of the 125th Pennsylvania was known as the "Huntington Bible Company" because the people of Huntington County gave each soldier a Bible.

899. McClellan ordered the Second Corps, commanded by Maj. Gen. E. V. Sumner, to advance to the aid of Hooker at 7:20 a.m.

900. The Second Corps was comprised of 15,200 men, divided into three divisions. It was bivouacked beyond McClellan's headquarters at the Pry House—about two miles marching distance from the battlefield.

901. Maj. Gen. Edwin Voss Sumner was the oldest active corps commander in the Civil War at age 65.

902. Sumner, the oldest major general at Antietam, was 36 years senior to the youngest major general, Jeb Stuart, the 29-year-old chief of the Confederate cavalry.

903. Gen. Sumner was the only corps commander at Antietam who was born in the 18th-century (1797).

904. Gen. Sumner's son-in-law, Armistead Long, served as Robert E. Lee's military secretary during The Maryland Campaign. He would later command Stonewall Jackson's Second Corps artillery.

905. Tradition holds that Gen. Sumner earned his nickname "Old Bull" or "Old Bull Head" because a musket ball once bounced off his head.

906. Sumner was one of only three brigadier generals in the Regular Army at the outset of the war.

907. Pry's Ford on Antietam Creek was the location where the Second Corps crossed the stream. Pry's Ford is located about midway between the Upper and Middle bridges.

908. Maj. Gen. Israel B. Richardson's division of the Second Corps was not permitted to move across the creek until a division of the Fifth Corps took its place as the tactical reserve east of the creek. As a result, Richardson was not released until nearly one hour and forty minutes after the remainder of the corps had moved forward.

909. The division leading the Second Corps into battle belonged to John Sedgwick.

910. Maj. Gen. John Sedgwick was a native of Connecticut and a graduate in the West Point class of 1837. Fellow classmates included Joseph Hooker and future Confederates Braxton Bragg and John C. Pemberton. Sedgwick served in the 1st US Cavalry prior to the war, and his commander was Robert E. Lee.

911. Sedgwick's men had an affection for their commander and they had christened him "Uncle John."

912. Sedgwick's division arrived in the East Woods encountering no opposition, with the exception of some Confederate artillery fire.

913. Gen. Sumner made no forward reconnaissance and obtained little information in a brief discussion with the wounded Hooker and the dysfunctional Gen. Ricketts. He brushed off Gen. Williams during a briefing.

914. Corps commander Sumner made three costly errors: 1) he acted like a division commander, riding in the van with Sedgwick, myopically focused on the front; 2) he was unavailable to direct the remainder of his corps into proper position on the field, thus creating confusion and consternation in his rear; and 3) his attack formation left Sedgwick's flanks exposed. (Sears, *Landscape Turned Red*, p. 222)

915. The formation of Sedgwick's division was "brigade front"—each of the three brigades was in parallel lines, facing west, each line 600 yards wide. There were two lines per brigade, with about 900 men per each of the six lines. Each brigade was separated by about 50 yards.

916. Holding Sedgwick's south flank were six men—one man per line. Holding his north flank were another six men. The formation worked well as long as all the Confederates were in front of Sedgwick—and none on his flanks.

917. Facing Sedgwick's front in the West Woods was his former West Point classmate Jubal Early.

918. Sedgwick, with 5,400 men, outnumbered Early's brigade of 1,200 Virginians by more than four to one.

919. An eerie silence—the first since dawn—fell over the battlefield as Sedgwick's men advanced toward the West Woods. "Not an enemy appeared," recalled Twelfth Corps commander Williams. "The Woods in front (the West Woods) were as quiet as any sylvan shade could be." (Alpheus Williams, *From the Cannon's Mouth: The Civil War Letters of General Alpheus S. Williams*, p. 127)

920. The only Confederate unit in Jackson's sector that had not been committed by 9:00 a.m. was Jubal Early's brigade. Jackson had no reinforcements available.

921. Early's brigade had been positioned west of the main fighting throughout the morning, in support of Jeb Stuart's horse artillery on Nicodemous Heights. Early was pressed forward to resist the Union thrust into the West Woods, but the 13th Virginia Infantry remained behind in support of the horse artillery.

922. Gen. Stuart repositioned the horse artillery, moving it south from Nicodemous Heights on to an adjoining elevation known as Hauser's Ridge. Stuart made the maneuver so that he could better see the federals in the woods, and thus fire "without danger of harming our own men." (*OR* 19 (1): 820)

923. A young lad named Randolph received special mention in Gen. Stuart's after-action report. The Fauquier County, Virginia, youth—apparently about 12-years-old— "brought me several messages from General Jackson," Stuart writes admiringly, "under circumstances of great personal peril, and delivered his dispatches with a clearness and intelligence highly creditable to him." Stuart did not indicate if Randolph was the first or last name of the youth. (*OR* 19 (1): 821)

924. Gen. Lee rushed reinforcements to Gen. Jackson's tenuous position from three different sectors: from his center near Sharpsburg—George T. Anderson's brigade; from his left near Burnside Bridge—John G. Walker's division; and from his rear, near his headquarters—Lafayette McLaws' division.

925. Brig. Gen. George Thomas Anderson was the first to receive orders from Lee to move toward the Confederate left to support Jackson. At 7:30 a.m., Anderson began pressing his brigade north from his Boonsboro Pike position, where he had been in support of the Washington Artillery. (*OR* 19 (1): 909)

926. "Tige" Anderson, the general's sobriquet, was one of three Confederate generals at Sharpsburg with the surname Anderson. George B. Anderson and Richard H. Anderson were the other two.

927. Gen. Lee ordered McLaws' division toward the West Woods between 8:30 and 9:00 a.m. McLaws was resting his men near Lee's headquarters west of Sharpsburg when the orders arrived. His force was located about one mile—cross country—from the West Woods.

928. McLaws had conducted an all-night march from Halltown, four miles west of Harpers Ferry, to Sharpsburg. His column reached Gen. Lee's headquarters at sunrise. (*OR* 19 (1): 857)

929. Gen. McLaws' men had received almost no sleep for 48 hours. They were awake throughout the night of the 14th and 15th holding their position against the Sixth Corps in Pleasant Valley; and during the night of the 16th and 17th they were marching toward Sharpsburg. Most of McLaws' men had had no provisions or time to cook the limited rations they carried in their haversacks. (*OR* 19 (1): 857)

930. McLaws recorded that his entire command was "very much fatigued" on the 17th, not only from the march and lack of provisions, but also by the fact that his troops did the heaviest fighting during the siege of Harpers Ferry, with severe actions on Maryland Heights and at Crampton's Gap. (*OR* 19 (1): 857)

931. John G. Walker's division was the last to receive orders to march to the Confederate left to support Jackson. His instructions arrived shortly after 9:00 a.m. (*OR* 19 (1): 914-915)

932. The largest shift in Confederate troop positions at Antietam occurred when Lee transferred Walker from the extreme right below Burnside Bridge to the Confederate left near the West Woods. Walker's shift covered 2½ miles from south to north.

933. McLaws' approach to the West Woods was from the southwest—nearly perpendicular to Sedgwick's unsuspecting and badly exposed left flank.

934. Stonewall Jackson was nearly killed near the West Woods. According to eyewitness Henry Lord Page King, an aide-de-camp to Lafayette McLaws, who wrote in his diary: "Met Gen. Jackson & he & Gen. McLaws had a conference. Shell fell at our feet, wounding one of the Gen's couriers—*did not explode or it would have killed both Gens.*" (emphasis added) (Trumpi, King Diary, p. 37)

935. Gen. Hood met McLaws south of the West Woods and pointed out the direction for McLaws' attack. (*OR* 19 (1): 858)

936. McLaws deployed his three brigades south and west of the West Woods with Kershaw anchoring the right, Barksdale holding the center, and Semmes positioned on the left.

937. Returns for three of the four brigades in McLaws' division showed 2,536 men engaged at Sharpsburg. Cobb's brigade was not included. (*OR* 19 (1): 861-862)

938. Shortly after 9:00 a.m., Union Gen. Sumner advanced into the West Woods with Sedgwick's lead brigade, commanded by Willis A. Gorman.

939. Brig. Gen. Willis Arnold Gorman was a former congressman from Indiana. He was appointed governor of the Minnesota Territory by President Franklin Pierce in 1853. He also served as a member of the Minnesota state constitutional convention and in the state legislature in 1859. He was the first colonel of the 1st Minnesota Infantry.

940. "Old Bull" Sumner moved forward with his first line, riding beside the 1st Minnesota Infantry, located on the extreme Union right.

941. The 1st Minnesota was the only regiment from that state in the Army of the Potomac at Antietam.

942. Gorman's brigade advanced to the western edge of the West Woods, stopping in front of an open field on a rock ledge. Here it encountered, to its front, fire from pieced-together remnants of Jackson's command and the repositioned cannon of Pelham on Hauser's Ridge.

943. The second federal brigade to enter the West Woods belonged to Brig. Gen. Napoleon J. T. Dana. It halted about midway into the woods, behind the stalled advance of Gorman's lead brigade.

944. The general with the most militaristic name at Antietam was Union Gen. Napoleon Jackson Tecumseh Dana. Dana's paternal grandfather was a Revolutionary War naval officer.

945. During the Mexican War, Dana was so severely wounded at Cerro Gordo that he was left for dead. He was discovered by a burial detail 36 hours later.

946. Two brigade commanders in Sedgwick's division—Dana and Gorman—had served as colonel of the 1st Minnesota Infantry.

947. The third and final Union brigade of Sedgwick's division, commanded by Brig. Gen. O. O. Howard, crossed the fences bordering the Hagerstown Pike and positioned itself along the eastern edge of the West Woods.

948. Oliver Otis Howard was a graduate of both Bowdoin College in Maine and West Point (class of 1854). Howard was an assistant professor of mathematics at West Point before the war.

949. Gen. Howard lost his right arm at the battle of Seven Pines outside of Richmond in May 1862. He returned to active service in 80 days and commanded the rear guard of the army during the retreat to Washington from Second Manassas.

950. Howard's brigade was known as the Philadelphia Brigade because its four Quaker State regiments were raised in the Philadelphia area.

951. McLaws crashed into Sedgwick's exposed left flank in the West Woods about 9:20 a.m., stunning the federals with a fierce and rapid lightening strike that drove Sedgwick's shocked soldiers north toward The Cornfield and the North Woods.

952. The first federals hit in the Confederate counterattack in the West Woods were three regiments on Sedgwick's left—the 125th Pennsylvania (already in position near the Dunker Church), the 34th New York, and the 78th New York. These men became detached from the main advance—separated by nearly 400 yards—in part because of a deep ravine in the West Woods. They were driven north in minutes by Kershaw's and Early's brigades, leaving behind heavy casualties.

953. Five bullets struck down the color bearer of the 34th New York, Sgt. Charles Burton, in the woods just west of the Dunker Church.

954. Kershaw's momentum was stymied by canister from six 12-pounder Napoleons in Lt. George A. Woodruff's Battery I, 1st US Artillery—located in a field 300 yards northeast of the Dunker Church—and from J. Albert Monroe's Battery D, 1st Rhode Island Battery—who had moved into a forward position near the junction of the Smoketown Road and Hagerstown Pike.

955. Capt. J. Albert Monroe's horse was shot six times when his rider charged impetuously into the West Woods near the Dunker Church. The badly wounded but devoted mount safely returned his rider back to his battery.

956. Kershaw's men had moved to within 25 yards of Tyndale's brigade of Ohioans, located behind the ridge east of the Dunker Church, when the Buckeyes rose up and fired a murderous volley that sent Kershaw reeling back toward the West Woods.

957. Brig. Gen. George Greene, Tyndale's division commander, personally led another battery—Capt. John A. Tompkins' Battery A, 1st Rhode Island—into a position upon the crucial hill east of the Dunker Church.

958. Kershaw's South Carolinians assaulted the Union left a second time, bolstered by the arrival of three regiments from Col. Van H. Manning's brigade of John Walker's division (coming up from the Burnside Bridge sector). Kershaw pushed toward the mouths of canister-loaded cannon and was wrecked by their discharges. The Union left held.

959. The highest casualties in McLaws' command were suffered by Kershaw's brigade—355 total—57 killed; 292 wounded; and six missing. (*OR* 19 (1): 862)

960. The 7th South Carolina charged to within 30 yards of Tompkins' battery before canister decimated them. The regiment sustained the highest regimental casualties within Kershaw's brigade—140 of 268 engaged (52%). As Kershaw wrote in his official report: "The Seventh . . . trailed their progress to the cannon's mouth with the blood of their bravest." (*OR* 19 (1): 862, 865)

961. Tompkins' Battery A, 1st Rhode Island, expended 83 rounds of canister, 68 rounds of solid shot, 427 rounds of shell, and 454 rounds of case shot—1,050 rounds in all. (*OR* 19 (1): 309)

962. A canister round hurls 27 iron balls, 1.5 inches in diameter, toward the enemy at 1,000 miles per hour.

963. Tompkins lost six horses killed and four wounded. Three single sets of harness were lost "by the horses getting among the burning timbers of the houses [Mumma farm] in the rear of the battery." (*OR* 19 (1): 309)

964. Every officer and man in the color company of the 7th South Carolina was killed or wounded. As Kershaw noted in his official report: "The colors of this regiment, shot from the staff, formed the winding sheet of the last man of the color company at the extreme point reached by our troops that day." (*OR* 19 (1): 866)

965. The 7th South Carolina lost its battle flag, but it was taken from the hands of a dead man following Kershaw's retreat. Corp. Jacob G. Orth, 28th Pennsylvania Infantry, received the Medal of Honor for grabbing the trophy and returning it to Union lines.

966. The 8th South Carolina, Kershaw's brigade, carried only 45 men into the West Woods fight and lost 23. (*OR* 19 (1): 865)

967. Pvt. Deas (first name not known), an orderly for Gen. Kershaw, received specific mention in Kershaw's battle report because his horse was shot in three places. (*OR* 19 (1): 866)

968. Capt. John P. W. Read's Pulaski Georgia battery, posted in a field south of the West Woods in support of Kershaw's attacks, lost 14 men, 20 horses, and two guns disabled. (*OR* 19 (1): 862; (2): 620)

969. The 30th Virginia Infantry, Manning's brigade, also experienced the violence of the federal artillery on the ridge east of the Dunker Church. The regiment charged in Kershaw's second assault and lost 160 of the 236 men it carried into battle.

970. The federals lost 13 men per minute during the 40 minute battle around the Dunker Church between 9:20-10:00 a.m. (John Priest, *Antietam: The Soldiers' Battle*, p.124)

971. Barksdale's Mississippians and Early's Virginians smashed into the center and right of Sedgwick's division, routing and pushing Howard's and Dana's brigades out of the West Woods, collapsing them from left to right "like a stand of dominoes." (Sears, *Landscape Turned Red*, p. 226)

972. Gen. Sumner recognized his predicament and attempted to save Sedgwick's division: "Back, boys, for God's sake, move back!" he shouted time and again. "You are in a bad fix!" (Sears, *Landscape Turned Red*, p. 227)

973. Howard's Philadelphia brigade lost 550 men in 10 minutes in the West Woods.

974. The federals in the front brigade (Gorman's) in the West Woods became trapped on three sides—Confederates to their front (Semmes); Confederates to their south (Barksdale); and Confederates to their rear (Early).

975. Friendly fire took its toll on the federals in the confusing cauldron of the West Woods. The 59th New York Infantry fired into the backs of the 15th Massachusetts. "Many of my men were . . . killed by our own forces," Lieut. Col. John Kimball recalled in his after-action report, "and my most strenuous exertions were of no avail either in stopping this murderous fire or in causing the second line to advance to the front." (*OR* 19 (1): 313)

976. The Union regiment that suffered the heaviest casualties in the West Woods was the 15th Massachusetts Infantry—318 dead and wounded out of 582 present (54.6%).

977. The 15th Massachusetts Infantry participated in 45 engagements during the Civil War, but Antietam was the regiment's bloodiest day.

978. Sixty-four folds of newspaper stuffed into the blouse of George Flectcher stopped a bullet from delivering a fatal chest wound. Fletcher, of Company H, 15th Massachusetts Infantry, owed his life to a copy of *Harpers Weekly*.

979. Capt. Oliver Wendell Holmes, Jr., of the 20th Massachusetts Infantry, was wounded in the neck and rendered unconscious by loss of blood in the West Woods. The bullet struck just off center in the back of his neck and excited through the front, barely missing his jugular vein and windpipe.

980. John Lemuel Stetson, cousin of John B. Stetson of "Stetson Hat" fame, was mortally wounded in the West Woods leading his regiment, the 59th New York Infantry.

981. The 59th New York, raised primarily in New York City, took part in 55 actions during the war, but its bloodiest day was at Antietam in the West Woods where it lost 224 killed and wounded of the 321 who went into action.

982. Sedgwick's division lost about 2,225 men in 20 minutes in the West Woods.

983. Gen. Sedgwick was wounded three times—once in the leg in the West Woods, and twice more while rallying his men near Woodruff's Battery just north of the Mumma farm.

984. The final federal assault against the West Woods was launched when reinforcements from the Twelfth Corps—the 2nd Massachusetts and 13th New Jersey infantry regiments—arrived about 9:45 a.m., charging east to west across The Cornfield toward the woods. The federals came to within 200 yards of the Woods before they were stopped by Confederates concealed behind a ridge of limestone in front of the woods.

985. One of Antietam's most unique reports counted the number of bullet holes piercing regimental flags. Filed by brigade commander Paul Semmes on October 27, 1862, Semmes discovered: 10th Georgia colors—46 shots; 32nd Virginia—17 shots; 15th Virginia—10 shots; and the 53rd Georgia—two shots. (*OR* 19 (1): 875-876)

986. Lieut. Col. C. C. Sanders, commanding Cobb's brigade, led his brigade too far to the right, consequently detaching itself from McLaws' advance into the West Woods. Cobb's men linked with the left of Rodes's brigade at the Sunken Road. (*OR* 19 (1): 871, 859)

987. Cobb's brigade carried 357 men into action at Sharpsburg. Still suffering from its tragic disaster at Crampton's Gap three days prior to Antietam, Cobb's brigade was less than half the size of McLaws' other three brigades. (*OR* 19 (1): 871)

Dunker Church—view looking toward the northwest (*USAMHI*)

D. R. Miller Farm—post-war—view from Union position (*ANB*)

Union burial detail near Miller's Cornfield (*USAMHI*)

Late Morning—Early Afternoon
Bloody Lane

988. Bloody Lane is also known as the battle of the Sunken Road.

989. Bloody Lane and its environs are the second bloodiest part of the Antietam Battlefield. Nearly 5,600 casualties occurred here in 3½ half hours of vicious fighting—second only to The Cornfield.

990. The battle for control of the Bloody Lane sector began about 9:15 a.m. and concluded just before 2:00 p.m.

991. George McClellan never ordered an attack against Bloody Lane. The uncontrollable circumstances of the battle led federal troops to move against this position.

992. The center of the Confederate line was at Bloody Lane. Had Robert E. Lee lost this position, his center would have been breached—the worst possible disaster for an army.

993. The two Confederate brigades defending Bloody Lane were never forced out of the road—instead, they abandoned it through misunderstood directions and by mistaken orders.

994. The Bloody Lane sector of the battlefield fell under the direction of Maj. Gen. James Longstreet—the right wing commander of Lee's army.

995. The Sunken Road was a dirt farm lane that connected the Hagerstown Pike with the Boonsboro Turnpike. The road entered the Hagerstown Pike about one mile north of Sharpsburg. It joined with the Boonsboro Pike about three-quarters of a mile east of Sharpsburg, or about midway between Sharpsburg and Antietam Creek.

996. Erosion had produced the Sunken Road. Years of travel by wagons, horses, and mules had eroded the soil away from the limestone floor of the Antietam Valley, carving a ditch into the earth—hence, the Sunken Road.

997. Most of the Sunken Road was *not* sunk into the ground. Only about three hundred yards (or 20% of the road) was carved three to six feet into the ground. The road was nearly one mile long, stretching from the Hagerstown Pike to the Boonsboro Pike.

998. The Confederates used the Sunken Road as a natural defensive position. The eroded section of the farm lane provided cover to only about one third of the Confederates initially holding the position. Split rail "worm-fences"—zigzagging along the north and south edges of the lane—were piled high by the Confederates on the north side of the road to provide additional cover. (*OR* 19 (1): 1023, 1037)

999. One half of the Sunken Road faces primarily north and generally runs east-west. This comprised the section from the Hagerstown Pike drawing east for 900 yards. The second half of the road, which connected with the Boonsboro Pike, ran perpendicular to the first, and for the most part, paralleled Antietam Creek (which flows north-south).

1000. The section of the Sunken Road where most of the fighting occurred was along the east-west section. Federal forces attacked the position from the north. Confederates defended the lane and rushed reinforcements forward from the south.

1001. Travelers using the Sunken Road could avoid Sharpsburg completely. The short cut between the Hagerstown and Sharpsburg pikes—which formed the short end of a triangle—reduced travel by nearly two miles.

1002. The 180-acre Roulette Farm was the northern border of the Sunken Road. William Roulette was 37 at the time of the battle, and his wife Margaret was 32. William was serving as a local Washington County commissioner. The farm had been in the hands of Margaret or her family since 1804. Roulette was of French Huguenot descent.

1003. A farm lane that ran north from—and perpendicular to—the Sunken Road connected the Roulette farm dwellings with the Sunken Road. The Roulette farm lane passed through a deep ravine near its junction with the Sunken Road.

1004. The Roulette farm buildings sat in a large hollow nearly 500 yards north of the Sunken Road. The buildings were invisible from most sections of the Sunken Road.

1005. On the south side of the Sunken Road was the 231-acre farm of Henry Piper. Bordering the road's southern edge was a 25-acre cornfield. Two hundred yards south of the road, Mr. Piper maintained a 48,000 square foot apple orchard.

1006. Maj. Gen. D. H. Hill commanded the troops holding Lee's center at the Sunken Road.

1007. D. H. Hill was Stonewall Jackson's brother-in law.

1008. Before the war, D. H. Hill was a professor of mathematics at Washington College in Lexington, Virginia (1849-1854) and then a mathematics professor at Davidson College until 1859. When the war began, he was superintendent of the North Carolina Military Institute.

1009. Only two of D. H. Hill's five brigades remained to defend the Confederate center. The other three brigades—Colquitt, Garland, and Ripley—had been sent north to fight in The Cornfield sector earlier in the morning. According to Hill, these brigades had been "broken and much demoralized." Some stragglers had been gathered and placed on Hill's left. (*OR* 19 (1): 1023)

1010. Holding the left of the Sunken Road was the Alabama brigade of Robert Rodes. Rodes had 700-750 men in his five (Yellowhammer's) regiments on the morning of the 17th. (*OR* 19 (1): 1023, 1037)

1011. Rodes' left initially did not extend to the Hagerstown Pike, falling 150 yards short. This gap was remedied when the small brigade of Howell Cobb, in charge of a lieutenant colonel, arrived. The brigade had been virtually annihilated at Crampton's Gap three days before. Rodes assumed command of Cobb's brigade and posted it on his left. (*OR* 19 (1): 1037)

1012. The 6th Alabama, under command of Col. John Brown Gordon, held the right of Rodes' brigade.

1013. Col. Gordon declared to Gen. Lee and Gen. Hill, who were inspecting the line along the center prior to the commencement of action on this front, "The men are going to stay here, General, until the sun goes down or victory is won!" (Gordon, *Reminiscences of the Civil War*, p. 84)

1014. Holding the right of the Sunken Road was the North Carolina brigade of George B. Anderson. Anderson had 1,153 men present for duty on the morning of the 17th. His men took up a position in the lane between 8:00-8:30 a.m. (*OR* 19 (1): 1023, 1037, 1051)

1015. Brig. Gen. George Burgwyn Anderson was born exactly 30 years prior to the bombardment of Fort Sumter. Anderson's birth occurred on April 12, 1831, at Hillsboro, North Carolina.

1016. Gen. G. B. Anderson graduated from West Point in 1852 and remained in the US Regulars, serving in the 2nd Dragoons on the frontier until the war began. He was wounded at Malvern Hill while leading a charge on July 1, 1862, but recovered in time to rejoin the army for The Maryland Campaign.

1017. The 30th North Carolina anchored Anderson's extreme right, and the extreme right of D. H. Hill's division at the Sunken Road.

1018. Generals Hill, Longstreet, and Lee were inspecting the Confederate center prior to the federal infantry attack. Hill remained mounted and was warned by Longstreet to dismount so as not to draw federal artillery fire. Hill stayed on his horse. Shortly after Longstreet's warning, "Old Pete" noticed a puff of smoke from a Union battery east of Antietam Creek. "There is a shot for you," he shouted to Hill. Seconds later a shell struck Hill's horse and carried off the forelegs of the animal. Hill was uninjured, but shaken by the incident. (James Longstreet, "The Invasion of Maryland," *Battles and Leaders of the Civil War*, Vol., 2, p. 671)

1019. The first Union division to attack the Confederates holding Bloody Lane was William H. French's division.

1020. French outnumbered D. H. Hill by more than two-to-one. French advanced with 5,740 in his three brigades. Hill defended with about 2,500, comprised of the brigades of Rodes and G. B. Anderson in the lane, with support from Cobb's brigade and remnants of Hill's three other brigades.

1021. Brig. Gen. William Henry French was a native of Baltimore, Maryland, born there on January 13, 1815. He graduated from West Point in 1837 with classmates Joseph Hooker and John Sedgwick.

1022. French was nicknamed "Old Blinky" because of his annoying habit of blinking furiously when he spoke.

1023. Gen. French was serving in the Regular Army in Texas when the state seceded. Instead of surrendering his garrison at Eagle Pass, Texas, French led his men 300 miles in 16 days to the mouth of the Rio Grande where his force sailed for Key West.

1024. French was the second of the Second Corps divisions to cross Antietam Creek at Pry's Ford. Sedgwick's division—which headed toward the West Woods—was first. (*OR* 19 (1): 323)

1025. French began crossing Antietam Creek about 7:30 a.m. with his three brigades in three columns. He continued marching in this formation for about a mile before reaching the William Roulette Farm. (*OR* 19 (1): 323)

1026. French became disoriented and "lost" while in the deep hollow on the Roulette Farm. He lost contact with Sedgwick—who was far in advance and who had disappeared into the East Woods and beyond. French's corps commander, Gen. E. V. Sumner, was not in the rear to place him into position—Sumner was with the advance of Sedgwick.

1027. Gen. French faced his division south and formed three lines of battle. His intent was to connect with and extend Gen. George S. Greene's left that was posted on a high ridge opposite the Dunker Church. French could see Greene's exposed left from his position on the Roulette Farm.

1028. The division of Gen. French had only recently been assembled. It included one brigade of raw-recruits and one brigade of troops that had experienced only garrison duty. Only one brigade in French's command included veteran soldiers.

1029. Of the ten regiments in French's division, only three had experienced combat—but nothing as intense or as deadly as the fire they were about to encounter at the Sunken Road. (Sears, *Landscape Turned Red*, p. 237)

1030. The first brigade leading French's division toward the Sunken Road was the brigade of Max Weber.

1031. Brig. Gen. Max Weber was born in 1824 in present-day Germany. He was born in the village of Achern near Baden-Baden, in the Grand Dutchy of Baden. Weber (pronounced veber) graduated from the military school at Karlsruhe, Germany, in 1843, but defected to the rebels in the 1848 revolution and emigrated to New York City. Weber operated the Hotel Konstantz at William and Frankfort streets in New York City—a rendezvous for refugees from southern Germany.

1032. Weber organized the "Turner Rifles"—a regiment of German-speaking New Yorkers—which was mustered into federal service as the 20th New York Infantry on May 9, 1861.

1033. The brigade of garrison troops in French's division was Weber's brigade. It had been on garrison duty at Fortress Monroe in Virginia.

1034. Weber made first contact with Confederates skirmishers near the Roulette farm buildings. He swept them away with little effort, and then turned south toward the Sunken Road in brigade front formation.

1035. Virtually all of the Sunken Road was invisible to Weber as he marched from north to south. His brigade ascended a steep rise as it moved out of the Roulette farm hollow. The Sunken Road was on the other side of this rise, completely hidden from the federals' view.

1036. Gen. D. H. Hill, from a commanding knoll behind the Sunken Road, watched Weber and French's other two brigades advance "with all the precision of a parade day." (*OR* 19 (1): 1023)

1037. Col. John Brown Gordon of the 6th Alabama described the Union advance as a "thrilling spectacle." Gordon recalled seeing white gaiters around the ankles of the federal soldiers, with the front line at "Charge bayonets," and the other lines at "Right-shoulder shift." As Gordon concluded, while marveling at "this magnificent array"—"What a pity to spoil with bullets such a scene of martial beauty!" (Gordon, *Reminiscences of the Civil War*, p. 85)

1038. Weber approached the Sunken Road with the 4th New York on his left, the 5th Maryland holding the center, and the 1st Delaware anchoring his right. His line had a 700-yard front.

1039. The color bearer of the 5th Maryland—at the center of Weber's advance—was a burly man who stood over six feet in height and weighed about 300 pounds.

1040. No cover was provided for the federals as they approached the Sunken Road. The ground was open pasture and clover fields.

1041. No Confederate artillery opposed the advance of Weber's troops. Boyce's battery was in a forward position on the left of Hill's line, but it retired before the Union attack. (*OR* (1): 1037)

1042. Confederates in the Sunken Road were told by their officers to hold their fire until the Union line got very close. Col. F. M. Parker of the 30th North Carolina ordered his men not to fire until they could see the belts of the enemy's cartridge boxes, and to aim for those belts.

1043. Weber's men arrived at the crest of the ridge paralleling the Sunken Road about 9:30 a.m. They were within 80 yards of Rodes' Alabamians on the Confederate left and 50 yards of G. B. Anderson's North Carolinians on the right. The order "Fire!" echoed down the rebel line and hundreds of bullets went flying toward the suddenly stunned Union targets. (*OR* (1): 1037)

1044. The 4th New York, opposite Anderson's position, lost 150 men in the first volley.

1045. Weber's brigade lost 450 casualties in five minutes. Brig. Gen. Weber was wounded seriously in the first volley

1046. Weber's brigade sustained the highest casualties of the six federal brigades that fought at Bloody Lane—131 killed; 623 wounded; and 48 missing—for a total of 802.

1047. Nearly one-third of the 1st Delaware fell in the opening volley from Rodes' brigade, and almost the entire color guard of the regiment was shot down.

1048. The colors of the 1st Delaware fell within 60 feet of the Confederate line. They were not recovered until over one hour later in a daring dash by Lt. Charles Tanner (Company H). Tanner received three wounds in covering the 80 yards to the colors and in his return.

1049. The second US brigade to advance against the Sunken Road was Col. Dwight Morris' brigade. It aligned on the crest of the ridge paralleling the lane and in immediate support of Weber's wrecked regiments. (*OR* (1): 332-333)

1050. Each of Morris' three regiments was comprised of raw-recruits—only in the army for about a month.

1051. Morris' brigade was aligned with the 14th Connecticut on his right; the 130th Pennsylvania standing in the middle; and the 108th New York positioned on the left.

1052. The raw-recruit 14th Connecticut mistakenly fired into the backs of the regiment on its front, the 1st Delaware. (*OR* (1): 337)

1053. Eight officers commanding companies in the 1st Delaware were either killed or wounded, both by enemy fire and friendly fire.

1054. The Union regiment that suffered the heaviest casualties at Bloody Lane was the 1st Delaware—62 killed; 356 wounded; 32 missing—for a total of 450.

1055. Losses in the 1st Delaware were more than double any of the remaining 23 Union regiments that fought in the Bloody Lane sector.

1056. Gen. French's 1,750 casualties (some maintain he suffered as high as 1,980) were the second highest division casualties sustained by a Union division at Antietam. Only Sedgwick suffered more in his ill-fated West Woods debacle.

1057. Gen. Longstreet ordered an attack by Rodes' brigade against the Union right. This attack failed because the 6th Alabama—not hearing the command to move forward—exposed Rodes' right, and because the left (comprised of Colquitt's remnants) did not advance far enough. (*OR* 19 (1): 1037)

1058. About 3,400 Confederate reinforcements in Maj. Gen. Richard H. Anderson's division arrived to support D. H. Hill's two brigades holding the Sunken Road.

1059. Richard Anderson's division had marched throughout the night from Harpers Ferry along with the command of Lafayette McLaws. It arrived at Sharpsburg about sunrise on the 17th. (*OR* 19 (1): 857)

1060. Maj. Gen. Richard Heron Anderson was a 41-year-old native of Sumter County, South Carolina. He graduated from West Point in the class of 1842—a class that ultimately furnished 22 Union and Confederate generals.

1061. Gen. R. H. Anderson was present during the reduction of Fort Sumter in April 1861, and assumed command of Charleston, South Carolina, following Gen. P. G. T. Beauregard's departure for the Virginia Theater in May 1861.

1062. R. H. Anderson's division was the last reserves present and available for Gen. Lee during the late morning of the 17th.

1063. R. H. Anderson was wounded shortly after his arrival on the field. His untimely loss—and the subsequent lack of leadership and direction—reduced the positioning and combat effectiveness of his four brigades.

1064. Anderson's second-in-command, Marcus Wright, was also wounded as his brigade pressed forward. The command of Anderson's division thus fell to Brig. Gen. Roger A. Pryor.

1065. Roger Atkinson Pryor was a 34-year-old native of the Petersburg, Virginia, area. Pryor was not a graduate of West Point and had no military experience prior to the Civil War. Pryor was valedictorian of his class when he graduated from Hampden-Sydney College in 1845. He then attended the University of Virginia where he received his law degree.

1066. Pryor was serving in the US House of Representatives six weeks before war began. He resigned from the Congress on March 3, 1861—one day prior to Abraham Lincoln's first inauguration.

1067. R. H. Anderson's division did not initially pour into the Sunken Road. Confused and slowed by the wounding of its commanders, the division stalled in the Piper cornfield south of the road and in Piper's orchard.

1068. Gen. French committed his third and final brigade shortly after receiving a message from Second Corps commander E. V. Sumner indicating that "his right divisions were being severely handled." The message referred to the attack of Sedgwick in the West Woods. French was instructed to "press the enemy with all my force." (*OR* (1): 324)

1069. The third Union brigade to launch an assault against the Sunken Road was Nathan Kimball's brigade of four regiments. (*OR* (1): 324)

1070. Nathan Kimball inflicted the only battlefield defeat suffered by Stonewall Jackson when he forced Jackson's forces to retire from the Kernstown battlefield in the Shenandoah Valley on March 23, 1862.

1071. Kimball commanded the most veteran regiments in French's division. The 14th Indiana and the 8th Ohio fought with him at Kernstown, where they helped defeat Stonewall Jackson. The 7th [West] Virginia had been in the service for about nine months.

1072. The 7th [West] Virginia was comprised of mostly loyal Unionists from the western Virginia counties of Preston, Monongalia, Marshall, Ohio, Tyler, and Hardy. These counties refused to follow Virginia into secession, remaining faithful to the federal government throughout the war.

1073. The 7th [West] Virginia was not designated officially by the title *West Virginia* until 1863, when West Virginia was established as a state. In December 1862, the regiment's name was officially designated 7th Union Virginia Volunteers.

1074. The fourth regiment in Kimball's brigade—the 132nd Pennsylvania—was a nine-month regiment that had been in the service for less than a month.

1075. The 132nd Pennsylvania's first combat at Antietam was with bees, not bullets. While passing through Mr. Roulette's farm, the regiment knocked over some of Roulette's beehives and the buzzing swarms created chaos in the ranks that were initially more disconcerting than rebel bullets.

1076. Col. Richard A. Oakford, commander of the 132nd Pennsylvania, was mortally wounded within moments after his regiment arrived on the battlefield. (*OR* 19 (1): 331)

1077. Kimball deployed and advanced in brigade front, with the 14th Indiana on his extreme right. Next to the 14th was the 8th Ohio. These two regiments advanced on the west side of Roulette's farm lane—the lane that ran perpendicular to the Sunken Road through a deep ravine. On the east side of Roulette's lane was the 132nd Pennsylvania, and on the extreme left, the 7th [West] Virginia. (*OR* 19 (1): 327)

1078. Kimball's attack stalled about 50-80 yards from the Sunken Road. He remained in this position, holding this ground for over three hours. His brigade helped defeat three Confederate counterattacks—one on the left flank by the 30th North Carolina; one against his center by Carnot Posey's brigade of Anderson's division; and one on his right led by John R. Cooke with the 27th North Carolina and 3rd Arkansas. (*OR* 19 (1): 1048, 1051)

1079. Kimball's brigade suffered the second highest casualty rate of the six Union brigades that fought at Bloody Lane—121 killed; 510 wounded; and eight missing—a total of 639.

1080. Nathan Kimball wrote his official report on September 18, 1862—less than one day after the battle, and while the two opposing lines were still in battle lines at Antietam. (*OR* 19 (1): 327)

1081. Union reinforcements under Maj. Gen. Israel B. Richardson—the last of the Second Corps troops—began crossing Antietam Creek at Pry's Ford about 9:30 a.m. (*OR* 19 (1): 277)

1082. Richardson's division was the smallest in the Second Corps with only about 4,000 men in its three brigades.

1083. Richardson's division had been delayed in arriving on the battlefield because McClellan ordered it to remain east of Antietam Creek until George W. Morell's division of the Fifth Corps took its place in the tactical reserve. Morell did not arrive until nearly 9:00 a.m.—almost 1½ hours after the Second Corps began crossing the creek.

1084. Israel Bush Richardson—known by his men as "Fighting Dick" or "Greasy Dick"— was born in Vermont one day after Christmas 1815. Gen. Richardson was the son of Revolutionary War Gen. Israel Putnam.

1085. Richardson graduated from West Point in 1841—a class that contributed 23 future generals to the Union and Confederacy.

1086. The Irish Brigade led Richardson's division onto the field. The brigade flag waved with an emerald background and a distinctive gold harp and shamrock embossed on the silk. (*OR* (1): 227, 293)

1087. Three of the four regiments in the Irish Brigade were recruited in New York City and were comprised almost exclusively of Irishmen. They included the 63rd, 69th, and 88th New York Infantry regiments.

1088. One regiment in the Irish Brigade—the 29th Massachusetts—was comprised of "colonial stock" from the Bay State that included almost no men of Irish descent.

1089. Commanding the Irish Brigade was Brig. Gen. Thomas Francis Meagher (pronounced mahr, so that it rhymes with far) or (muh-HAR). (Quigley, *Civil War Spoken Here*, pp. 112-113)

1090. Gen. Meagher was born in Waterford, Ireland, on August 3, 1823. He participated in various Irish independence movements, and was banished by the British to Tasmania in 1849. He escaped from Tasmania three years later and eventually migrated to New York City, where he recruited and organized the Irish Brigade.

1091. Meagher's Irish Brigade arrived on the ridgeline paralleling the Sunken Road and extended Kimball's line on the Union left. The 69th New York and 29th Massachusetts formed the brigade's right, and the 63rd and 88th New York regiments anchored Meagher's left. The entire brigade fronted George B. Anderson's brigade of North Carolinians. (*OR* (1): 294)

1092. Father William Corby bestowed unconditional absolution upon all in the Irish Brigade who would fall in the coming battle, except those who displayed cowardice.

1093. The weapons used by the Irish Brigade were smoothbore muskets that fired a .69 caliber buck and ball. Weapons of this type—that are like shotguns and do not have the accuracy of rifles—required close-order combat to be effective.

1094. The Irish Brigade moved to within 50 paces of the Confederate right in the Sunken Road. It then delivered five to six volleys before Meagher ordered the front ranks to charge. The lines pushed to within 30 paces of the Confederates in the Sunken Road before the federals were stopped and forced to retire to the cover of the ridge. (*OR* (1): 294)

1095. The Confederates poured a devastating fire into the Irish Brigade, "literally cut[ting] lanes through our approaching line," Meagher reported. The 63rd New York and 69th New York lost 60% of their respective commands in only a few minutes. (*OR* (1): 294)

1096. Sixteen color bearers of the 63rd New York were shot down in the action at Bloody Lane. (*OR* (1): 296)

1097. Gen. Meagher's horse was shot from beneath him, and "from the shock which I myself sustained," he wrote in his official report, "I was obliged to be carried off the field." Some accused Meagher of being drunk and toppling from his horse in his stupor. (*OR* 19 (1): 295; Sears, *Landscaped Turned Red*, p. 244)

1098. Gen. George B. Anderson, commanding the North Carolina brigade holding the Confederate right in the Sunken Road, was mortally wounded in the ankle. He was taken to Raleigh, North Carolina, where his foot was amputated. He failed to recover from the wound and died on October 16, 1862.

1099. G. B. Anderson was the only Confederate general killed or mortally wounded during the Bloody Lane phase of the battle. He would be the last Confederate general to die from wounds received at Antietam—dying only one day short of the battle's one-month anniversary.

1100. Col. Charles C. Tew of the 2nd North Carolina Infantry rose to command of G. B. Anderson's brigade, but only momentarily—Tew was killed by a bullet through the brain shortly after he took command. The brigade then fell into the hands of Col. R. T. Bennett of the 14th North Carolina Infantry.

1101. Charles Corutenay Tew was born in Charleston, South Carolina, on October 17, 1827. He graduated from the South Carolina Military Academy in 1846, and taught at the academy for 11 years. He established the Hillsboro Military Academy in North Carolina in 1858.

1102. Confederate reinforcements from R. H. Anderson's division pressed forward from the Piper cornfield and orchard to support the Confederate right in the Sunken Road. Col. R. T. Bennett, now in command of G. B. Anderson's North Carolina brigade holding the lane, described the approach as "masses of Confederate troops in great confusion." (*OR* 19 (1): 1048)

1103. Col. Risden Tyler Bennett of the 14th North Carolina Infantry was an antebellum lawyer who began his Civil War career as a corporal in the 14th regiment. At age 22, he was promoted to colonel of the regiment.

1104. Col. Bennett was wounded four times during the war—first at Antietam, with subsequent wounds at Gettysburg in 1863; Spotsylvania in May 1864; and Cold Harbor in June 1864.

1105. Two regiments of Carnot Posey's Confederate brigade—the 16th Mississippi and the 2nd Florida—recklessly passed over and through the Sunken Road and attempted to drive a wedge between the right of the Irish Brigade and the left of Kimball's brigade. The attack was unsupported and resulted in a complete failure. (*OR* 19 (1): 1048)

1106. The 16th Mississippi lost nearly 55.7% of its strength in the ill-fated charge north of Bloody Lane.

1107. The Irish Brigade nearly expended all of its ammunition and was relieved by the arrival of Brig. Gen. John C. Caldwell's brigade.

1108. Both the Irish Brigade and Caldwell's brigade performed a maneuver that permitted one to pass through the other without disrupting the lines. When leaving the battle front, the Irish Brigade broke into companies that marched to the rear. Caldwell's brigade formed companies that proceeded to the front. This was accomplished under some Confederate fire, but in relative safety behind the ridge that paralleled the Sunken Road. (*OR* 19 (1): 227, 285)

1109. Caldwell's brigade advanced to within 30 yards of the Sunken Road—at the crest of the ridge paralleling the road. On the brigade's right was the 61st and 64th New York regiments (consolidated). In the middle stood the 7th New York and 81st Pennsylvania. Holding the left was the 5th New Hampshire Infantry. (*OR* 19 (1): 227, 285)

1110. Eleven of the 20 Union regiments that fought at Bloody Lane were New York regiments.

1111. Col. Francis Channing Barlow commanded the consolidated 61st and 64th New York regiments.

1112. Col. Barlow was the 27-year-old son of a Brooklyn minister. He graduated from Harvard in 1855 and then studied law in New York, where he was admitted to the bar in 1858. He enlisted as a private in the three-month 12th New York at the outset of the war and then reentered the army as a lieutenant in the 61st New York.

1113. Barlow enlisted at the outbreak of the war just one day after his marriage.

1114. Barlow's advance coincided with the confused withdrawal of Posey's brigade from the Sunken Road on the Confederate right. The appearance of a general Confederate withdrawal—in addition to the advance of Caldwell's legions along the Confederate right and, for the first time, overlapping their extreme right—sent one half of G. B. Anderson's regiments in flight, leaving only the 2nd and 14th North Carolina to defend the position. (*OR* 19 (1): 289)

1115. Col. Francis Marion Parker of the 30th North Carolina miraculously escaped death when a bullet sliced a deep groove in his skull. The missile did not penetrate the membrane encasing his brain.

1116. Barlow's New Yorkers encountered a slackening of Confederate resistance due to the partial evacuation of the Sunken Road on the Confederate right. Barlow immediately took advantage of the reduced enemy fire, advancing to the crest of the ridge overlooking the lane. From this advanced position, his men poured an enfilading fire into the road itself. (*OR* 19 (1): 289)

1117. Confusion on the Confederate left resulted from the enfilading fire of Barlow's New Yorkers. The 6th Alabama—holding the extreme right of Rodes' brigade—came under a severe and deadly fire. (*OR* 19 (1): 289)

1118. Col. John B. Gordon, commander of the 6th Alabama, was wounded for the fifth time. The first bullet struck Gordon in the calf of his right leg. A second ball hit the same leg, but did not break any bone. A third bullet pierced his left arm. A fourth ball smashed into his shoulder. (Gordon, *Reminiscences of the Civil War*, p. 89)

1119. The fifth wound Col. Gordon received was a bullet in the face that barely missed the jugular vein on its exit. Gordon fell forward, unconscious from this wound, with his face buried in his cap. He later claimed that he would have suffocated in his own blood had it not been "for the act of some Yankee, who, as if to save my life, had at a previous hour during the battle, shot a hole through the cap, which let the blood out." (Gordon, *Reminiscences of the Civil War*, p. 90)

1120. Lieut. Col. James Newell Lightfoot of the 6th Alabama sought guidance from Gen. Rodes following Col. Gordon's incapacitation. To protect the regiment from the enfilading fire of Barlow's New Yorkers, Rodes ordered him to "refuse" his right wing in order to face the enemy. (*OR* 19 (1): 1037)

1121. The Confederate line at Bloody Lane was abandoned by a mistaken order. Lieut. Col. Lightfoot misunderstood Gen. Rodes' command to turn his right flank so that it was parallel to the enfilading fire of Barlow's regiments. Instead, Lightfoot ordered a retreat. (*OR* 19 (1): 1037)

1122. Six words effectively ended the Confederate defense of Bloody Lane—"Sixth Alabama, about face; forward march." This was the mistaken order Col. Lightfoot gave to his regiment. (*OR* 19 (1): 1037)

1123. Maj. E. L. Hobson, commanding the 5th Alabama located to the left of the 6th, asked Lightfoot if the order to retreat was intended for the entire brigade. Lightfoot then made another mistake telling Hobson "Yes." At that point, all of Rodes' brigade abandoned the Sunken Road. (*OR* 19 (1): 1038)

1124. Gen. Rodes was not present at the Sunken Road when his Alabama brigade withdrew. Rodes was several hundred yards to the rear near the Piper farm buildings, aiding a wounded assistant. (*OR* 19 (1): 1038)

1125. Rodes attempted to rally his brigade, but it retreated in such confusion he found only 40 men. The remainder, Rodes wrote in his report, had "completely disappeared from this portion of the field." (*OR* 19 (1): 1038)

1126. Rodes rallied about 150 men and placed them in line on a small ridge running parallel to the Sunken Road—but to its rear some 150 yards. The men were comprised of remnants of his own brigade (about 40 men), as well as scattered troops from Mississippi and North Carolina.

1127. Many Confederate casualties occurred not in the Sunken Road itself, but on the high ground south of the road. This resulted as the retiring Confederates were exposed to a murderous infantry fire from Union regiments on the paralleling ridge north of the road—some 200 yards distant. (*OR* 19 (1): 291)

Confederate Dead in Bloody Lane (*USAMHI*)

1128. Gen. McClellan witnessed the rupture in Lee's center from his headquarters at the Pry House. "It is the most beautiful field I ever saw, and the grandest battle!" he exclaimed. "If we whip them today it will wipe out Bull Run forever." (Sears, *Landscape Turned Red*, p. 24)

1129. Barlow's New York regiments captured nearly 300 Confederates of G. B. Anderson's brigade following the sudden departure of Rodes' brigade on the Confederate left. The evacuation of Rodes' men exposed the remainder of Anderson's North Carolinians holding the right. (*OR* 19 (1): 289)

1130. Two Confederate battle flags were seized by the 61st New York. A third was captured by the 64th New York but was subsequently lost when the captor was shot. (*OR* 19 (1): 289)

1131. The Confederate casualties in Bloody Lane left an indelible impression upon Lt. Thomas Livermore of the 5th New Hampshire: "In this road there lay so many dead rebels that they formed a line which one might have walked upon as far as I could see." (Thomas Livermore, *Numbers and Losses in the Civil War in America, 1861-1865*, p. 140)

1132. Barlow's New York regiments pressed south into Piper's cornfield after the Confederates abandoned the Sunken Road. Barlow reported: "[N]o enemy appeared in this field." (*OR* 19 (1): 290)

1133. Confusion struck the federal ranks following the seizure of Bloody Lane. "Our troops were joined together without much order," Barlow recalled. "[S]everal regiments in front of others, and none in my neighborhood having very favorable opportunities to use their fire." This confusion stalled the federal advance. (*OR* 19 (1): 290)

1134. One of the greatest understatements of the battle of Antietam was recorded by Gen. Longstreet following the collapse of the Confederate line at Bloody Lane: "From this moment our center was extremely weak . . ." Longstreet wrote in his official report, dated October 10, 1862. (*OR* 19 (1): 840)

1135. Gen. Longstreet attempted to relieve pressure against the Confederate center by ordering a flank attack against the exposed right of the Union forces massed at Bloody Lane. (*OR* 19 (1): 915)

1136. Longstreet ordered Col. John R. Cooke—in position just south of the West Woods, and holding the ground on the right of John Walker's division—to lead the 27th North Carolina (his own regiment), the 3rd Arkansas, and the remnants of Cobb's brigade in an assault against the Union center near Bloody Lane. (*OR* 19 (1): 915)

1137. The 3rd Arkansas was the only regiment from the Razorback state at Antietam.

1138. Col. John R. Cooke was the brother-in-law of Jeb Stuart. Cooke was also the son of Union Maj. Gen. Philip St. George Cooke, who commanded McClellan's cavalry in the Peninsula Campaign in the spring of 1862.

1139. Longstreet's counterattack against the Union center at Bloody Lane only employed about 675 men. Longstreet had no other infantry reinforcements available.

1140. The route of Cooke's attack was from west to east. It began from the area south of the West Woods, then crossed the Hagerstown Pike, and then drove east toward the Roulette farm.

1141. Kimball's and Caldwell's brigades united to protect the Union right flank and to halt Cooke's attack. Kimball turned the 130th Pennsylvania, 14th Indiana, and 8th Ohio at right angles to the Sunken Road. Extending the line on Kimball's left were Barlow's New York regiments, as well as the 52nd New York Infantry. (*OR* 19 (1): 290-291, 327)

1142. Cooke's regiments advanced to within 200 yards of the reformed federal line—now running perpendicular to the Sunken Road. According to Brig. Gen. John G. Walker, in his official report: "Battery after battery, regiment after regiment opened their fire upon them, hurling a torrent of missiles through their ranks, but nothing could arrest their progress." (*OR* 19 (1): 915)

1143. After firing about 20 rounds, Cooke ran out of ammunition and retired rapidly back to the vicinity of the Hagerstown Pike, under a severe artillery and infantry fire. Cooke lost about half of his detachment in his ill-fated attack. (*OR* 19 (1): 291, 916)

1144. Longstreet personally led two guns of Capt. M. B. Miller's Battery forward to the edge of the Piper orchard to fire upon the federal force that had seized the Piper cornfield and Bloody Lane. (*OR* 19 (1): 849-850)

1145. Longstreet's staff aided in firing Miller's 12-pounder Napoleons after many of Miller's artillerymen were shot down. Longstreet remained near Miller's guns, holding the horses of his staff, standing on the battlefield with one foot in a carpet slipper. (*OR* 19 (1): 849-850)

1146. A third cannon from Miller's battery, under Sgt. William H. Ellis, arrived in support of Miller's two other Napoleons. This piece was serviced by infantrymen from the 6th Virginia Infantry. (*OR* 19 (1): 850)

1147. Gen. D. H. Hill discovered Capt. R. Boyce's South Carolina battery concealed in a cornfield near the Piper farm buildings. He ordered it forward to fire on the federals holding the Sunken Road and the Piper cornfield just south of the road. The battery had one of its caissons explode during the advance, but it unlimbered and "with grape and canister [drove] the Yankees back." (*OR* 19 (1): 1024)

1148. Boyce's artillerymen were positioned within easy canister range of the federals in the Piper cornfield. According to Capt. Boyce, the enemy line showed a front of several hundred yards that was plainly visible to the right and center, but partly concealed by corn on the left. Boyce cut down two enemy flags in his second and third discharges and, he reported, the federal right and center "soon gave way and retired." (*OR* 19 (1): 943)

1149. The effective fire of Boyce's battery convinced D. H. Hill that the time had arrived for a Confederate counterattack. "I was now satisfied that the Yankees were so demoralized, Hill claimed in his official report, "that a single regiment of fresh men could drive the whole of them in our front across the Antietam." (*OR* 19 (1): 1024)

1150. Gen. Hill personally grabbed a musket and led about 200 men—most of them from Rodes' broken command—through the Piper orchard in an attack against the federals at the Sunken Road. Hill's effort failed because, as he reported, it was met "with a warm reception, and the little command [was] broken and dispersed." (*OR* 19 (1): 288, 1024)

1151. A second Confederate attack, comprised of another 200 men from remnants of 5th, 20th, and 23rd North Carolina regiments, attacked the federal left flank. The 5th New Hampshire, holding the extreme federal left in the Piper cornfield and at the Sunken Road, saw Hill's flanking column and repulsed it, capturing the state colors of the 4th North Carolina in the process. (*OR* 19 (1): 288, 1024)

1152. Both of Hill's desperate attacks failed, but Hill reported both attacks "have a most happy effect." "The Yankees were completely deceived by their boldness," Hill explained, "and induced to believe that there was a large force in our center. They made no further attempt to pierce our center, except on a small scale." (*OR* 19 (1): 1024)

1153. Col. Cooke's command of the 27th North Carolina and the 3rd Arkansas added to this charade of Confederate strength in the center. Without a cartridge in hand, according to Longstreet, Cooke "stood with his empty guns, and waved his colors to show that his troops were in position." This deception—along with Boyce's and Miller's cannon, and the two small infantry attacks by Hill—helped to halt federal movements against the Confederate center. (*OR* 19 (1): 840)

1154. The mortal wounding of division commander Israel B. Richardson contributed to the federal failure to exploit the breach in the Confederate center. Richardson was wounded by case shot that struck him in the leg while he was positioning Capt. William Graham's artillery on his left near the eastern end of Bloody Lane.

1155. Gen. Richardson was the only Union general that was mortally wounded in the Bloody Lane sector of the battlefield.

1156. Israel Richardson was the last general—of the eight shot down at Antietam—to die from mortal wounds received at Antietam. Richardson died at the Pry House on November 3, 1862—nearly seven weeks after the battle.

1157. Col. Francis Barlow was badly wounded in the groin by a spherical case shot, and the loss of his aggressive leadership contributed to the Union failure to exploit the collapse of the Confederate center. Barlow was succeeded by Lieut. Col. Nelson A. Miles. (*OR* 19 (1): 290-291)

1158. Barlow wrote his official report on September 22, 1862, from his hospital bed. His report was addressed from: "General Hospital, Keedysville, Md." (*OR* 19 (1): 289)

1159. Brig. Gen. Winfield Scott Hancock was ordered by McClellan to take command of Richardson's division following Richardson's wounding. Hancock was a brigade commander in the Sixth Corps. (*OR* 19 (1): 279)

1160. Hancock was born on Valentine's Day 1824 near Norristown, Pennsylvania. He graduated from West Point in 1844 and was serving as chief quartermaster in Los Angeles when the war began in 1861.

1161. Hancock received instructions from McClellan that emphasized defense rather than offense: "My instructions were to hold that position [Piper cornfield and Bloody Lane] against the enemy," Hancock noted in his official report, written 12 days after the battle. (*OR* 19 (1): 279)

1162. Hancock discovered his command numbered about 2,100 men, *with no artillery support*. Hancock applied for two batteries of artillery, in addition to a plea to the chief of artillery, but "none could be spared at that time." Less than one mile north of Hancock's position were 44 federal cannon massed from seven different batteries. (Sears, *Landscape Turned Red*, p. 253)

1163. Confederate casualties in the Bloody Lane sector were nearly 2,600. Union casualties numbered about 3,000.

1164. At 1:20 p.m. on the 17th—shortly after the federal breakthrough in the Confederate center—Gen. McClellan sent a message to General-in-Chief Halleck in Washington: "We are in the midst of the most terrible battle of the war—perhaps of history," McClellan adroitly observed. "Thus far it looks well, but I have great odds against me. . ." (*OR* 19 (1): 312)

Bloody Lane (*USAMHI*)

Roulette House (*USAMHI*)

Late Afternoon
Burnside Bridge and A. P. Hill's Attack

1165. Burnside Bridge received its name from Union Maj. Gen. Ambrose E. Burnside, whose forces attacked and carried the bridge during the late morning and early afternoon of September 17.

1166. Lincoln offered Burnside command of the Army of the Potomac on two occasions. First after the President's disillusionment with McClellan's failed Peninsula Campaign and second, just before the onset of The Maryland Campaign. Burnside, although flattered, refused both offers: "I had always unreservedly expressed that I was not competent to command such a large army as this." (Sears, *Landscape Turned Red*, p. 79)

1167. Phase three of Antietam occurred on the southern end of the battlefield. This area constituted the Union left and the Confederate right. Fighting there began at 10:00 a.m. and continued in earnest until 6:00 p.m.

1168. The only combat at Antietam adjacent to the creek itself occurred at or near Burnside Bridge.

1169. The only location where Confederate infantry defended against the crossing of Antietam Creek was between Burnside Bridge and nearby Snavely's Ford, one mile south of the bridge.

1170. No other Union force at Antietam faced terrain as difficult as Burnside's men. First, the creek functioned as a moat. Second, the steep bluffs towering over the creek's west bank acted like castle turrets. Beyond the bluffs toward Sharpsburg, the ground "seesaws" into broken, undulating ridges and ravines.

1171. Burnside was the *only* Union commander at Antietam to carry the position he was instructed to assault (the bridge).

1172. Burnside Bridge is a three-arch, 125-foot limestone structure constructed in 1836 by master bridge builder John Weaver. The cost was $2,300.

1173. Much of the limestone used in the bridge's construction was quarried from a steep 100-foot eminence overlooking the structure's western terminus. These excavation pits were used by the Confederates during their defense of the position. They remain visible today.

1174. Before the battle, the bridge was known as the Lower Bridge—situated "lower" or further downstream than any of the three bridges in close proximity to Sharpsburg. The bridge also appeared as the Rohrbach Bridge, named after Henry Rohrbach, whose farm lies east of the bridge.

1175. The dirt roadway crossing the bridge was twelve feet wide. The road connected Sharpsburg with the village of Rohrersville, five miles to the east.

1176. Wooden shingles capped the bridge's vertical retaining walls to shield them from rain, snow, and ice. This prevented water penetration and freeze/thaw action that injured the stability of the stone and mortar.

115

Burnside Bridge viewed from the Confederate position *(USAMHI)*

1177. A Confederate brigade under Brig. Gen. Robert A. Toombs held the vertical bluffs spiraling above the bridge along the west bank of Antietam Creek. Toombs's force consisted of the 2nd, 20th, and 50th Georgia regiments—about 400 men. *(OR* 19 (1): 888-889)

1178. Toombs's brigade represented the advance position on the extreme Confederate right. The primary position, held by Maj. Gen. David R. Jones's division, was on a linear ridge nearly three-quarters of a mile north of Toombs. *(OR* 19 (1): 886)

1179. Robert Augustus Toombs was age 52 at Antietam. Born July 2, 1810, in Wilkes County, Georgia, he had a career in politics as a Whig and Democrat, including service in the US House and Senate. Toombs resigned as a US Senator in 1861 to help lead Georgia through secession.

1180. When the new Confederate government formed in February 1861, Toombs was among the frontrunners for the office of president. He was embittered when the appointment went to Jefferson Davis.

1181. Toombs served as the first Secretary of State of the Confederacy until July 19, 1861, when he resigned to accept an appointment as a brigadier in the Confederate army.

1182. As a politician with no military experience, Toombs viewed old army discipline and procedure with some disdain. He once proclaimed the epitaph of the Confederate army would be: "Died of West Point." (Warner, *Generals in Gray*, p. 307)

1183. Ambrose Everett Burnside was age 38 at Antietam. Born on May 23, 1824, at Liberty, Union County, Indiana, Burnside was the son of a former South Carolina slave owner.

1184. Burnside graduated from West Point in 1847, one year behind McClellan's class. He and McClellan developed a close friendship at the Point, and in the late 1850s, he worked for McClellan at the Illinois Central Railroad.

1185. McClellan and Burnside affectionately referred to each other as "Mac" and "Burn."

1186. Burnside invented the "Burnside carbine" while in the army, and moved to Rhode Island in 1853 to open a factory to produce the weapon. The initial venture failed when Burnside did not receive a government contract, forcing him into bankruptcy.

1187. The Burnside carbine was the first US military weapon to use a metallic cartridge. Over 55,000 Burnside carbines were delivered to the government during the Civil War, second only to the Spencer and Sharps carbines.

1188. Other than McClellan, Burnside was the only Union officer at Antietam who had experience as an independent army commander. Burnside led the very successful North Carolina coastal expedition in the spring and early summer of 1862, seizing Albemarle and Pamlico sounds, and capturing Roanoke Island, New Bern, Beaufort, and Fort Macon.

1189. The McClellan-Burnside friendship was strained during The Maryland Campaign. Reasons included: 1) "Little Mac's" jealousy over Lincoln's offer to Burnside to command the army; and 2) the insidious machinations of Fitz John Porter—McClellan's closest friend—who attempted to demean Burnside and present him as a threat to McClellan. (Sears, *Landscape Turned Red*, pp. 170-171, 259)

1190. McClellan effectively diminished Burnside's authority by splitting his "wing command" in half when the army arrived at Antietam. McClellan assigned Hooker's First Corps operations to the extreme north end of the field. The Ninth Corps held the far southern end of the Union line. Separated by nearly three miles, this arrangement made it impossible for Burnside to command his entire wing.

1191. McClellan apologists blamed Burnside for sulking in his demoted role, thus purposely delaying the readiness of his troops and implementation of orders on the 15th through the 17th.

1192. Burnside became McClellan's scapegoat for his failure to snare a complete military victory at Antietam. In his August 1863 report on the campaign—compiled after 11 months of reflection—McClellan unjustly accused Burnside of repeated delays. Had it not been for his procrastination, "Little Mac" opined, "[o]ur victory might thus have been much more decisive." (*OR* 19 (1): 64)

1193. Maintaining his position as wing commander, Burnside assigned Maj. Gen. Jacob D. Cox to temporary command of the Ninth Corps. (*OR* 19 (1): 418)

1194. Jacob Dolson Cox, at age 33, was the youngest Union corps commander at Antietam.

1195. Cox was born in Montreal, Canada, on October 27, 1828. He was an attorney and state senator from Warren, Ohio, prior to the war. Gen. Cox was a strong abolitionist who helped organize the Ohio Republican Party.

1196. Cox, a political appointee who had no previous military experience, served as a brigadier under McClellan in "Little Mac's" successful western Virginia campaign in 1861. Cox remained in command in western Virginia until August 1862.

1197. The Ninth Corps comprised approximately 12,000 men. It included four divisions, eight brigades, and 29 infantry regiments.

1198. The Confederate opposition to the Ninth Corps, defending the bluffs overlooking the Lower Bridge, was 220 men in Col. John B. Cumming's 20th Georgia and 120 soldiers in Lieut. Col. William R. Holmes's 2nd Georgia infantry.

1199. Gen. Toombs ordered Col. Henry Benning, commander of the 17th Georgia, and Toombs's most capable subordinate, to defend the bridge. (*OR* 19 (1): 889)

1200. "Old Rock " Benning was a former justice on the Georgia Supreme Court.

1201. Col. Benning deployed the 20th Georgia opposite the mouth of the bridge and to its left (or north) 200 yards. Extending south of the bridge for about 300 yards was the 2nd Georgia regiment.

1202. Burnside received orders from McClellan to *prepare for attack* at 7:00 a.m. on the 17th. Burnside promptly conveyed the alert to Cox, and the temporary commander moved the Ninth Corps into position. McClellan later claimed in his August 3, 1863, report that he ordered Burnside *to attack*. This was a fabrication designed to blame Burnside for impertinent delay. (*OR* 19 (1): 424)

1203. Burnside received McClellan's order *to attack* three hours after the preparatory order. The attack order was dated 9:10 a.m. and hand-delivered by Lt. John M. Wilson of "Little Mac's" staff. Burnside immediately instructed Cox to initiate the assault and Cox complied immediately. (*OR* 19 (1): 419; *OR* 51 (1): 884)

1204. The 11th Connecticut Infantry, commanded by Col. Henry W. Kingsbury, Jr., was the first Union force to advance against the bridge. (*OR* 19 (1): 419, 425)

1205. Kingsbury charged over a knoll directly opposite the eastern entrance to the bridge. Three hundred yards separated the top of the slope from the creek. The Nutmeg boys reached the eastern bank, but were subject to a withering fire from the Georgians. Ten minutes after its advance, the 11th withdrew, losing 139 of its strength of 440 men— 31.5%.

1206. The 11th Connecticut suffered the highest casualty rate in the fight for Burnside Bridge.

1207. The highest number of killed in action for any Union regiment in combat at Burnside Bridge was 36 men—the loss suffered by the 11th Connecticut.

1208. Col. Kingsbury was shot four times and mortally wounded near the eastern mouth of the bridge. He died at the Henry Rohrbach farm house.

1209. Kingsbury was married to a daughter of former president and Mexican War hero Zachary Taylor.

1210. Kingsbury's brother-in-law was Maj. Gen. David R. Jones—commander of the far right of the Confederate line at Antietam—a ridge only three quarters of a mile from Burnside Bridge.

1211. Attempts to ford the stream by Capt. John Griswold of Company A, 11th Connecticut, proved deadly, as the Georgians chopped down the attackers in the four-foot water. Griswold struggled across the creek, but died from his wounds on the west bank. Griswold's valiant effort proved the futility of fording the creek.

1212. Col. George Crook badly bungled the second assault against the bridge. First, he held the largest of his three regiments, 800 men of the 36th Ohio, in reserve. Second, disaster struck when only four companies of the 28th Ohio moved forward, with the remainder staying behind to guard a two-gun battery. Third, the 11th Ohio split in half, with the right wing completely missing the bridge. Fourth, Crook himself got lost when advancing with half of the 28th Ohio, emerging nearly 400 yards north of his target, where he became pinned down for two hours.

1213. Of the brigades engaged at the bridge, Crook suffered the fewest casualties—only 67 out of 2,005 men—or just 3.3 percent.

1214. The third assault on the bridge ended in failure. The 2nd Maryland and the 6th New Hampshire, with 300 men, formed in a column of fours and followed the Rohrersville Road—exposing their flank to the murderous fire of the Georgians—only 100 yards away on the paralleling bluffs. The head of the column reached to within 250 feet of the bridge before the men broke for cover. (*OR* 19 (1): 444)

1215. The 2nd Maryland, commanded by Lieut. Col. Jacob Duryea, suffered 44% casualties—the highest percentage loss of any regiment attacking Burnside Bridge.

1216. Benning's Georgians fended off three attacks in 2½ hours. The narrow gorge separating the warring opponents effectively canceled Burnside's numerical advantage i.e., any approach to the bridge crammed limited Union regiments into the throat of a bottle.

1217. While Burnside hammered the bridge with frontal assaults, Maj. Gen. Isaac P. Rodman's division searched for an avenue to flank Benning's Georgians out of their stronghold. (*OR* 19 (1): 425)

1218. Gen. Rodman had just recently rejoined the Ninth Corps. He was at home in Rhode Island throughout the summer of 1862 recuperating from an apparent bout with typhoid fever.

1219. Rodman's search for a suitable crossing of Antietam Creek was hampered by poor advice from McClellan's staff engineers. On September 16, the engineers identified a ford about two thirds of a mile south of the bridge; but when Rodman marched there about 10:30 a.m. on the 17th, he discovered skirmishers of the 50th Georgia guarding the position from their perch 160 feet above the stream. Another crossing had to be found.

1220. Rodman discovered another ford—known locally as Snavely's Ford—one mile south of the Lower Bridge.

1221. Gen. Rodman's 3,200 man division had to march a circuitous two-mile route to gain access to Snavely's Ford. Nearly two hours passed. Finally, sometime between noon and 12:30 p.m., Rodman reached the ford.

1222. Maj. Gen. John G. Walker's Confederate division guarded Snavely's Ford and the extreme Rebel right until about 9:00 a.m. on the 17th. The division was then moved north by Gen. Lee to support weakened Confederate positions in the vicinity of the West Woods on the army's left. (*OR* 19 (1): 914)

1223. Walker's vacated position at Snavely's Ford remained a Confederate void because Gen. Lee did not have the troops to replace Walker.

1224. Rodman would have faced stiff resistance from Confederates protecting Snavely's Ford—holding high ground and in a strong defensive position—had Walker not been transferred to another sector of the battlefield. Rodman's crossing and flanking movement became problematic.

1225. The 50th Georgia and a company of South Carolinians—totaling about 125 men under Col. Benning's command—attempted to fill the void at Snavely's Ford following the removal of Walker. (*OR* 19 (1): 889)

1226. When Rodman arrived at Snavely's Ford he received resistance from Confederate skirmishers perched atop a 185-foot bluff. Rodman called upon Col. Harrison Fairchild's brigade of New Yorkers to clear the area.

1227. The 9th New York "Hawkins Zouaves" Infantry, with 373 in its ranks, splashed across at Snavely's Ford—the first federal regiment to breach the Antietam moat in the southern sector of the battlefield.

1228. The Georgians and South Carolinians attempted to stall Rodman's crossing by defending a stone wall 165 yards from the ford, but the outgunned Confederates were no match for the bluecoats and were quickly pushed back from the position.

1229. Once across Snavely's Ford, Rodman rapidly extended his line north toward the Lower Bridge. Fairchild's brigade began pressing the right flank of the Georgians' overlooking the bridge.

1230. Burnside staged his fourth and final frontal assault against the bridge at 1:00 p.m. (*OR* 19 (1): 419, 425)

1231. Gen. Burnside selected Brig. Gen. Samuel Davis Sturgis' division to carry the bridge. Sturgis was a classmate of McClellan's at West Point, and one year ahead of Burnside at the academy. A native of Shippensburg, Pennsylvania, Sturgis was age 40 at Sharpsburg.

1232. Sturgis was famous for uttering one of the most insubordinate, insulting, and inflaming comments in American military lore: "I don't care for John Pope one pinch of owl dung!" Sturgis voiced this declaration just prior to Second Manassas in late August 1862 after learning his division must wait in line to use the railroad supplying Pope. (Warner, *Generals in Gray*, p. 487)

1233. The "two 51sts"—the 51st Pennsylvania and the 51st New York—were selected by division commander Sturgis to drive the Rebels away from the bridge. (*OR* 19 (1): 444)

1234. When Col. Edward Ferrero informed his brigade that the "two 51sts" had been chosen for the honor of storming the bridge, Cpl. Lewis Patterson of Company I, 51st Pennsylvania, bellowed: "Will you give us our whiskey, colonel, if we take it?" Ferrero answered back: " Yes, by God! You shall have as much as you want, if you take the bridge." (Murfin, *The Glean of Bayonets*, pp. 274-275)

1235. Edward Ferrero was born in Spain to Italian parents. Col. Ferrero *literally* followed in the steps of his father—a dance-master in New York City. Ferrero taught dancing, waltz, and fencing lessons to cadets at West Point before the war.

1236. Ferrero aligned the "two 51sts" behind the cover of a knoll, the base of which was 100 yards east of the bridge. The Pennsylvanians of Col. John Hartranft formed on the right; the New Yorkers of Col. Robert Potter on the left. Each regiment brought 335 men into the fight.

1237. Col. John Frederick Hartranft was a trained civil engineer who became a practicing lawyer. He was a 31-year-old native of Pottstown, Pennsylvania.

1238. Hartranft commanded a 90-day Pennsylvania militia regiment on the eve of First Manassas whose time expired one day prior to the battle. Despite personal pleas, the regiment refused to fight at Manassas and instead marched to the rear.

1239. Col. Robert Brown Potter, commander of the 51st New York, began his Civil War military career as a private in the New York state militia.

1240. Potter was promoted to colonel of the 51st on September 10—only seven days prior to Antietam.

1241. The two colonels who led the successful assault against Burnside Bridge were both lawyers before the war.

1242. Three hundred yards of open field separated the crest of the knoll, behind which were the "two 51sts," from the eastern entrance to the bridge.

1243. A five-foot high chestnut rail fence—running parallel to the Sharpsburg-Rohrersville Road and the creek—proved an obstacle to the momentum of the "two 51sts" as they charged toward the yawning eastern opening of the bridge. The fence's connection with the upper abutment of the bridge prohibited entry from the adjoining field. The fence effectively stalled the attack of the two regiments, creating mass congestion.

1244. The bridge-blocking fence forced the 51st Pennsylvania to the right, where it sought cover behind a stone wall paralleling the creek.

1245. The 51st New York veered left, crowding and stretching along the post and rail fence. This fence barrier—and the massed concentration it produced—provided the best opportunity for the Georgians to inflict casualties.

1246. Col. J. F. Hartranft of the 51st Pennsylvania, positioned near the upper wing wall of the bridge, had two panels of the fence nearest the bridge torn down, thus opening an outlet at the choke point.

1247. Hartranft admitted "the most fatal act" of the 51st Pennsylvania was stopping and returning the enemy's fire. "If we had not stopped, we would have returned with little loss." (Murfin, *The Gleam of Bayonets*, pp. 275-276)

1248. The "two 51sts" suffered 207 dead and wounded in their attack on the bridge, or about one in three of the 670 men in action.

1249. Confederate fire from the bluffs above the bridge suddenly slackened as colonels Hartranft and Potter attempted to breach the stubborn fence. Both colonels seized the opportunity, and with the New York and Pennsylvania colors leading the way, side by side, the two columns sprinted across the stone span. The bridge belonged to Burnside!

Burnside Bridge from the Union Position *(USAMHI)*

1250. Lieut. Col. William R. Holmes of the 2nd Georgia—waving his sword in a last and desperate act of defiance—attempted to lead a Confederate counterattack, but was killed in a shower of Union bullets near the west entrance of the bridge. (*OR* 19 (1): 892)

1251. Benning evacuated his position above the bridge because he was almost out of ammunition and Rodman's division was threatening to overrun his right flank.

1252. Benning's defenders retired approximately one half of a mile to a stone wall, where they joined other regiments of Toombs's brigade and replenished their ammunition. Benning's day was not yet over. (*OR* 19 (1): 890-891)

1253. Col. Benning and his 340 Georgians delayed Burnside's crossing of the Lower Bridge for three hours. Burnside seized the position shortly after 1:00 p.m.

1254. Benning's defense of Burnside Bridge and Snavely's Ford cost the Confederates 120 dead and wounded—about one in four Rebel defenders. They inflicted a toll four times as great within Burnside's bluecoats.

1255. Confederate artillery stopped any further advance by Sturgis once across the bridge. After scaling the bluffs formerly held by the Confederates, Sturgis discovered Confederate batteries to the north some 500 to 600 yards. "We could only lie down and await reinforcements," Sturgis reflected in his official report, filed five days after the battle. (*OR* 19 (1): 444)

1256. Railroad iron was being fired from some Confederate cannon. Sturgis recalled the railroad iron, along with canister and shell, as "vehicles of destruction [that] fell like hail." (*OR* 19 (1): 444)

1257. Burnside's seizure of the bridge did not break the Confederate right. D. R. Jones's division of 2,430 men held the high ground three quarters of a mile north of the Lower Bridge. Antietam's climax occurred here. (*OR* 19 (1): 886)

1258. D. R. Jones would receive approximately 400 reinforcements early in the afternoon, expanding his force to nearly 2,800. The reinforcements were the 15th and 17th Georgia—that had been detached from Toombs's brigade—and five companies from the 11th Georgia. (*OR* 19 (1): 886)

1259. Half of the 11th Georgia was at Martinsburg on the 16th and 17th, guarding Gen. D. H. Hill's commissary train. This "left wing" of the regiment did not make it to Sharpsburg. (*OR* 19 (1): 911)

1260. If Burnside crushed Jones and collapsed the Rebel right, Lee's umbilical cord—his line of retreat to the Potomac and Virginia—would become exposed to the Union knife.

1261. Gen. Lee could not shift troops to strengthen Jones's position. Lee's *modus operandi* throughout the day—moving brigades and even divisions to shore up holes at Union pressure points—worked only when extra men were available or relief occurred along the front. Neither relief nor more men were present options for Gen. Lee. Jones must stand alone—unless help arrived from afar.

1262. Maj. Gen. David Rumph Jones was a classmate of George McClellan at West Point.

1263. D. R. Jones was a 37-year-old South Carolina native who served as General P. G. T. Beauregard's chief of staff at Charleston during the opening bombardment of the war. Witnesses reported D. R. Jones hauled down the US flag after Fort Sumter's surrender.

1264. Jones' friends called him "Neighbor," a sobriquet he received while at West Point for his gracious demeanor and genial disposition.

1265. Jones died of heart disease just four months after Antietam. The two Virginia brigades in his division (Garnett's and Kemper's) stormed Cemetery Ridge on the third day of Gettysburg as part of George Pickett's division.

1266. The Lower Bridge remained Burnside's enemy even after he seized it. The narrow twelve-foot roadway arching between the stone abutments constricted troops, artillery, wagons, horses, mules—and any other moving part of the army.

1267. It required two hours, from 1:00 p.m. to 3:00 p.m., for Burnside to funnel three corps across the bridge—approximately 9,000 men—and to place them in attack formation on a ridge parallel to Jones's Confederate position. (*OR* 19 (1): 425)

1268. Gen. Burnside himself was present at the bridge directing traffic and facilitating the movement of troops and guns.

1269. Twenty-two cannon, or four batteries, crossed the bridge. Each cannon normally required a six-horse team, or 132 horses for 22 guns. Each cannon usually had a separate caisson, also hitched to six horses, for another 132 horses. All records are silent on the length of time necessary to move Burnside's artillery across the bridge, but the sheer volume of horses, cannon, and caissons stole many minutes away from Father Time.

1270. Burnside's quickness was further hampered by empty cartridge boxes in Sturgis' division. As the ammunition came forward—more horses and more wagons crossing the bridge—General Cox asked Burnside to call upon Orlando B. Willcox's division to relieve Sturgis. Burnside immediately complied. (*OR* 19 (1): 425)

1271. Brig. Gen. Orlando Bolivar Willcox graduated with Burnside in 1847 from West Point. Willcox, a 39-year-old native of Detroit, was a prisoner of war for 13 months following his capture at First Manassas on July 21, 1861. Antietam was his first action since his release from captivity.

1272. Willcox's division, in reserve during the three hours of action at the bridge, had not yet fired a shot. Although fresh troops, they had remained stationary three-quarters of a mile east of the bridge, under cover to avoid Confederate artillery. Willcox did not reach the bridge until 2:00 p.m.

1273. Twenty-seven US infantry regiments were across the bridge by 3:00 p.m.

1274. The widest battle formation of the day at Antietam was just over one mile in breadth. It occurred when Rodman linked with Willcox's left, extending the Union battle line south.

1275. Burnside, in his assault against D. R. Jones, was the only Union commander at Antietam who did *not* throw his divisions piece-meal at the enemy. Unlike Hooker, Mansfield, and Sumner—who met disaster by fighting their divisions as separate detachments—Burnside coordinated his advance, tying his troops together for a unified assault. (*OR* 19 (1): 425)

1276. The Ninth Corps advance against the Confederate right began about 3:00 p.m. (*OR* 19 (1): 425)

1277. Burnside's battle formation involved three divisions: Willcox's two brigades held the right; Rodman's two brigades constituted the left; Cox's two brigades were in immediate support just behind Willcox and Rodman. (*OR* 19 (1): 425)

1278. Willcox's target was Sharpsburg. Rodman's objective was the Harpers Ferry Road and the ridge south of Sharpsburg. (*OR* 19 (1): 425)

1279. Burnside outnumbered D. R. Jones by more than three to one—9,000 vs. 2,800 men in the ranks.

1280. Jones had 28 pieces of artillery facing Burnside when the Union attack began. Many were posted on the high knoll just east of Sharpsburg (today the location of the Antietam National Cemetery).

1281. Burnside received no infantry support on his right. McClellan made no major advance via the Boonsboro-Sharpsburg Pike and committed almost none of his reserves posted on the east bank of Antietam Creek near the Middle Bridge.

1282. Battalions of US Regulars in George Sykes's division—about 1,500 men total—did cross the Middle Bridge, but not in support of Burnside. They were advanced only to protect Union batteries operating in that sector. (*OR* 19 (1): 362, 356-357, 359)

1283. Captain Hiram Dryer, 4th US Infantry, assumed command of all Regulars on the west side of the Antietam. Dryer deployed his Regulars on both the right and left sides of the Boonsboro-Sharpsburg Pike and advanced to within 250 yards of the Confederate positions on the eastern slope of the hill east of Sharpsburg (Antietam National Cemetery location today). (*OR* 19 (1): 356-357)

1284. The fire of the US Regulars on the left of the Boonsboro-Sharpsburg Pike, under the command of Lt. John S. Poland, forced Confederate gunners to "leave their guns." The guns were withdrawn soon afterward, under protection of a Confederate regiment. (*OR* 19 (1): 362)

1285. Fitz John Porter reportedly said to McClellan, when he gave consideration to committing the Fifth Corps into action: "Remember, General! I command the last reserve of the last Army of the Republic." This account was related by Thomas M. Anderson and published as a footnote in Volume II of *Battles and Leaders of the Civil War.* (Jacob Cox, The Battle of Antietam," *Battles and Leaders of the Civil War*, Vol. 2, p. 656)

1286. The first contact with the Confederates in Burnside's assault against Sharpsburg occurred on the Union right, just west of the Joseph Sherrick house. (*OR* 19 (1): 438)

1287. Col. Benjamin C. Christ's brigade, anchoring the extreme right of Burnside's line, encountered stiff resistance from the Confederate battery of Capt. H. R. Garden, commanding the South Carolina Palmetto Artillery. (*OR* 19 (1): 438, 926)

1288. Garden was called upon at 2:00 p.m. to hold the Sharpsburg-Rohrersville Road. He placed his four smoothbores on the north side of the road on the hill that today is the location of the National Cemetery. (*OR* 19 (1): 836, 926)

1289. Christ advanced to within 350 yards of Garden's battery, when he discovered that his left flank was in danger because his support had not yet advanced. Christ stopped under cover of a hill behind the Sherrick house. (*OR* 19 (1): 438, 926)

1290. Leading Christ forward was the 79th New York "Highlanders." This regiment received its sobriquet because it began the war wearing Scottish kilts. None of the regiment was wearing kilts at Antietam.

1291. A second Confederate battery under Capt. J. S. Brown—which included three rifled pieces—was positioned on the south side of the Sharpsburg-Rohrersville Road. It was in a location where it managed to enfilade Christ's brigade on the Sherrick farm at a distance of only 400 yards. (*OR* 19 (1): 438, 926)

1292. Christ was delayed by murderous Confederate artillery from his front and flank for 30 minutes. "It was impossible to move forward," he wrote in his official report, filed only four days after the battle. "[N]o place in the neighborhood afforded any cover." (*OR* 19 (1): 438)

1293. Christ received relief when the brigade of Col. Thomas Welsh advanced in support of Christ's exposed left flank. This movement forced the retirement of Brown's annoying cannon. (*OR* 19 (1): 438, 440)

1294. Thomas Welsh was a native of Columbia, Pennsylvania, where in the antebellum days he prospered as a merchant, canal boat owner, justice of the peace, and lock superintendent.

1295. Federal long-range artillery destroyed the carriage of one of Capt. Garden's guns. Another was rendered useless by "the bursting of a shell." The guns that remained in service were without ammunition. (*OR* 19 (1): 926)

1296. Christ charged Garden's battery with the 17th Michigan in the lead. When the federals drew within 100 yards of the Confederate cannon, Garden limbered up his guns and retired. An intervening hill between the Confederate cannon and the battery's horses saved the animals from the bullets of Christ's men. (*OR* 19 (1): 439)

1297. The Confederate guns facing Christ were run to the rear by hand. Lt. John A. Ramsey then hurried forward with a section of rifled-cannon and helped stall the Union advance into the streets of Sharpsburg. (*OR* 19 (1): 926)

1298. Col. F. W. McMaster of the 17th South Carolina Infantry moved forward with his regiment and the Holcombe Legion—all totaled about 100 men—confronting the Union advance in an orchard west of the Sherrick house. Here McMaster held for about 30 minutes before Christ and Welsh renewed their push forward. (*OR* 19 (1): 946)

1299. McMaster retired to a stone house astride the Sharpsburg-Rohrersville Road that he temporarily converted into a "fort." After losing support on his flanks, he abandoned the house, but Capt. H. D. D. Twiggs and 10 of his men were captured "in three minutes after I left." (*OR* 19 (1): 946)

1300. D. R. Jones called upon the brigades of Jenkins, Drayton, and Kemper to defend his endangered left flank and to block the advance of Willcox's division.

1301. Jenkins' brigade of South Carolinians, under the command of Col. Joseph Walker, was the first to strike Willcox's advance. The timely arrival of the Palmetto State troops onto the southeastern flank of the hill east of Sharpsburg (National Cemetery location) halted any further forward movement of Christ's brigade. (*OR* 19 (1): 907)

1302. Welsh's Union brigade continued toward the crest of the ridge, outdistancing any support on its right or left. Seeing Welsh's exposed right, Walker changed the front of his South Carolina brigade so that it could enfilade Welsh's unprotected right. This maneuver helped break the momentum of Welsh's advance, and forced him to retire. (*OR* 19 (1): 144, 907)

1303. Welsh's brigade suffered the fewest casualties in Burnside's drive against Sharpsburg—143 men.

1304. Burnside's right wing (Willcox's division) sustained only one third the casualties of Burnside's left wing (Rodman's division) in the attack against the Confederate right.

1305. The remainder of D. R. Jones' right—James Kemper's and Thomas Drayton's brigades—were outflanked on their right and driven in confusion into the outskirts of Sharpsburg by the arrival of Rodman's division. (*OR* 19 (1): 886)

1306. Only three regiments of Kemper's brigade came onto the field—the 1st, 11th, and 17th Virginia. Only one report exists in the *Official Records* from Kemper's brigade. No brigade report was found, and the only regimental report was filed by Montgomery D. Corse of the 17th Virginia Infantry. (*OR* 19 (1): 905)

1307. The 17th Virginia held the extreme right of Kemper's brigade, and went into battle with only 46 enlisted men and nine officers. (*OR* 19 (1): 905)

1308. Casualties for the 17th Virginia at Sharpsburg were 24 men and seven officers, or a 67% loss. (*OR* 19 (1): 905)

1309. Col. Montgomery D. Corse, commander of the 17th Virginia, was wounded in the foot and was not able to retire with his line. He was temporarily captured, but was rescued by the advance of Toombs and Archer. (*OR* 19 (1): 905)

1310. The first brigade to move forward in Rodman's division belonged to Col. Harrison S. Fairchild.

1311. Fairchild drove his three New York regiments up the slope toward Kemper's and Drayton's brigades in an attempt to connect with and extend the left of Willcox's division. (*OR* 19 (1): 451)

1312. Accurate artillery fire from 12 Confederate cannon on the ridge south of Sharpsburg took its toll on Fairchild's brigade as it advanced the 800 yards across open fields. Nearly one-quarter of Fairchild's men were hit before they encountered the enemy's infantry. (*OR* 19 (1): 451)

1313. One Confederate shell exploded in the midst of 9th New York "Hawkins' Zouaves" Infantry, killing eight men.

1314. The 9th New York Zouaves were outfitted in slightly baggy dark blue trousers, short blue jackets, and fezzes. (Michael McAfee, *Zouaves: The First and the Bravest*, pp. 65, 90)

1315. Kemper and Drayton's men fired from behind a stone wall near the Harpers Ferry Road when the federals drew within 50 yards. The sheet of flame and tornado of lead stunned the New Yorkers, but only temporarily.

1316. The Confederate right flank became overwhelmed as the 89th, 103rd, and 9th New York rushed forward, engaging briefly in some hand-to-hand combat.

1317. The colors of the 103rd New York were captured by Lt. William W. Athey, Company C, 17th Virginia Infantry. The 17th Virginia also captured the colors of the 11th Pennsylvania Infantry at Second Manassas. (*OR* 19 (1): 905; (2): 677)

1318. The 9th New York advanced further west against the Confederate right than any other federal regiment. It came within 150 yards of the Harpers Ferry Road.

1319. The 9th New York Infantry lost 235 of 373 engaged—or 63% casualties. This regiment had the second highest casualty count in the entire Ninth Corps.

1320. Fairchild's brigade suffered a loss of 455 of its 940 men—or 63 % casualties.

1321. Only Toombs's and Jenkins' brigades remained as cohesive and effective fighting units on the Confederate right following the collapse of Kemper and Drayton.

1322. Gen. Lee sent no reinforcements to D. R. Jones from other sectors of his line. Instead, the commanding general looked south toward Harpers Ferry, anxiously awaiting the arrival of his last division from that post—A. P. Hill's "Light Division."

1323. A. P. Hill received orders to march from Harpers Ferry to Sharpsburg at 6:30 a.m. on the 17th. Hill commenced moving his division at 7:30 a.m., one hour after orders arrived from Gen. Lee at Sharpsburg. (*OR* 19 (1): 981)

1324. Not all of Hill's six brigades marched north to Sharpsburg. Col. Edward L. Thomas' brigade remained behind at Harpers Ferry to "complete the removal of the captured property." (*OR* 19 (1): 981)

1325. The forced march of A. P. Hill's "Light Division" covered 17 miles in seven hours, which included crossing the Potomac River at Boteler's Ford. (*OR* 19 (1): 981)

1326. Hill's men were the only troops in Jackson's Harpers Ferry expedition who received two days of rest. Nearly 48 hours passed from the time of the surrender until Hill began his march to Sharpsburg.

1327. Hill's division began crossing Boteler's Ford about 2:00 p.m. The distance from the Potomac to the southern end of the battlefield is about two miles.

1328. Gen. Lee first saw Hill's arrival from a knoll near his headquarters, just west of Sharpsburg.

1329. Lee asked Lt. John Ramsay to use a scope to identify the column moving on his right near the Harpers Ferry Road. "They are flying the United States flag," Ramsay reported. Lee then saw another column further to the south and west. Ramsay lifted his scope and joyously announced: "They are flying the Virginia and Confederate flags." Lee quietly observed: "It is A. P. Hill from Harpers Ferry." (Sears, *Landscape Turned Red*, pp. 170-171, 259)

1330. The head of Hill's column arrived at Sharpsburg at 2:30 p.m. According to Hill, in his official report dated February 25, 1863, "My troops were not in a moment too soon." (*OR* 10 (1): 981)

1331. The arrival of A. P. Hill saved Lee's army from certain destruction at Sharpsburg.

1332. Gen. Lee, in delirium on his deathbed in 1870, called out clearly: "Tell A. P. Hill he must come up!" (More recent scholarship debunks this as mythology, suggesting that General Lee's stroke incapacitated him so severely that he was unable to speak.)

1333. The first written use of Hill "coming up" appeared in the October 1, 1862 account of Maj. B. W. Frobel, chief of artillery for Hood's division. In an understatement regarding the desperate situation of the Confederate right, Frobel wrote: "At this time General A. P. Hill came up, and charging, drove them from the field." (*OR* 19 (1): 925; James I. Robertson, *General A. P. Hill: The Story of a Confederate Warrior*, p. 148)

1334. Gen. Lee himself directed Hill to take a position on the Confederate right, in support of D. R. Jones. (*OR* 19 (1): 981)

1335. The first Union soldiers to see Hill's advance were the signalmen at the Red Hill signal station. At 3:00 p.m., they flagged a message to Burnside's headquarters: "Look out well on your left; the enemy are moving a strong force in that direction." (*OR* 19 (1): 138)

1336. Burnside was not at his headquarters when the signal station message arrived warning him to watch out for his left. Burnside's headquarters was on the east bank of Antietam Creek and Burnside himself was somewhere on the west bank when the message was sent. It was unlikely the message reached him—certainly not in time to adjust his left flank.

1337. Hill and Burnside were classmates at West Point, both graduating in 1847.

1338. Burnside owed Hill $8,000—a sum he borrowed before the war, and never repaid.

1339. The battery of D. G. McIntosh was the first of Hill's men to go into action. McIntosh was sent forward in advance of Hill's infantry to help strengthen Jones' position. The battery arrived about 3:00 p.m. (*OR* 19 (1): 981, 984)

1340. McIntosh's battery took position to the right and rear of Toombs's brigade, anchoring Jones's right on the Harpers Ferry Road. (*OR* 19 (1): 984)

1341. Col. Edward Harland's brigade of Rodman's division formed the extreme left of the entire federal line at Antietam. His position was about three miles south of the extreme Union right, located on the Joseph Poffenberger farm, just north of the North Woods. (*OR* 19 (1): 453)

1342. Harland's brigade did not advance in concert with Fairchild's brigade on the Union left. Only the 8th Connecticut Infantry moved forward on the right, while the 16th Connecticut and 4th Rhode Island remained stationary in a cornfield. (*OR* 19 (1): 453)

1343. The 8th Connecticut advanced without support on its left, aiming directly at the three newly arrived guns in McIntosh's battery just east of the Harpers Ferry Road. (*OR* 19 (1): 453)

1344. Double canister failed to halt the 8th Connecticut and the regiment's fire disabled many of McIntosh's horses, making it impossible to remove the cannon from the field. When the 8th drew within 60 yards of his battery, McIntosh ordered his men to abandon the guns.

1345. The 8th Connecticut seized McIntosh's guns—but only temporarily. The 8th had no support on its right or left, and was isolated. It had outdistanced its support by nearly a half a mile.

1346. The first Confederate infantry in Hill's column to arrive in "the actual presence of the enemy" was Maxcy Gregg's brigade of South Carolinians. (*OR* 19 (1): 988)

1347. Brig. Gen. Maxcy Gregg was a 38-year-old native of Columbia, South Carolina, who was practicing law at the outbreak of the war.

1348. Gregg's five Palmetto State regiments arrived on the battlefield at 3:40 p.m. (*OR* 19 (1): 988)

1349. The first Confederate infantry regiment in Hill's column to arrive on the battlefield was the 14th South Carolina of Gregg's brigade. (*OR* 19 (1): 988)

1350. The 14th South Carolina Infantry was posted on the extreme Confederate right. It did not become engaged since the enemy, "checked in his flank movement," never drove against the position held by the regiment. (*OR* 19 (1): 988)

1351. Gregg deployed the remainder of his brigade as follows: on the right the 1st South Carolina; in the middle, the 12th South Carolina; and on the left the 13th South Carolina. (*OR* 19 (1): 988)

1352. Gregg's brigade clashed—in a 40-acre cornfield—with Burnside's extreme left, positions held by the 16th Connecticut and the 4th Rhode Island.

1353. Col. Edward Harland, holding the extreme left of the Union army, was first informed about a Confederate brigade deploying on his left (Gregg's South Carolinians) from his acting aide-de-camp, Maj. Lion. (*OR* 19 (1): 453)

1354. Edward Harland was a grandson of an English watchmaker and a graduate of Yale University. He was practicing law in Connecticut when the war began.

1355. Col. Harland notified Gen. Rodman of the danger to his left. Rodman hurried off toward the 16th Connecticut and the 4th Rhode Island to secure the army's left flank. (*OR* 19 (1): 453)

1356. Gen. Rodman changed the front of the 16th Connecticut—shifting it from facing west toward D. R. Jones's line along the Harpers Ferry Road—to facing south toward Gregg's rapidly approaching South Carolinians. (*OR* 19 (1): 453)

1357. Isaac Rodman was mortally wounded in the chest as he galloped away from Harland's left to warn his other brigade, Gen. Fairchild's, of a Confederate flanking maneuver against the left. (*OR* 19 (1): 426)

1358. Rodman was the ninth Union general at Antietam to be mortally wounded or wounded during the battle.

1359. Rodman's middle name was "Peace." He was a Quaker from South Kingstown, Rhode Island. He died at age 40.

1360. Harland saw the Confederate infantry advancing against his vulnerable left. He "put the spurs" to his horse to hasten the arrival of the 16th Connecticut, but his horse was almost immediately shot, delaying his contact with the regiment. (*OR* 19 (1): 453)

1361. The 16th Connecticut advanced into a deep ravine in the 40-acre cornfield, moving against Gregg's left. The Nutmeg state boys failed to dislodge the 13th South Carolina, which was ensconced behind a stone wall along the western edge of the cornfield. (*OR* 19 (1): 988)

1362. Antietam was the first battle of the war for the 16th Connecticut—a raw-recruit regiment that had been in the army for only three weeks.

1363. Confusion over who was friend or foe stalled the movement of the 4th Rhode Island as it attempted to turn Gregg's right flank. (*OR* 19 (1): 456)

1364. The 4th Rhode Island ceased fire while it determined what regiment—apparently displaying US colors, but with uniforms invisible in the corn—was approaching from its front. The color bearer of the 4th, Cpl. Tanner, accompanied by two lieutenants, carried the regiment's flag forward through the corn. Confederates opened fire when the flag came within 20 feet of the Rebel position, killing the corporal, and positively identifying the regiment as the enemy. (*OR* 19 (1): 456)

1365. The 12th South Carolina charged the position of the 16th Connecticut three times. The 16th was positioned behind a stone fence within the ravine of the 40-acre cornfield, but the South Carolinians broke through the Union line on the third try, sending the 16th retreating in great confusion. (*OR* 19 (1): 988, 996)

1366. Col. Dixon Barnes, commander of the 12th South Carolina and a wealthy planter before the war, described as "a quiet gentleman with a long white beard," was mortally wounded in the 40-acre cornfield. He died 10 days after the battle. (*OR* 19 (1): 997; Robert Krick, *Lee's Colonels: Biographical Register of the Field Officers of the Army of Northern Virginia*, p. 40)

1367. Gen. Jackson had Barnes placed under arrest five days before the battle for permitting his hungry men to take apples from trees adjacent to the road over which Barnes was marching en route to Harpers Ferry.

1368. Gen. Gregg was wounded in the hip and knocked off his horse. The wound was not severe, but badly bruised the general. (*OR* 19 (1): 981)

1369. Gregg sat down to breakfast on an ear of corn on the morning of the 18th, and when he pulled a handkerchief from his hip pocket to use as a napkin, a flattened bullet fell out.

1370. The final assault that wrecked Harland's left flank occurred when Orr's Rifles (the 1st South Carolina Rifles), under Lieut. Col. James M. Perrin, swept forward against the left of the 4th Rhode Island, driving the regiment back from the 40-acre cornfield. Perrin stated in his official report dated September 30, 1862, "We delivered a destructive fire into [the 4th] before our presence seemed to be realized." (*OR* 19 (1): 988, 994)

1371. Only one man was killed in the Orr's Rifles during the regiment's successful flank assault against the 4th Rhode Island. (*OR* 19 (1): 989, 994)

1372. Nearly half of the total casualties in A. P. Hill's division were incurred by Gregg's brigade. In its fight for the 40-acre cornfield, the brigade lost 28 killed, 135 wounded, and two missing—for a total of 165 casualties. (*OR* 19 (1): 981, 989)

1373. The 16th Connecticut suffered the highest casualty count in the Ninth Corps—302 casualties.

1374. The 16th Connecticut also sustained the highest number of missing in action in the Ninth Corps—78.

1375. Harland's brigade incurred the heaviest losses during Burnside's attack against the Confederate right—596 casualties: 102 killed; 393 wounded; 101 missing.

1376. Harland's 101 missing in action was second only to the 104 missing in Dana's brigade during the West Woods action.

1377. The three Connecticut regiments in Harland's brigade—8th, 16th, and 11th—suffered 635 casualties. Nearly 22% of this total (139 men) resulted when the 11th Connecticut attacked Burnside Bridge.

1378. Harland suffered more casualties in his defense of Burnside's left flank than all the federal regiments *combined* who attack Burnside Bridge.

1379. The second of Hill's five brigades to arrive on the battlefield was James J. Archer's. (*OR* 19 (1): 1000)

1380. James Jay Archer was a native of Bel Air, Maryland, and a graduate of Princeton University. He studied law at the University of Maryland and became an attorney, but in 1855, he entered the Regular Army as a captain in the 9th Infantry. He resigned from the army at the outbreak of the war and joined the Confederacy as colonel of the 5th Texas Infantry.

1381. Archer's brigade was reduced to only 350 men by the time it reached the battlefield. "This was a long and fatiguing march," Archer explained in his official report, dated March 1, 1863. "[M]any of the men fell, exhausted from the march." (*OR* 19 (1): 1000)

1382. The only Tennessee regiments that fight at Antietam—the 1st, 7th, and 14th infantry regiments—were in Archer's brigade.

1383. Archer, suffering from illness, relinquished command of his brigade at Harpers Ferry on the 16th and rode to Sharpsburg in an ambulance the next day. Archer resumed brigade command as it prepared to go into battle at Sharpsburg. (*OR* 19 (1): 1000)

1384. Archer's brigade aligned on the Harpers Ferry Road, facing east, with Toombs's reconstituted brigade posted on his left.

1385. A countercharge by Archer's brigade—with Toombs's bigger brigade along side—against the 8th Connecticut Infantry saved McIntosh's guns from capture and secured the ridge along the Harpers Ferry Road for the Confederates. (*OR* 19 (1): 891-892, 984)

1386. The terrible converging fire on the front and left flank of the 8th Connecticut produced extensive casualties—173 of the 350 men engaged (49%).

1387. Archer once again relinquished brigade command at 9:00 a.m. on the 18th because, "the little strength with which I entered the fight being completely exhausted." (*OR* 19 (1): 1001)

1388. Archer's command suffered nearly one third of the total casualties in Hill's division—15 killed and 90 wounded. (*OR* 19 (1): 1001)

1389. The 11th Georgia Infantry—which was separated from its own brigade of George T. Anderson—joined Toombs's brigade and their fellow Georgians in the assault against the 8th Connecticut. At 8:00 a.m. on the 17th, the "right wing" of this regiment—140 men in five companies under Maj. F. H. Little—left Shepherdstown on the [West] Virginia shore, arriving on the battlefield in the early afternoon. (*OR* 19 (1): 911)

1390. The third of Hill's brigades to arrive at Sharpsburg was Branch's brigade, which pulled into line to the left of Archer. (*OR* 19 (1): 1001)

1391. Brig. Gen. Lawrence O'Bryan Branch was a native of North Carolina and an 1838 graduate of Princeton.

1392. Salmon P. Chase, President Lincoln's Secretary of Treasury and later Chief Justice of the United States Supreme Court, tutored Lawrence Branch in his early life.

1393. Branch served in the US Congress representing North Carolina from 1855-1861.

1394. President James Buchanan offered Branch positions in his cabinet as Secretary of Treasury and Postmaster General, but Branch declined both.

1395. Gen. Branch was killed with a bullet through the head as he was pressing his brigade forward at Sharpsburg.

1396. Branch was the tenth general and the last Confederate general to be gunned down during the battle.

1397. Burnside's reserves—the Kanawha division, under temporary command of Col. Eliakim P. Scammon—attempted to halt the breach on the left flank. (*OR* 19 (1): 466)

1398. The extreme left of the Union line, following the collapse of Rodman's division, was held by three Ohio regiments in Hugh Ewing's brigade. (*OR* 19 (1): 463)

1399. Ewing's brigade crossed Antietam Creek about one mile downstream from Burnside's Bridge, probably at Snavely's Ford. (*OR* 19 (1): 465)

1400. Ewing advanced to a stone wall where he was only 100 yards from the enemy in his front. (*OR* 19 (1): 466, 470)

1401. Ewing ordered the 12th Ohio to face south, perpendicular to the rest of the brigade, when he discovered a flanking column moving against his left—Gregg's South Carolina brigade. (*OR* 19 (1): 466)

1402. Maj. J. M. Comly of the 23rd Ohio believed the column advancing against the 30th Ohio's left were federal troops. Comly ordered his men not to fire. (*OR* 19 (1): 468)

1403. Comly soon discovered, as he wrote in his official report dated four days after the battle, "the enemy had uniforms similar to ours." In addition, Comly stated the Rebels "used the national colors on the occasion." Comly later learned from a prisoner that Confederates had taken Union clothing at Harpers Ferry and were wearing it at Antietam. (*OR* 19 (1): 468)

1404. On two separate occasions, federal officers ceased firing because they believed the column approaching on their left was a Union force. It happened first with the 4th Rhode Island and again with the 23rd Ohio. (*OR* 19 (1): 468)

1405. In both cases where federal uniforms and the US colors were reported on display by the Confederates, the unit involved was Gregg's South Carolina brigade. (*OR* 19 (1): 456, 468)

1406. Weapons in Companies A and B of the 30th Ohio proved defective during the fight. After only five rounds, the men could scarcely ram their projectiles down the rifle barrel. Maj. George Hildt recommended "a change of arms." (*OR* 19 (1): 470)

1407. Ewing was attacked on both front and flank. Gregg's South Carolinians hit his left flank and the 15th and 20th Georgia of Toombs's brigade struck his front. (*OR* 19 (1): 892)

1408. The last Confederate colonel mortally wounded at Sharpsburg was Col. William Terrell Millican of the 15th Georgia. Millican was hit while leading the final charge of his regiment against Ewing's brigade. (*OR* 19 (1): 892)

1409. Ewing's aides suffered deadly consequences during the brigade's fight on the Union left. Lt. Furbay was shot by three balls and mortally wounded. Lt. Duffield was shot twice and killed. Lt. Headington had his horse shot from under him. (*OR* 19 (1): 463)

1410. Forty Confederate cannon, collected from 15 batteries, commanded the ridge east and south of Sharpsburg near the end of Burnside's assault.

1411. Since 4:00 p.m., about 40 cannon shots per minute had been heard in Hagerstown—13 miles north of Sharpsburg. (*OR* 19 (1): 321)

1412. Only 40 rounds were issued to Samuel Benjamin's battery on the 17th. After he had expended his rounds, between 5:00-5:30 p.m., Gen. Burnside ordered him to fire blank cartridges to "draw the enemy's fire from our infantry." (*OR* 19 (1): 436)

1413. Gen. Cox, commanding the Ninth Corps, ordered the divisions to retire from exposed ground "to the cover of the curved hill above the bridge." (*OR* 19 (1): 426)

1414. Cox gave the following reasons for the Ninth Corps withdrawal, listed in his official report, filed six days after the battle: 1) enemy strength continued to increase on the left; 2) new batteries placed by the enemy in position along the ridge paralleling the Harpers

Ferry Road and on the hill east of Sharpsburg; and 3) no prospect of reaching Sharpsburg without reinforcements. *(OR* 19 (1): 426)

1415. Near twilight, Gen. Sturgis was ordered forward to protect Burnside's position on the west side of Antietam Creek. His division remained in this position throughout the night of the 17th and the next day. *(OR* 19 (1): 444-445)

1416. The newly recruited 35th Massachusetts Infantry held the advance of Sturgis' position, and was subjected to a converging and massive Confederate artillery bombardment during the final hour of the battle.

1417. The 35th Massachusetts sustained nearly as many casualties—214 while under artillery bombardment—as the rest of Ferrero's brigade suffered on its successful attack against Burnside Bridge.

1418. The Confederates did not attempt to drive Burnside back across the bridge. Burnside maintained a strong defensive position on the west side of Antietam Creek the following day. *(OR* 19 (1): 444-445)

1419. Total casualties for A. P. Hill's division were 374—64 killed, 304 wounded, and six missing. This total was 28 higher than Hill listed in his official report.

1420. Burnside's losses during his attack against the Confederate right are just over 1,800 casualties.

1421. A. P. Hill and George McClellan both courted Miss Ellen Marcy in the mid-1850s. Miss Marcy eventually broke her engagement with Hill in 1856 and married McClellan.

1422. McClellan missed the opportunity to watch most of Burnside's attack from his headquarters. Although Burnside's assault was clearly visible from the Pry House, McClellan was absent from headquarters at the time, being away conferring with Sumner.

1423. McClellan returned to headquarters in time to see Burnside's left collapse. He then rode toward Burnside's position, but was intercepted by a courier near the Boonsboro-Sharpsburg Pike. McClellan went no further.

1424. Burnside asked for reinforcements. McClellan replied to a courier: "Tell General Burnside this was the battle for the war. He must hold his ground till dark at any cost. . . . I can do nothing more. I have no infantry." (Sears, *Landscape Turned Red*, pp. 291-292)

The Aftermath:
Retreat, Hardship, and Postwar

1425. Nearly 4,000 unburied corpses covered the Antietam battlefield's three-mile front.

1426. Over 19,000 wounded struggled for survival between the lines on the 18th. No flags of truce were honored, so it remained too dangerous to offer aid to the suffering.

1427. The first message from McClellan to Washington regarding the outcome of the battle on the 17th was sent at 8:00 a.m. on the 18th. "Little Mac" told General-in-Chief Halleck: "The battle will probably be renewed today." (*OR* 19 (2): 322)

1428. McClellan launched no attack on the 18th. "I should have had a narrow view of the condition of the country had I been willing to hazard another battle with less than an absolute assurance of success," he wrote in his official report. He concluded: "[W]ith Virginia lost, Washington menaced, Maryland invaded—the national cause could afford no risks of defeat. One battle lost and almost all would have been lost." (*OR* 19 (1): 65)

1429. Gen. McClellan had nearly 32,000 fresh troops to hurl at the Confederates on the late morning of the 18th. This included 26,300 veterans in the Fifth and Sixth Corps, and 6,000 raw-recruits who had just arrived on the field in Brig. Gen. Andrew A. Humphreys' division.

1430. Gen. Lee attempted an offensive maneuver against McClellan's right on the 18th. Gen. Jeb Stuart led the effort, but he abandoned the movement after he discovered federal batteries were massed on the Union right within 800 yards of the Potomac River. It thus became impossible to drive north between the river and the guns. (*OR* 19 (1): 820, 841)

1431. Gen. McClellan called for more ammunition about 9:30 p.m. on the 17th in a direct plea to the army's Chief of Ordnance, Brig. Gen. James W. Ripley. McClellan's first message asked for 20-pounder Parrott ammunition. It was followed quickly by a second message requesting replenishment rounds for five different types of artillery. (*OR* 19 (1): 313)

1432. A special train loaded with 20-pounder ammunition departed from Washington about 1:00 a.m. on the 18th and traveled to Baltimore, then Harrisburg, Chambersburg, and then to Hagerstown, where it arrived on the early afternoon of the 18th. By order of the President of the United States, the ammunition train must "run through at the fastest possible speed," and must "have the right of way throughout" so that the ammunition can arrive to sustain McClellan's expected fight on the 18th. (*OR* 19 (1): 313-314, 322-323)

1433. The 20-pounder Parrott ammunition train was delivered to the North Central Railroad at Baltimore at 6:57 a.m. on the 18th. It was transferred to the Cumberland Valley Railroad at Harrisburg at 10:20 a.m. The train traveled 84 miles in two hours and fifty-three minutes during its first leg. At the conclusion of its second leg, it arrived in Hagerstown by 2:30 p.m. on the 18th. The ammunition still had to be transported, via wagon, to McClellan's army, which was 13 miles away. (*OR* 19 (1): 327, 329)

Confederate Dead Prepared for Burial (*USAMHI*)

1434. Mary W. Lee of the Philadelphia Refreshment Saloon distributed home made apple dumplings, bread, and cups of water on the Boonsboro Turnpike—behind the lines—on the day of the battle.

1435.   Gen. Longstreet recommended, via a note to the commanding general, a withdrawal about 2:00 p.m. on the 18th. At about the same time, Gen. Lee rode up to "Old Pete" and the two agreed a withdrawal was necessary because it was "impossible to make any move except a direct assault upon some portion of the enemy's line." (*OR* 19 (1): 841)

1436. Gen. Lee retreated across the Potomac on the night of September 18-19, 1862, unmolested by Union pursuers. He informed President Davis on September 20 that he withdrew because "our position [was] a bad one to hold with the river in rear..." (*OR* 19 (1): 142)

1437. Longstreet ordered, before the retreat on the 18th, that one of his batteries with rifled guns, "be left in the main street of Sharpsburg for General Stuart's cavalry." Longstreet further directed the battery horses be "heading to the rear." (*OR* 19 (1): 620)

1438.   The first command to leave the battlefield was Longstreet's, commencing its withdrawal at 2:00 a.m. on the 19th. (*OR* 19 (1): 841)

1439. Burial of the Union dead began on September 19, and details then began burying Confederate corpses on the 20th. The burial parties did not complete their ghastly work until September 22. Seven hundred bodies were buried on the Roulette Farm just north of Bloody Lane.

1440. Horse carcasses were burned, generally in the area whey they were killed or mortally wounded.

1441. The first American battlefield ever photographed was Antietam. Alexander Gardner, working for the Matthew Brady studio, arrived on the battlefield on September 19 and photographed scenes in The Cornfield, along the Hagerstown Pike, at the Dunker Church, Bloody Lane, and Burnside Bridge.

1442. Gardner photographed only the Confederate dead at Antietam.

1443. The Confederate army retreated into [West] Virginia at Boteler's Ford. Confederates also referred to this as Shepherdstown Ford, since it is located 1½ miles south of the [West] Virginia village.

1444. Shepherdstown became a hospital center for the Confederate wounded following the battle. Only the most severely wounded remained there however, as the Potomac River town was too close to federal artillery and not secure from federal raids.

1445. Three brigades from A. P. Hill's division—Branch, Gregg, and Archer—formed the rear guard of Lee's army, departing from their position on the Antietam battlefield at 3:00 a.m. on the 19th. The brigades retired in line of battle facing the enemy. Infantry, artillery, cavalry, wagons, and ambulances were all safely across the Potomac by mid-morning of the 19th. The rear brigade of the army was Maxcy Gregg's. (*OR* 19 (1): 986, 988)

1446. The last fight on Maryland soil in The Maryland Campaign occurred about 9:00 a.m. on the 19th when two companies of the 14th South Carolina, Gregg's brigade, drove away and dispersed a Union cavalry detachment in a cornfield about one mile from Boteler's Ford. (*OR* 19 (1): 988-989)

1447. Hill's division completed the passage over Boteler's Ford about 10:00 a.m. on the 19th. His division then bivouacked about five miles from the river. (*OR* 19 (1): 981)

1448. McClellan's first message to Washington announcing the Confederate withdrawal from its forward position on the battlefield was at 8:30 a.m. on the 19th. McClellan noted the enemy had abandoned the field, but he did not know "whether he is falling back to an interior position or crossing the river." (*OR* 19 (2): 330)

1449. The first notification of the Confederate retreat sent to Washington appeared in a 10:30 a.m. message from McClellan to Halleck on September 19: "Pleasanton is driving the enemy across the river. Our victory was complete. The enemy is driven back into Virginia. Maryland and Pennsylvania are now safe." (*OR* 19 (2): 330)

1450. Fear of a back door attack on Washington continued to concern General-in-Chief Halleck on the morning of September 19. "Letters received here give it as a part of Lee's original plan to draw you as far as possible up the Potomac," Halleck warned McClellan at 12:30 p.m. on the 19th, "and then move between you and Washington." Halleck took some consolation in the fact that Lee's defeat "may be such as to prevent the attempt." (*OR* 19 (2): 330)

1451. Gen. Lee intended to *continue the offensive* following his withdrawal back into Virginia. The army "immediately [was] put in motion toward Williamsport," Lee informed

President Davis on September 20, "in order to threaten the enemy on his right and rear and make him apprehensive for his communications." (*OR* 19 (1): 142)

1452. To inaugurate Lee's new offensive, Jeb Stuart forded the Potomac at an obscure ford on the evening of the 18th, taking Wade Hampton's cavalry brigade with him. The cavalry marched all night and re-crossed the Potomac above Williamsport at Mason's Ford on the 19th. Meanwhile, a part of the 12th Virginia Cavalry, aided by a battalion of the 2nd Virginia Infantry, dashed directly into Williamsport on the 19th. Stuart then moved his entire force to commanding ridges overlooking Williamsport, where it encountered the advance of the enemy on the 20th. (*OR* 19 (1): 820, 824)

1453. McClellan responded to the threat at Williamsport with alacrity and force. He sent two brigades of cavalry and one battery of artillery to Jones's Cross Roads on September 20, then to Williamsport. "That force will be amply sufficient for any rebels to be met in that quarter," reported Pleasanton. McClellan remained unconvinced, and also ordered Couch's division of 6,000 men to the river town. In support of both the cavalry and Couch, McClellan directed Franklin's corps to Williamsport on the 21st. All totaled, McClellan sent nearly 18,000 men toward Williamsport to protect his extreme right. (*OR* 19 (1): 68; (2): 334-335)

1454. Stuart maintained his position at Williamsport throughout the 20th, but realizing he was vastly outnumbered, withdrew to the south bank of the Potomac that night, without loss. Lee's new offensive abruptly ended, less than 36 hours after it began. Gen. Lee expressed disappointment to President Davis that he was unable to sustain his proposed offensive at Williamsport. "It was my intention to recross the Potomac at Williamsport, and move upon Hagerstown," he wrote on September 25, "but the condition of the army prevented [it]." (*OR* 19 (1): 821; (2): 626-627)

1455. The offensive at Williamsport "is arrested" not only because of the federal show of strength, but also because of events at Boteler's Ford on the 19th and 20th. Gen. Lee turned Jackson's corps back toward Shepherdstown "to rectify occurrences in that quarter." (*OR* 19 (1): 141)

1456. Lee selected Brig. Gen. William Nelson Pendleton, his chief of artillery, to hold the position at Boteler's Ford. Pendleton was familiar with the area, as he had been coordinating movements on the [West] Virginia bank of the Potomac throughout the 17th and 18th. (*OR* 19 (1): 830-831)

1457. Pendleton massed 44 cannon on the bluffs overlooking Boteler's Ford. The short-range cannon were concentrated in the middle of the line, with the longer range, and more accurate rifled cannon positioned on the flanks. In support of the guns were Armistead's and Lawton's small infantry brigades—numbering no more than 600 men—and Thomas Munford's cavalry brigade. (*OR* 19 (1): 831)

1458. Fitz John Porter's Fifth Corps cautiously moved towards the Potomac, arriving on the Maryland side of Boteler's Ford in the early afternoon of the 19th. Skirmishers from the 1st US Sharpshooters took position along the riverbank and C & O Canal. Federal artillery arrived and began exchanging fire with the enemy across the river. (*OR* 19 (1): 39, 344-345)

1459. The Union cavalry was sent *to the rear* on the 19th by order of Fifth Corps commander Fitz John Porter, thus "interfer[ing] most materially with a proper pursuit of the enemy," cavalry commander Alfred Pleasanton complained bitterly to Gen. McClellan on the 20th: "I trust . . . [you] will not permit corps commanders to interfere with the cavalry under my command, for it breaks up all my system and plans." (*OR* 19 (1): 334)

1460. Pendleton discovered that ammunition for many of his batteries at Boteler's Ford was exhausted near dusk, and he ordered a systematic withdrawal of his guns during the night. At about dusk, 500 handpicked men from George W. Morell's Fifth Corps division suddenly splashed across the ford. In the darkness and confusion, Morell's men captured five cannon—the Confederates listed only four—two caissons, 2 caisson bodies, 2 forges, and about 400 stand of arms. The Union party withdrew back across the Potomac during the night. Gen. Pendleton spent the night searching for Gen. Lee, whom he found about 1:00 a.m. seeking reinforcements. (*OR* 19 (1): 832, 339-340)

1461. Gen. Porter ordered a larger federal force across the river on the morning of the 20th. Three brigades from Brig. Gen. George Sykes's division began crossing the ford at 7:00 a.m. In support of Sykes was Col. James Barnes's brigade from Morell's division. About 8:00 a.m., one mile west of the ford, Sykes's lead brigade encountered A. P. Hill's Confederates—reinforcements from Jackson sent forward to secure the ford. Sykes informed Fifth Corps commander Porter, who ordered a general withdrawal, but Barnes's brigade of 1,711 men—operating north of the ford—initially remained and took position on the bluffs overlooking the river. (*OR* 19 (1): 340, 346, 351-352)

1462. The federal batteries of Weed, Randol, and Van Reed, on the Maryland side, poured a very destructive fire into A. P. Hill's division as it advanced toward the bluffs overlooking the ford. Hill labeled the Union missiles as "the most tremendous fire of artillery I ever saw." Samuel McGowan, a brigade commander under Hill, recalled the cannon "practice was remarkably fine, bursting shells in the ranks at every discharge." (*OR* 19 (1): 352, 982, 989)

1463. Hill approached rapidly against Barnes's left, front, and right, with a force that outnumbered Barnes almost two to one. Barnes wisely ordered a withdrawal. Every regiment but one—the recently mustered 118th Pennsylvania Infantry (Corn Exchange Regiment) from Philadelphia—evacuated the position. (*OR* 19 (1): 346-347)

1464. A. P. Hill smashed into the unlucky 118th Pennsylvania on the bluffs above the Potomac, driving them "pell-mell into the river." Hill waxed eloquent on his thumping success: "Then commenced the most terrible slaughter that this war has yet witnessed. The broad surface of the Potomac was blue with the floating bodies of our foe. But few escaped to tell the tale." (*OR* 19 (1): 982)

1465. In its baptism of fire, the 118th Pennsylvania lost 63 killed, 101 wounded, and 105 missing—a total of 269 casualties of the 737 men who went into action (36%). A. P. Hill's division suffered 261 casualties—many resulting, no doubt, from the accurate and galling Union artillery fire.

1466. The bloodiest fight in what became the State of West Virginia occurred at Boteler's Ford on September 20, where the total losses for both sides were 624 casualties.

1467. First Sgt. Daniel W. Burke, Company B, 2nd US Infantry, volunteered to return across the Potomac to spike a piece of artillery that was left behind on the Shepherdstown side of the river. He succeeded in disabling the cannon "in the face of the enemy's sharpshooters." (*OR* 19 (1): 364)

1468. A. P. Hill issued a special congratulations to his men one week following the battle of Antietam: "You saved the day at Sharpsburg and at Shepherdstown. You were selected to face a storm of round shot, shell, and grape such as I have never before seen. [Y]ou have a reputation in this army which it should be the object of every officer and private to sustain." (*OR* 51 (2): 627)

1469. Pennsylvania Governor Andrew Curtin arrived in Hagerstown at noon on the 18th to personally supervise transport of supplies arriving from Pennsylvania and to join Pennsylvania militia gathering in town. Prior to his arrival at Hagerstown, Governor Curtin requested, on the evening of September 17, that two million buck and ball cartridges and one million .58 caliber cartridges be shipped to him immediately. The US Chief of Ordnance, James W. Ripley, ordered the cartridges shipped from the arsenal at Governor's Island, New York, on the 19th. (*OR* 19 (1): 329, 321, 331)

1470. About 4,000 Pennsylvania militiamen in Hagerstown refused to march to Sharpsburg to join McClellan's army on the 18th and 19th. "What will be done, or can be done, with the force here I cannot say," Maj. Gen. John F. Reynolds reported to General-in-Chief Halleck. "[I] do not think much can be expected of them—not very much." "The Governor will take [the state militia] to the field, if it is necessary, tomorrow," stated Gen. Reynolds. (*OR* 19 (1): 329, 332)

1471. Destruction of the pontoon bridge at Harpers Ferry about 5:00 p.m. on the evening of September 18 was one of the final actions taken by the Confederates during their last hours of occupation. The railroad bridge at Harpers Ferry was burned on the 18th, but the piers remained in good condition. The Confederates tried to blow up the piers five times, but did not succeed. (*OR* 19 (1): 325, 333)

1472. Citizens of Sandy Hook buried Union dead on Maryland Heights, beginning on the 18th. (*OR* 19 (2): 325)

1473. Supplies and ammunition became a major concern of Union quartermasters and ordnance officials. On the 18th, Quartermaster Gen. Montgomery C. Meigs informed McClellan's quartermaster, Lieut. Col. Rufus Ingalls, that 600,000 rations had been sent to Frederick and another 500,000 rations were on the way to Hagerstown. Chief of Ordnance James W. Ripley informed McClellan on September 18 that 414 wagonloads of field and small-arms ammunition had been sent to Frederick in the past five days. (*OR* 19 (2): 323)

1474. McClellan listed five reasons why he did not pursue Lee across the Potomac in an explanatory message to Halleck on September 22: 1) loss of ten general officers, many regimental officers, and large number of enlisted men as casualties; 2) army corps cut up and scattered and the army exhausted by "unavoidable overwork, hunger, and want of sleep and rest; 3) no transportation to furnish a single day's subsistence; 4) placing the

Potomac River between the army and its base of supply; and 5) "old skeleton regiments" must be filled and officers appointed to fill vacancies. (*OR* 19 (2): 343-344)

1475. Gen. Lee explained to President Davis on September 23 that casualties, desertions, and straggling were "the main cause[s] of [the army's] retiring from Maryland, as it was unable to cope with advantage with the numerous host of the enemy." Lee desired to renew offensive operations—even with his diminished numbers—he informed Davis on the 25th. He hesitated, however, because the army did not "exhibit its former temper and condition." As a result, Lee concluded, "the hazard would be great and a reverse disastrous. I am, therefore, led to pause." (*OR* 19 (1): 622-627)

1476. Jefferson Davis informed Gen. Lee on September 28 that "the feverish anxiety to invade the North has been relieved by the counter-irritant of apprehension for the safety of the capital [Richmond] in the absence of the army." (*OR* 19 (2): 634)

1477. Lee labeled the campaign into Maryland an "expedition" in a September 25 letter to Maj. Gen. W. W. Loring, commander of the Confederate Army of Kanawha operating in western Virginia. (*OR* 19 (2): 626)

1478. President Lincoln hailed Antietam as a military victory, thus issuing the Preliminary Emancipation Proclamation on September 22—five days after the battle. The emphasis of the Administration changed—no longer was the only goal the preservation of the Union; rather the abolition of slavery and the destruction of the culture it supported became a major goal.

1479. Lee's defeat and withdrawal from Maryland, in conjunction with emancipation, swayed the British against intervening in the war.

1480. The camps of the Confederate army following Antietam were primarily below Martinsburg, along the Opequon Creek, in Berkeley County, [West] Virginia. Lee listed the headquarters address on his correspondence as "near Smoketown." (*OR* 19 (2): 624, 626)

1481. Confederate strategy following Antietam was outlined by Gen. Lee in a September 24 letter to the commander of the defenses of Richmond: "If we cannot advance into Maryland, I hope to draw him [McClellan] into the valley, where I think we can operate to advantage, and at least have the benefit of the bountiful grain crops of this season." (*OR* 19 (2): 625)

1482. A second strategy by Lee was announced in the September 25 letter to Maj. Gen. Loring in western Virginia: "I hope to be able to retain them on the Potomac, or if they cross, to draw them up the valley." By freezing the Union army along the river, Gen. Lee concluded "it will give them but little time before winter to operate south of the Potomac," thus reducing the threat to Virginia or Richmond during the remainder of 1862. (*OR* 19 (2): 626)

1483. A third strategy option was explained by Lee in a September 25 message to President Davis. "In a military point of view, the best move . . . would be to advance upon Hagerstown and endeavor to defeat the enemy at that point." (*OR* 19 (2): 627)

1484. The Confederate army had plenty of beef and flour for the troops, and hay for the horses following the retreat from Sharpsburg, but Gen. Lee complained his army suffered from a great deficiency of clothing—especially under-clothing and shoes. (*OR* 19 (2): 623)

1485. Gen. Lee worried about the condition of the army's horses. "Our horses have been so reduced by labor and scant food," he informed President Davis on September 28, that "unless their condition can be improved before winter, I fear many of them will die." Lee concluded with a wish: "Rest would be extremely advantageous to men and horses, and yet I see no way of affording it." (*OR* 19 (2): 633)

1486. About 1,200 barefooted men were at Winchester on September 27. Four thousand (4,000) pairs of shoes arrived for the Confederate army on October 1, and another 2,000 were expected on the following day. (*OR* 19 (1): 629-630, 644)

1487. Gen. Lee's first request for the artillery captured at Harpers Ferry came on September 21 when he was "particularly anxious" to have four 20-pounder Parrott rifles sent forward to the army from Winchester "if ammunition of a suitable character can be obtained." Lee desired the long-range pieces to help counter the federal advantage in this area. (*OR* 19 (2): 613)

1488. Brig. Gen. George H. Steuart was ordered to Winchester on September 21 to systematize operations at Lee's base of operations in the Shenandoah Valley. Steuart was instructed to: 1) establish a provost guard to keep order; 2) organize the commissary and quartermaster's departments; 3) forward all stragglers, recruits, and convalescents to the front; and 4) establish hospitals for sick and wounded. (*OR* 19 (2): 614-615)

1489. Gen. Lee instituted a daily roll call at reveille on September 22 in an attempt to interject discipline into his ranks, hoping thereby to reduce depredations committed by the army and the "daily diminution by straggling." (*OR* 19 (2): 618-619)

1490. An abstract of field returns for the Army of Northern Virginia on September 22—five days after the battle—showed 41,250 officers and men present. This return did not include the cavalry or the reserve artillery. The largest division in the Confederate army, according to the September 22 returns, was Richard H. Anderson's, with 6,298 present. The smallest was Jackson's own division, with only 2,367 reporting. (*OR* 19 (2): 621)

1491. A sweep of the Lower Shenandoah Valley by Gen. J. R. Jones herded between 5,000 and 6,000 stragglers back into the Army of Northern Virginia by September 27. The number of Confederate officers absent from the ranks and in the Lower Shenandoah Valley was "most astonishing," according to J. R. Jones. To remedy the problem, Jones ordered the cavalry to arrest all officers and men found in the rear without proper leave. The result—"It created quite a stampede in the direction of the army." (*OR* 19 (2): 629)

1492. To help combat bad conduct by regimental and company grade officers, Gen. Lee recommended a law that would degrade officers for the following offenses: 1) bad conduct in the presence of the enemy; 2) leaving their posts in time of battle; or 3) deserting their commands or the army in march or in camp. "There is great dereliction of duty among the regimental and company officers," Lee informed Secretary of War George

W. Randolph on September 23, "and unless something is done the army will melt away." (*OR* 19 (2): 622)

1493. The total present in the Army of Northern Virginia swelled to 62,713 by September 30. This number included the reserve artillery of 1,027 men, but not the cavalry, which had not reported. This increase of 20,436 men occurred in just eight days. Longstreet's corps reported 33,126 present on September 30—an increase of 10,445. Jackson's corps reported 28,738 present on September 30—an increase of 9,899. (*OR* 19 (2): 639)

1494. The largest division in the Confederate army on September 30 was A. P. Hill's division, boasting a strength of 9,103—an increase of 3,635 (66.5%) in eight days. The division showing the largest percentage increase on September 30 in total present was Jackson's division, which leaped 102% in eight days. (*OR* 19 (2): 639)

1495. Gen. Lee acknowledged his increase in strength to President Davis on October 2, but he stressed, "our ranks are still thin, notwithstanding that all the stragglers within my reach have been restored to [the ranks]." (*OR* 19 (2): 639)

1496. Lee expressed concern over the large number of sick in the army. "[A]ll the care and attention I can give to the subject do not seem to diminish the number." Until the regimental officers attended to the wants and comforts of their men—including enforcing cleanliness—Lee informed Davis on October 2, "I fear the sanitary condition of the army will not improve." (*OR* 19 (2): 643)

1497. Confederate strength on October 8 increased to 78,204. By October 20, the army's size had increased by only an additional 1,301 men. Longstreet's and Jackson's corps had expanded by an additional 9,113 men between September 30 and October 8. (*OR* 19 (2): 660, 674)

1498. The first cavalry returns filed since returning from the invasion of Maryland showed 6,378 men present for duty on October 8. (*OR* 19 (2): 660)

1499. Gen. A. P. Hill's division remained the largest division in the Confederate army on October 8, counting 10,596 present for duty—an increase of 1,493 men in eight days. The second largest division belonged to Richard H. Anderson, with 10,264 answering the roll. (*OR* 19 (2): 660)

1500. A request for 204 horses to transport the artillery in Jackson's division was filed by the division's chief of artillery, Maj. L. M. Shumaker. This number was reduced to 128 horses by Jackson's corps artillery chief, Stapleton Crutchfield: "I know how scarce [horses] are," Crutchfield admitted to Jackson, "and you will find it impossible to supply fully all the demands made on you for them." (*OR* 19 (1): 95)

1501. Sharpsburg's economy, ecology, health, and community psyche suffered as a result of The Maryland Campaign. Three distinct factors helped produce this suffering: 1) the unexpected and uninvited occupation of nearly 120,000 soldiers around a community of 1,300; 2) the destruction of buildings, crops, livestock, fences, and cultivated and pastured fields; and 3) the presence of dead, dying, and wounded men and animals in the midst of

Confederate dead southeast of town near the Sherrick farm (*USAMHI*)

the community for days, weeks, and months. (Ted Alexander, "Destruction, Disease, and Death: The Battle of Antietam and the Sharpsburg Civilians," *Civil War Regiments*, pp. 143-173)

1502. About 100 civilians sought refuge in the basement of the substantial stone house owned by John Kretzer on Main Street on the day of the battle. Among the refugees was a mother with a three-day old child.

1503. Buildings in the village of Sharpsburg, although screened from the battle by a ridge, did suffer from artillery damage. Projectiles from long-range Union batteries often flew over the ridge and struck or pierced the east walls of homes, churches, and businesses in the town.

1504. The farm that suffered the most damage on the Antietam battlefield was the Samuel Mumma Farm. His house and outbuildings—burned by the Confederates early on the morning of the battle—were the only civilian structures in the heart of the battlefield destroyed. Damage to his farm amounted to $10,000, and included the loss of 35 tons of hay and several hundred bushels of wheat, corn, and rye. Mumma was never completely compensated for his loss since the US government blamed most of it on the Confederates.

1505. Joseph Sherrick's house, located about one half-mile north of Burnside Bridge, suffered $8.00 damage from an artillery shell. His farm sustained $1,351 damage from occupying federal troops.

The Ruins of the Samuel Mumma Farm (*LC*)

1506. Henry Piper's farm buildings, located just south of Bloody Lane, suffered only $25.00 in damages. During the post-battle occupation by the Union army, however, Piper claimed more than $2,000 in damages caused by the 3rd and 4th Pennsylvania Cavalry and the 8th New York Cavalry, camped on the property after the battle. Livestock lost included: one roan mare; eight milk cows; two steers; 14 other cattle; 40 hogs; 18 sheep; 200 chickens; 15 geese; and 24 turkeys. The Pipers also lost: 100 bushels of Irish potatoes; 30 bushels of sweet potatoes; 200 bushels of apples; 200 bushels of wheat; 800 pounds of bacon; 3,000 pounds of lard; and 20 acres of corn. (Alexander, "Destruction, Disease, and Death," p. 155)

1507. Maj. Gen. Israel B. Richardson died at the Philip Pry house, McClellan's headquarters during the battle, on November 3, 1862. Richardson was one of three Union generals killed or mortally wounded at Sharpsburg—and was the last to die from his wounds.

1508. The Philip Pry family was so devastated by the Union occupation in the aftermath of the battle that they sold their farm in 1873 and moved to Tennessee.

1509. Dr. Thomas T. Ellis mentioned in his diary that a young girl in Sharpsburg was killed on the day of the battle. Her name remains unknown, and no corroborative evidence has been found to substantiate this claim.

1510. John Keplinger was mortally wounded by an unexploded shell as he attempted to diffuse it. Keplinger had disarmed 99 unexploded projectiles from fields around Bloody Lane before the fatal accident.

1511. Diseases brought by the armies into the Antietam Valley proved more dangerous to the population than the battle. Although the number of civilians who died from disease after Antietam remains unknown, disease killed the wife of Henry Mumma, the wife and daughter of Adam Michael, and Raleigh Showman—to name only a few.

1512. Supplies for the Union army accumulated at Monocacy and Frederick, but Quartermaster Gen. Montgomery C. Meigs was concerned for their safety: "The country roads between Frederick and Washington offer rare temptations to cavalry and infantry raids." Two hundred loaded railroad cars—full of supplies—were at Frederick by September 21. No artillery was present, and virtually no infantry was available to protect the cars. The Potomac River was reported fordable in 20 places between Washington and Harpers Ferry, making supply depots and supply lines unsafe according to a September 22 message from Meigs to Lieut. Col. Rufus Ingalls, McClellan's chief quartermaster. (*OR* 19 (2): 341, 342)

1513. The first Union force to enter Harpers Ferry following the surrender—elements of Brig. Gen. George Stoneman's division, who had been guarding river crossings near Point of Rocks—arrived on September 19. Stoneman's men found no enemy, but did discover 300 sick and wounded US troops left behind by the Confederates. (*OR* 19 (2): 335-336)

1514. Alpheus Williams' division of the Twelfth Corps was the first federal force to reoccupy Maryland Heights following the surrender of Harpers Ferry. Williams' men arrived on the mountain on September 20 after marching from their bivouac near the northeast end of the Antietam battlefield. (*OR* 51 (1): 855-856)

1515. Unburied Confederate dead who fought on Maryland Heights—unburied for a week since the September 13 fight—were *burned* by Union forces rather than buried. These human remains were burned because the stony, almost soil-less summit made burial nearly impossible. "[T]he only thing we could do was to gather brush and logs and burn the bodies of the dead," recalled Miles Clayton Huyette of the 125th Pennsylvania Infantry. (Frye & Frye, "Maryland Heights: Archeological & Historical Resources Study," 1989, p. 65)

1516. Surgeon Jonathan Letterman was the Medical Director of the Army of the Potomac. He established Frederick as the primary hospital center for wounded in The Maryland Campaign. Working in Frederick in October were 62 surgeons; 15 medical cadets; 22 hospital stewards; 539 nurses; and 127 cooks. (*OR* 19 (1): 106, 110-111)

1517. Jonathan Letterman was the son of a prominent western Pennsylvania surgeon. He graduated from Jefferson Medical College in Philadelphia in 1849 and then joined the army as a surgeon. He was appointed McClellan's Medical Director in July 1862.

1518. Seventy-one field hospitals were established in Antietam based on the following requisites: 1) they must be far enough to the rear to be secure from enemy artillery fire; 2) barns were preferable to houses because they provided better ventilation and more commodious space; 3) plenty of straw and hay must be available; and 4) a good source of water must be present. (John Schildt, *Antietam Hospitals*, p. 9)

Union hospital site at the Smith Farm (*LC*)

1519. Amputated limbs at the Mount Vernon German Reformed Church in Keedysville were thrown into a large hole excavated just outside the rear windows of the church. Large quantities of wastewater are also thrown into the hole, which eventually caused structural failure of the walls, necessitating the use of iron rods to hold the walls together.

1520. Clara Barton began tending to the wounded about 9:00 a.m. on the day of the battle. She unloaded her wagon near the Smoketown Road and began treating wounded men—mostly from the Twelfth Corps—near an old barn northeast of the Union right. She was practically at the front, within a few hundred yards of a federal battery. Being so close to the battle, a stray bullet passed through her sleeve and killed a man she was helping. Barton never mended the hole in her dress.

1521. Mary Hartwell of Frederick was wounded in the neck on the federal right while looking for her beloved, a young lieutenant in the 3rd Wisconsin. Mary, who was wearing a Union uniform, laid on the battlefield for 36 hours before federal soldiers found her. They did not realize she was a young woman and took her to a field hospital. Eventually, she came under the care of Dr. F. H. Harwood, who asked Clara Barton for assistance. Harwood removed the ball from her neck and Barton helped nurse the woman so that she could return to Frederick.

1522. Five hundred hospital tents were sent to Frederick on September 27. Supplying hospital tents to the Union army became a serious problem. There were only 1,250 in the depot, and to produce 4,000 to 5,000 more would require a lengthy procurement time and cost $400,000 to $500,000. (*OR* 19 (2): 396, 406)

147

1523. Approximately 2,500 Confederate wounded from South Mountain, Crampton's Gap and Antietam received US medical treatment. Immediately after Antietam, the Confederate wounded were gathered from fields, houses, and barns. "Everything [was] done to alleviate their sufferings that was done for our own men," Dr. Letterman wrote in his official report. "Humanity teaches us that a wounded and prostrate foe is not then our enemy." (*OR* 19 (1): 111)

1524. Dr. Letterman established two principal hospitals at Antietam for the long-term care of wounded whose injuries were too severe for a move to Frederick. Six hundred hospital tents were set up at the Hoffman farm near Smoketown for those taken off the battlefield from the Union right. The Locust Spring hospital—also known as the Geeting hospital and the Crystal Farm hospital—was established about one mile southwest of Keedysville for those carried off the field from the Union left. (*OR* 19 (1): 112)

1525. Alexander Gardner's photographs of a Union field hospital at Antietam were taken at the Hoffman farm hospital located about two miles north of Keedysville and about one mile north of the Upper Bridge on the Williamsport-Keedysville Road.

1526. Gen. Meade, commanding the First Corps in place of the wounded Joseph Hooker, reported an increase of 8,875 officers and men from returns on September 18—the day after the battle—through returns on September 22. Meade explained these absences were due to straggling and abandonment of commands. "How this serious and terrible evil can be cured is a difficult question to solve," he informed McClellan, "inasmuch as the disease seems to pervade the whole body." (*OR* 19 (1): 348-349)

1527. Pennsylvania Governor Curtin reported the militia force had been disbanded by September 23, and the men returned to their homes. (*OR* 19 (2): 352)

1528. Gen. Fitz John Porter attempted to quash rumors circulated in early October that Burnside and Pleasonton had presented charges against him "for refusing re-enforcements asked of me at the battle of Antietam." (*OR* 19 (2): 404)

1529. On September 22, McClellan asked the president of the Chesapeake & Ohio Canal to repair damages to the canal at once: "That he should do so is indispensably necessary for ulterior military operations." Canal repairs were slow and frustrating for McClellan's plan to move supplies via the canal to his depot at Harpers Ferry. Two weeks after McClellan's initial request to reopen the canal, 65 men were working on the only break, which was at the mouth of the Monocacy. Attempts were underway on October 6 to increase the workforce to 150 men, but "there is great difficulty in employing laborers." All the government's useful contractors had been sent to the depots or had been absorbed as teamsters. (*OR* 19 (2): 343, 388)

1530. Gen. McClellan, on September 22, asked the president of the Baltimore & Ohio Railroad, John W. Garrett, to fully repair the destroyed railroad bridge spanning the Potomac at Harpers Ferry: "I beg to assure you that so long as I remain in command, no harm shall again occur to this bridge from the hands of the enemy." (*OR* 19 (2): 343)

1531. Pontoons for a new pontoon bridge arrived at Harpers Ferry on September 23. The bridge was laid by September 25. (*OR* 19 (2): 353, 358)

1532. McClellan decided to establish his new base of operations at Harpers Ferry on September 24—one week after the battle. (*OR* 19 (2): 354-355)

1533. The Confederate army changed its positions on September 27. Longstreet's "right wing" passed beyond Mill Creek and encamped on the waters flowing into the Opequon, extending to Lick River or Red Bud Run. Jackson's "left wing" halted on Mill Creek and closed on Longstreet's command. Gen. Lee shifted the position of the army, partly in response to a large build up of federal forces at Harpers Ferry. He informed President Davis on the 28th that he moved to the Mill Creek-Lick River line "to be prepared for any flank movement the enemy might attempt." (*OR* 19 (2): 628-629, 633)

1534. Gen. Lee expressed disappointment that McClellan did not advance. "I have been in hopes that he would cross the river and move up the valley," Lee noted to Jefferson Davis on October 2, "where I wish to get him, but he does not seem so disposed." Lee concluded that "General McClellan's army is apparently quiescent." (*OR* 19 (2): 644)

1535. No advance against the Confederates was possible McClellan informed Halleck on September 24, until a permanent double-track bridge was built over the Potomac at Harpers Ferry and a wagon bridge constructed over the Shenandoah at the same place. "Until this . . . railroad bridge is finished, it is scarcely possible to advance from Harpers Ferry, in force, as that is clearly our true line of operations." McClellan further stressed the importance of the bridge in an October 1 message to Halleck in which he predicted engineer Roebling could build the bridge in three or four weeks. General-in-Chief Halleck objected to McClellan's bridge-building plan: "[T]he War Department wishes to be informed more definitely of your plans," he informed "Little Mac" on September 26, "before authorizing the expenditure of large sums of money for rebuilding bridges on the Potomac." As a follow up to McClellan's October 1 assertion that the bridge could be built in three to four weeks, Halleck scolds: "I know the Government does not contemplate the delay in your movements for the length of time required to build permanent bridges." (*OR* 19 (1): 10 (2): 354-355, 360)

1536. President Lincoln directed McClellan—in no uncertain terms—to advance against Lee. "The President directs that you cross the Potomac and give battle to the enemy or drive him south," Halleck asserted in an October 6 dictate. "Your army must move now while the roads are good." McClellan did not begin an advance until 20 days later. (*OR* 19 (1): 10)

1537. McClellan determined on October 7 that his offensive strategy would "adopt the line of the Shenandoah [Valley] for immediate operations against the enemy." This ran counter to President Lincoln's suggestion that the army move south, east of the Blue Ridge. McClellan believed that operations west of the Blue Ridge would prevent the enemy from moving against Maryland or Pennsylvania. McClellan made this decision "after a full consultation with the corps commanders in my vicinity." (*OR* 19 (1): 11, 14)

1538. Gen. McClellan established a new headquarters approximately three miles south of Sharpsburg on September 25. The headquarters location was at the home of widow Keziah Showman and her son, Otho Showman. McClellan then moved his headquarters to the east side of South Mountain, just north of Knoxville, on October 8. He informed

General-in-Chief Halleck he was "pushing everything as rapidly as possible to get ready for the advance." (*OR* 19 (2): 403; The author discovered McClellan's headquarters site while examining the Otho and Raleigh Showman damage claim in the National Archives.)

1539. Gen. Burnside established his headquarters at the home of Raleigh Showman, about four miles south of Sharpsburg near Antietam Furnace, during the last week of September. Burnside moved his command and headquarters into Pleasant Valley, just north of Harpers Ferry, on October 7. (*OR* 19 (1): 394, 402; Burnside's post-Antietam headquarters is the home of the author)

1540. William and Margaret Roulette—owners of the farm over which the Second Corps attacked Bloody Lane—lost their daughter Carrie May Roulette on October 26—five weeks after the battle.

1541. McClellan considered supplying the Army of the Potomac—during an expected advance toward Winchester and with its base at Harpers Ferry—via the Winchester & Potomac Railroad. The W & P Railroad, that runs 32 miles from Harpers Ferry to Winchester (and was built in 1834-1835), was "perhaps the worst in the Union," according to W. P. Smith, superintendent of the B & O Railroad. (*OR* 19 (1): 408-409, 411-412)

1542. Repair of the Winchester & Potomac Railroad will require, at a minimum, installation of 30 miles of "T-rail," as well as new ties. At least six weeks was required to purchase iron, cut ties, and reconstruct the track. Gen. McClellan decided against efforts to make the Winchester & Potomac Railroad operational because it "cannot be reconstructed now so as to benefit a movement this autumn." (*OR* 19 (2): 412, 414)

1543. McClellan personally reconnoitered Maryland Heights on September 26 and determined to fortify them "in order to avoid a similar catastrophe to the one which happened to Colonel Miles." (*OR* 19 (2): 360-361)

1544. "Contraband" slaves were requisitioned by McClellan for the purpose of constructing fortifications at Harpers Ferry. McClellan requested 2,000 "contrabands"— slaves who have sought refuge behind Union lines—to be sent from the Washington area to Harpers Ferry. (*OR* 19 (2): 360-362)

1545. Lt. Cyrus B. Comstock of the engineer staff surveyed and laid out the fortifications on Maryland and Loudoun Heights. Comstock developed an ambitious plan for Harpers Ferry that fortified the crests of Maryland and Loudoun Heights by "a line of stone blockhouses or redoubts" stretching for at least 1½ miles from the Potomac. This plan developed an "entrenched camp" for 3,000 men, with one side comprised of stone blockhouses, and the other side log blockhouses, which also furnishes quarters for the troops. The total estimated cost of the Comstock plan: $50,000. According to Comstock, his scheme would: 1) prevent enemy crossings into Maryland at this point; 2) protect the B & O Railroad bridge crossing the Potomac; and 3) furnish a strong post for the protection of the railroad in the vicinity. (*OR* 19 (2): 360-362)

1546. Delays and expense were the price of McClellan's Harpers Ferry proposal. "This project of extensively fortifying Harpers Ferry, and constructing a permanent bridge at that point," General-in-Chief Halleck maintained, "involves a very considerable

expenditure of money, a larger garrison, and a long delay, perhaps extending into winter."
(*OR* 19 (2): 442-443)

1547. A difference of opinion developed between Gen. McClellan and General-in-Chief Halleck with regard to the utilization of Harpers Ferry as a base of operations. McClellan argued on October 18: "I look upon the permanent and secure occupation of Harpers Ferry as a military necessity." Halleck countered on the 19th that Harpers Ferry was "at best, an exterior line of operations upon our proper objective point—Staunton, Lynchburg, or Richmond." (*OR* 19 (2): 442-443)

1548. Halleck argued the proper base of operations for McClellan was Washington, D.C., and *not* Harpers Ferry. "Old Brains" contended on October 19 that Union operations should commence east of the Blue Ridge, not west in the Shenandoah Valley, thereby threatening Confederate communications and supplies and compelling Lee "to evacuate the vicinity of Harpers Ferry." The General-in-Chief concluded on October 20: "Harpers Ferry is not, in my opinion, a proper base of military operations, and it would be an error to expend time and money there for such an object." (*OR* 19 (2): 442-443, 451)

1549. Halleck's plan of operations for the army—penetrating Virginia east of the Blue Ridge and reducing Harpers Ferry to "field defenses, with a moderate garrison"—was approved by Secretary of War Stanton on October 20. (*OR* 19 (2): 442-443)

1550. Staunton, Virginia—in Augusta, County, in the Upper Shenandoah Valley, and about 60 miles south of Winchester—became Lee's primary base of operations. Winchester served as his forward base. By the first week of October, Lee was attempting to move to Staunton everything captured at Harpers Ferry, as well as "all of value" in Winchester, in addition to his sick and wounded. This process was slowed considerably, Gen. Lee reported, "from our weakness in transportation." The number of Confederate wounded sent to Staunton for recovery—from the battles of around Manassas and in Maryland—numbered 4,500 by October 8. (*OR* 19 (1): 657, 664)

1551. The number of Confederate sick at Winchester numbered between 4,500 and 5,000 on October 8. Most of the sick were conscripts or new recruits. Most of the sick were suffering from contagious diseases, such as measles, mumps, and camp fever, that infect new soldiers who were exposed to army life for the first time. Gen. Lee recommended no more conscripts or recruits be sent to the army until they were assembled in camps of instruction "so that they may pass through the inevitable diseases, and become a little inured to camp life." (*OR* 19 (2): 657, 660)

1552. Gen. Lee surmised, based upon the federal build up at Harpers Ferry, that McClellan intended to advance up the Shenandoah Valley, and that his "great object" would be the destruction of the Virginia Central Railroad, with its depot at Staunton, "upon which they think we depend for our supplies." (*OR* 19 (2): 641)

1553. A congratulatory order to the Army of Northern Virginia was issued by Gen. Lee on October 2. It expressed admiration for the "indomitable courage" the army had displayed and its "cheerful endurance of privation and hardship on the march." Lee concluded with valedictory praise: "History records few examples of greater fortitude and endurance than this army has exhibited." Regarding Sharpsburg, Lee made a proud declaration: "[W]ith less than one-third his numbers, you resisted from daylight until dark the whole army of the enemy, and repulsed every attack along his entire front of more than 4 miles." (*OR* 19 (2): 644-645)

1554. Construction of fortifications began on Maryland Heights by late October, commencing with the earthworks known as the 30-pounder Battery—equipped with 30-pounder Parrott rifles—and at the "Stone Fort." The "Stone Fort" was a dry-laid masonry blockhouse that stood upon the highest point on Maryland Heights (1448 feet). It was designed by Lt. Charles R. Suter, and the original plan appeared in the diary of Cyrus B. Comstock. Monthly returns for November-December 1862 revealed 28 masons and one master mason employed in construction of the "Stone Fort" on Maryland Heights.

1555. Twenty new regiments, totaling 18,667 men, arrived at Frederick between September 29 and 30 to reinforce McClellan's army. These new regiments were assigned to five different corps and Couch's division. Gen. Lee observed on October 9 that McClellan's army was "filled almost to bursting with new recruits and regiments." (*OR* 19 (2): 368-369, 373-374, 659)

1556. From September 16 to October 26, nearly 120,000 Union soldiers were camped in the Sharpsburg-Harpers Ferry area.

1557. Straggling and marauding in the Union army remained a problem after Antietam. McClellan's headquarters issued a circular on October 1 that reminded the army it was "now occupying a country inhabited by a loyal population, who look to us for the preservation of order and discipline, instead of suffering our men to go about in small parties, lawlessly depredating upon their property." Punishment for Union stragglers or marauders would be hard labor on the defenses of Harpers Ferry. (*OR* 19 (2): 376)

1558. Abraham Lincoln visited the Army of the Potomac from October 1-4, 1862. The president left Washington at 6:00 a.m. on the 1st and then proceeded by railroad to the pontoon bridge at Harpers Ferry. Lincoln reviewed the Second Corps on Bolivar Heights and spent the evening of the 1st at Harpers Ferry with Gen. Sumner.

1559. President Lincoln visited and reviewed federal troops on Maryland Heights on October 2, but he did not reach the summit: "I showed the way until we got to a patch where it was right straight up, when Abraham backed out," noted guide Charles F. Morse of the 2nd Massachusetts Infantry. Lincoln was riding horseback when he reached the steep incline and determined it was best to return back down the mountain. (Frye & Frye, *Maryland Heights: Archeological & Historical Resources Study*, p. 66)

1560. Lincoln arrived at McClellan's headquarters at the Keziah and Otho Showman property, three miles south of Sharpsburg, on the afternoon of October 2. Gen. Burnside was the first to greet the president, and "Old Burn" escorted him to "Little Mac's" headquarters. McClellan escorted Lincoln over the Antietam battlefield during the afternoon of the 2nd.

1561. President Lincoln spent the nights of October 2 and October 3 in a tent at McClellan's headquarters at the Keziah and Otho Showman farm.

President Lincoln and General McClellan at the Grove Farm on October 3, 1862
(*USAMHI*)

1562. First on President Lincoln's itinerary for October 3 was a 10:00 a.m. review of Burnside's Ninth Corps, that occurred about four miles south of Sharpsburg near the mouth of the Antietam Creek. During the afternoon, he traveled to the Stephen P. Grove farm, where Fitz John Porter was headquartered. Here Lincoln shook hands with both Union and Confederate wounded. The President also reviewed the First Corps beginning at 3:00 p.m. on the 3rd, followed by a quick review of the Sixth Corps at the end of the day.

1563. The famous Lincoln-McClellan photographs, taken by Alexander Gardner on October 3, were reportedly taken at the Grove farm. There is little question that the photograph of Lincoln and McClellan with Porter and Fifth Corps staff members was at the Grove farm. The close-up interior tent pictures of Lincoln and McClellan may, however, have been photographed at McClellan's headquarters at the Keziah and Otho Showman property.

1564. On October 4, Lincoln's final day of visit to the Army of the Potomac, he departed McClellan's headquarters at 10:00 a.m., visited the wounded Gen. I. B. Richardson at the Pry House, and then departed for Boonsboro and South Mountain, where McClellan and the president parted. Lincoln then proceeded to Frederick, where he re-boarded a train and returned to Washington at 10:00 p.m.

1565. President Lincoln displayed frustration with McClellan 11 days after completing his visit to the army. "You remember my speaking to you of what I called your overcautiousness," Lincoln began an October 13 letter. "Are you not overcautious when you assume that you cannot do what the enemy is constantly doing?" Lincoln was referring to Lee's ability to supply his army from Culpeper Court House, while McClellan complained that he cannot supply his force at half the distance. (*OR* 19 (1): 13)

1566. Artillery in the Army of Northern Virginia was reorganized and consolidated in October for the following reasons: 1) too many artillery companies existed, with some never reaching their full complement of men or guns; 2) inadequate officers in some companies; and 3) companies so reduced in men and horses that little hope remained for "their restoration to efficiency." (*OR* 19 (2): 647-654)

1567. Brig. Gen. William Nelson Pendleton, Lee's chief of artillery, had the difficult task of examining the batteries, reducing their number, and increasing the efficiency of the artillery organizations. Pendleton established three standards of evaluation to guide his assessment of existing artillery companies: 1) laudable past service; 2) thoroughly efficient officers; and 3) existing conditions and future prospects for the battery. Pendleton's October 2 report to Gen. Lee recommended reducing the current 72 batteries by 18 batteries. He also suggested eliminating 10 more batteries and consolidating their men, guns, and horses into other batteries. (*OR* 19 (2): 647, 652)

1568. Five hundred men from Maryland had been organized into five Confederate infantry companies at Winchester by October 13. More Marylanders were arriving, and Brig. Gen. George H. Steuart, who was organizing the command, soon hoped to have enough to fill a regiment. (*OR* 19 (2): 664)

1569. Five hundred barrels of potatoes and onions were requested to be sent to the Hagerstown depot on October 22. (*OR* 19 (2): 468)

1570. One hundred and twenty thousand small arms were on hand in the Army of the Potomac according to an October 11 inventory. The arms count broke down as follows: 80,000 rifles (calibers .57 and .58); 20,000 rifles (caliber .54); 10,000 rifles (caliber .69); 5,000 smoothbore muskets (caliber .69); and 5,000 carbines. Each small arm in the Army of the Potomac had available about 140 rounds of ammunition by the second week of October. In addition, about 2,300,000 rounds were available at the Frederick depot. (*OR* 19 (2): 412)

1571. Due to a shortage of Confederate wagons and horses, Gen. Lee fixed transportation in his army as follows: division headquarters—three four-horse wagons; brigade headquarters—two four-horse wagons; for each regiment—one wagon for headquarters; one for hospital and medical stores; one for ordnance; and one wagon for every 100 men in the regiment. (*OR* 19 (2): 641)

1572. By October 13, 7,000 pounds of bread were baked daily in the Confederate ovens at Winchester. (*OR* 19 (2): 655)

1573. Frustration became intense over the failure to deliver clothing to the Union army in a timely manner. "There is no clothing at Hagerstown, and an entire corps is waiting for it," declared an exasperated Rufus Ingalls, McClellan's chief quartermaster, on October 10. "What is the matter? The operation is becoming painful. . . . In mercy's name, get after this clothing." A portion of clothing began arriving in Hagerstown on October 14, but incomplete delivery further frustrated First Corps commander John Reynolds. His quartermaster procured overcoats and pants, as well as a few socks, coats, and drawers. No shoes, tents, blankets, knapsacks, or other clothing had yet arrived. (*OR* 19 (1): 408, 429-430)

1574. Gen. Reynolds reported on October 15 that he had requisitioned 5,251 pairs of shoes but by mid-October, "many of the men [are] yet without a shoe." Army headquarters instructed the First Corps commander on October 16 to draw his clothing from Harpers Ferry. "At least 10,000 suits, 20,000 blankets, and 10,000 shelter-tents were ordered from New York some time ago, and should soon be at Harpers Ferry." The Quartermaster General dispatched 10,000 pairs of shoes, via special wagon train, from the depot in Washington to McClellan's headquarters on October 22. The wagons carrying the shoes would be added to McClellan's supply trains. . (*OR* 19 (1): 430, 437, 464-465)

1575. Supplies on hand at Harpers Ferry on October 22 included: 24,000 booties; 1,800 blankets; 3,000 stockings; 4,000 infantry trousers; 4,000 infantry overcoats; 7,500 knit jackets; 1,500 cavalry trousers; and 3,000 cavalry overcoats. (*OR* 19 (2): 466)

1576. Transportation via the Cumberland Valley Railroad, servicing Hagerstown from the north, became so inept that the Secretary of War ordered Brig. Gen. Herman Haupt— military superintendent of railroads—to personally inspect the line and "take such measures as may be necessary to enforce promptness and efficiency." Haupt received permission to take military possession of the railroad. (*OR* 19 (2): 439)

1577. Gen. Lee, in a letter to President Davis on October 1, perceived two reasons for McClellan's failure to advance against him: 1) "[He] is only able to procure supplies for his army from day to day"; and 2) "[H]e is employing his time in recuperating his army from the effects of the recent battles." (*OR* 19 (2): 641)

1578. Gen. Lee recommended Longstreet and Jackson for promotion to the newly created rank of lieutenant general on October 2. Lee informed President Davis that he only desired two corps commander and two corps in the Army of Northern Virginia. (*OR* 19 (2): 643)

1579. A. P. Hill—next to Longstreet and Jackson—"is the best commander with me," Gen. Lee observed in his October 2 message to President Davis. (*OR* 19 (2): 643)

1580. On October 8, Gen. Lee ordered Jeb Stuart and his cavalry to carry out a raid into Maryland and Pennsylvania. Lee instructed Stuart to proceed as far north as Chambersburg to destroy the Cumberland Valley Railroad bridge across the Conococheague Creek. Gen. Lee also asked Stuart to determine the position, force, and intention of the enemy and to seize as many horses as practicable. (*OR* 19 (2): 55)

1581. In one of his most unusual stipulations of the war, Lee granted Stuart the authority during his raid to arrest Pennsylvanians who hold state of federal offices so that "they may be used as hostages, or the means of exchanges, for our own citizens that have been carried off by the enemy. (*OR* 19 (2): 55)

1582. Stuart launched his cavalry raid with three brigades of 1,800 men and four pieces of horse artillery at noon on October 9. He crossed the Potomac River at McCoy's Ferry near Clear Spring at dawn on the 10th, and then crossed the Pennsylvania line to Mercersburg, where he arrived at noon. The cavalry then pushed rapidly toward Chambersburg, where it arrived after dark on the 10th—riding 40 miles without opposition. It rained all night of the 10th and 11th. On the 11th, Stuart proceeded east toward Gettysburg, but altered direction after crossing South Mountain, zigzagging southwest toward Hagerstown, and then southeast toward Frederick. Before reaching Frederick, the Confederates crossed the Monocacy and headed east, marching throughout the night through Liberty, New Market, and Monrovia. At daylight on the 12th, Stuart arrived at Hyattstown, and then headed for Poolesville near the Potomac. The cavalry recrossed the Potomac at White's Ford and returned to Virginia by late morning on the 12th. (*OR* 19 (2): 52-54)

1583. In three days, Stuart's cavalry command covered 180 miles—80 during the last 24 hours of the raid. The Confederates captured over 1,200 horses, and suffered no men killed and only one wounded. (*OR* 19 (2): 52-54)

1584. Stuart's Confederates failed to destroy the Conococheague railroad bridge because it was an iron span. They also failed to capture any Pennsylvania public officials, all of whom had fled. According to Stuart, "no one could be found who would admit that he held office." The Confederate cavalry did destroy extensive machine shops and railroad depot buildings at Chambersburg, which resulted in the loss of 5,000 muskets, pistols, and sabers, as well as a large assortment of clothing. Stuart also burned several trains of loaded cars. Frederick, Maryland, "with great army stores, our cars, engines, and bridges at Monocacy" made a narrow escape from Stuart's cavalry, as they passed within three miles of the town. (*OR* 19 (2): 52-54, 415)

1585. Brig. Gen. Alfred M. Pleasonton, McClellan's cavalry commander, learned about Stuart's raid at 4:00 a.m. on the 11th. Pleasonton immediately began the chase, marching some 400 cavalrymen 78 miles in 24 hours. By the time he arrived at White's Ford on the 12th, with a command that was "not well closed up," Stuart had escaped. (*OR* 19 (2): 38-40)

1586. McClellan attempted to cut off Stuart's avenues of escape across the Potomac by alerting George Stoneman's infantry division, on duty near the mouth of the Monocacy. Stoneman failed to end Stuart's adventure, offering as excuses too much river to cover and "the rapidity and uncertainty of the enemy's movements." Stoneman was censored by McClellan, accusing him of failing to obey an order by not supporting Pleasonton's cavalry. In the aftermath of Stuart's raid, McClellan ordered Burnside to deploy his infantry along the Potomac from the mouth of the Monocacy to Harpers Ferry.

1587. Gen. Lee prepared for a federal cavalry raid around his army in the Shenandoah Valley, mimicking the one recently completed by Stuart. Evidence of this concern appeared in an October 18 warning to Brig. Gen. George H. Steuart, commanding at Winchester: "I wish you would be on the alert," directed Lee, "and keep your Maryland troops and others with your prepared for any emergency." (*OR* 19 (2): 671)

1588. McClellan blamed his want of adequate and effective cavalry for Stuart's raid. His quartermaster requested 1,500 fresh horses on October 13—the day after the raid ended. (*OR* 19 (2): 417, 421)

1589. President Lincoln directed this reflection to General McClellan regarding Stuart's cavalry raid: "[I]f the enemy had more occupation south of the river, his cavalry would not be so likely to make raids north of it." (*OR* 19 (2): 421)

1590. Secretary of War Stanton noted McClellan's complaint of an "inadequate supply of horses for his cavalry command," and demanded an explanation from the Quartermaster General on October 13. Quartermaster Gen. Meigs responded to Secretary Stanton's inquiry about horses within a day. He informed the Secretary on October 14 that 10,254 horses had been sent to McClellan's command—a weekly average of 1,709 animals—in six weeks, beginning September 1. Meigs revealed his exasperation with McClellan's constant cry for new horses: "I do not understand," he wrote Secretary Stanton, "how General McClellan has fallen into such an error as to the number of horses issued." (*OR* 19 (2): 416, 422-423)

1591. The cost of the 10,254 horses issued to McClellan's army in those weeks was not less than $1,200,000. (*OR* 19 (2): 423)

1592. Meigs blamed the "waste and destruction" of the horses on "abuse, suffering, overwork, or neglect." He informed Secretary Stanton that "every commander, from the highest to the lowest in rank . . . has a direct interest in the condition of the stock. Upon the efficiency of the animals depend the precision, rapidity, and success of [the army's] marches, and thence of all [its] military operations." Quartered at the Washington depot on October 14 are 2,671 unserviceable horses, "broken down by hard usage, by insufficient food and care." At one point, the broken down horses reached 3,300. Many died, some were shot, and some sold. The majority, however, after rest and good feed, recovered and returned to the army within one or two weeks. (*OR* 19 (2): 423-424)

1593. Confederate forces in the Lower Shenandoah Valley began the systematic destruction of the Baltimore & Ohio Railroad the third week of October. Ties were taken up and burned, bridges collapsed, and the station houses at Martinsburg destroyed. Rails were heated and bent into "Confederate bow ties." (*OR* 19 (2): 675)

1594. President Lincoln showed great impatience with McClellan's failure to advance against the enemy in correspondence dated October 25. First, the President reviewed a dispatch forwarded by McClellan to the War Department in which the colonel of the 1st Massachusetts Cavalry complained about his broken-down horses. Lincoln directed his response to McClellan: "I have just read your dispatch about sore-tongued and fatigued horses," the President began. "Will you pardon me for asking what the horses of your army have done since the battle of Antietam that fatigues anything?" (*OR* 19 (2): 484)

1595. McClellan responded matter-of-factly to Lincoln's sarcastic question about fatigued cavalry. "Little Mac" shared some statistics with the president, such as six cavalry regiments traveling 200 miles in pursuit of Stuart during his raid, including a march of 55 miles in one day. McClellan then offered a second reason to the president for his worn-out mounts: picketing and scouting 150 miles of river front since Antietam, as well as repeated reconnaissances. As McClellan summarized: "[The cavalry] has performed harder service since the battle than before." (*OR* 19 (2): 485)

1596. President Lincoln concluded the debate over "fatigued" horses with this message to McClellan on October 27: "To be told, after more than five weeks' total inaction of the army, and during which period we have sent to the army every fresh horse we possibly could . . . that the cavalry horses were too much fatigued to move, presents a very cheerless, almost hopeless, prospect for the future, and it may have forced something of impatience in my dispatch." (*OR* 19 (2): 486)

1597. Horses in the Confederate army were also in a broken-down condition. In Orders No. 115, issued by Gen. Lee on October 1, he proposed five regulations: 1) no teams will be overdriven, misused, or neglected; 2) artillery horses especially, must be kept in good condition through sufficient and suitable food—"sparing no effort or reasonable expense"; 3) halting places on the march for battery horses must be where there is food and water, and in the vicinity of the enemy, every opportunity provided for resting, feeding, and watering; 4) horses worn down must be turned over to the chief quartermaster for pasturage; and 5) battery horses will not be ridden. (*OR* 19 (2): 642-643)

1598. Gen. Lee returned the effects of US Maj. Gen. Philip Kearny to Gen. McClellan on October 4. Kearney was killed on September 1 in the battle of Chantilly, during the federal retreat from Second Manassas. Lee returned Kearny's sword, horse, and saddle, at the request of his wife, which had fallen into Confederate hands at the time of his death. (*OR* 19 (2): 381)

1599. Confederate wounded, nurses, and doctors on the Maryland side of the river in the vicinity of Sharpsburg should be "sent away at once," declared Gen. Fitz John Porter in an October 14 message to army headquarters. Porter recommended this action because the Confederate wounded and those tending to them "communicate with their friends on the opposite side of the river, and are well posted in regard to the position of our troops." (*OR* 19 (2): 425)

1600. The US Army returned 27 wagons and teams captured at Harpers Ferry to the Confederates on October 20. The wagons and teams were loaned to Gen. Julius White by Gen. A. P. Hill as part of the surrender terms to transport officers' baggage. The wagons were removed, under Union escort, from Bolivar Heights, and handed over to the Confederates near Charles Town. (*OR* 19 (2): 378, 388, 396-397, 450)

1601. Forty thousand rations a day were delivered to depots at Harpers Ferry and Sandy Hook beginning the third week of October. To supply animals, 5,000 bushels of oats and 50 tons of hay *daily* were delivered to the Harpers depot by the last week of October. To supply the animals servicing the entire Army of the Potomac required 200 tons of hay and 10,000 bushels of grain daily. (*OR* 19 (2): 456, 480, 492)

1602. Resistance to the recently instituted military draft became a serious problem in Schuylkill, Luzerne, and Carbon Counties, Pennsylvania the last week of October. Pennsylvania Governor Curtin informed the Secretary of War that there were several thousand armed men—he later reported 5,000—in these counties who refuse to be drafted and who will not permit the drafted men to leave. Governor Curtin requested 1,000 soldiers be sent to him "to crush the [draft] resistance so effectually that the like will not occur again." The governor reported the rebellion over by October 27. (*OR* 19 (2): 473, 479, 500)

1603. In a six week period between September 12 and October 29, 1862, the Army of the Potomac was shipped 97,700 drawers; 17,000 ponchos; 34,500 forage caps; 123,425 stocking pairs; 28,229 canteens; 45,301 flannel shirts; 33,889 haversacks; 13,800 pairs of boots; 44,060 infantry coats; and 86,440 booties, and this represented only a partial list. (*OR* 19 (2): 488)

1604. Small pox broke out in the Confederate army the third week of October. Twenty-five cases were reported by October 23 with two deaths resulting from the disease. (*OR* 19 (2): 679)

1605. Gen. Lee began transferring his army toward the Blue Ridge on October 23. The division leading the advance belonged to Maj. Gen. John G. Walker, who was ordered to cross the mountain via Ashby's Gap and take up a position at Paris or near Upperville. (*OR* 19 (2): 676)

1606. Stonewall Jackson's corps established its new camp on the west side of the Blue Ridge along Long Marsh Run, just north of Berryville. Jackson's force, in addition to a brigade of cavalry, would be the only Confederate presence remaining in the Shenandoah Valley. Gen. Lee authorized Jackson on October 28 to "regulate the movements of your corps as circumstances may require . . . without referring to me for authority." Lee kept Jackson in the northeastern Shenandoah Valley to watch for movements of the enemy along the Potomac and to discover his intentions, should he move. Jackson also posed a threat to the flank of any Union force moving south on the east side of the Blue Ridge. (*OR* 19 (2): 685-686)

1607. Gen. Lee established his new headquarters at Culpeper to thwart any move of the enemy south toward Fredericksburg or Richmond. (*OR* 19 (2): 685)

1608. Longstreet's corps was summoned to Culpeper, and he began his march on October 28, leaving the Valley via Front Royal and Chester Gap, and proceeding across the piedmont through Washington (Virginia in Rappahannock County), then to Sperryville, and finally to Culpeper. (*OR* 19 (2): 686)

1609. The two brigades in Gen. Hood's division that have been separated on account of small pox were directed to take a different route across the Blue Ridge—first to Front Royal then south to Luray and across the Blue Ridge on the road to Madison Court House and Gordonsville. (*OR* 19 (2): 686)

1610. Thirty-nine days after Antietam, on October 26, McClellan launched the Army of the Potomac on the offensive into Virginia. (*OR* 19 (2): 485-486)

1611. The first Union division across the Potomac, to spearhead McClellan's late October offensive, was A. W. Whipple's division of the Twelfth Corps. It crossed the river at Berlin (modern-day Brunswick, Maryland) on October 26 via a pontoon bridge and occupied ground on the Virginia side between the bridge and Lovettsville. William M.

Fenton's division of Burnside's Ninth Corps was the second Union division to cross at Berlin, following Whipple's division on the 26th. Pleasonton's cavalry then followed. (*OR* 19 (2): 485-486, 494)

1612. On October 30, McClellan ordered Fitz John Porter and the Fifth Corps to advance from near Sharpsburg toward Harpers Ferry, "being careful to proceed by such back roads as will effectually conceal your movement from the enemy." (*OR* 19 (2): 511)

1613. The last Union corps to cross the Potomac in McClellan's offensive into Virginia was William B. Franklin's Sixth Corps. It advanced across the river on November 2—six days after the offensive commences. (*OR* 19 (2): 531-532)

1614. All stragglers working on the defenses of Harpers Ferry were ordered to return to their regiments on October 29, with this warning—"If any of the delinquents are detected again in straggling, they will be put at special hard labor for three months." (*OR* 19 (2): 509)

1615. The Union Twelfth Corps, by orders from General McClellan on October 29, established positions on Maryland, Loudoun, and Bolivar Heights, and did not join the general advance of the army. (*OR* 19 (2): 506)

1616. Gen. McClellan warned President Lincoln and Governor Curtin that the troops left behind to guard the upper Potomac above Harpers Ferry was "not a force sufficient to prevent raids." (*OR* 19 (2): 510)

1617. All clothing, teams, and quartermasters' property on hand at the depots at Harpers Ferry, Frederick, and Hagerstown was to be sent to Washington, as ordered in a November 6 directive from Rufus Ingalls, chief quartermaster of the Army of the Potomac. (*OR* 19 (2): 548)

1618. McClellan warned President Lincoln on October 27 that many of his old regiments had been greatly reduced, and it was necessary "to fill up these skeletons *before taking them again into action.*" (emphasis added). McClellan requested that the president use drafted men to fill the ranks of these depleted regiments. (*OR* 19 (2): 496)

1619. The "skeleton regiments" missive McClellan sent to Lincoln severely tested the president's patience: "Is it your purpose not to go into action again," Lincoln asked pointedly, "until the men now being drafted in the States are incorporated into the old regiments?" "Little Mac" informed the president on the evening of the 27th that the phrase *before taking them into action again* was an error. An aide inadvertently added the phrase, McClellan explained—"not authorized or intended by me." (*OR* 19 (2): 497)

1620. President Lincoln fired McClellan as commander of the Army of the Potomac on November 5, 1862. He was instructed to proceed to Trenton, New Jersey, to await orders. He received no other command during the war. Two days after Lincoln issued the orders, McClellan discovered he had been relieved. McClellan was at his headquarters near Rectortown, Virginia, when word arrives on the 7th, during a heavy snowstorm that struck north-central Virginia. (*OR* 19 (2): 545, 551)

1621. Gen. McClellan issued a brief farewell address to the army. "In parting from you," he began, "I cannot express the love and gratitude I bear to you. As an army, you have grown up under my care." "Little Mac" concluded by throwing his support behind the president's authority to make his decision: "We shall ever be comrades in supporting the Constitution of our country and the nationality of its people." (*OR* 19 (2): 551)

1622. McClellan's official report of The Maryland Campaign is dated August 4, 1863— nearly eleven months after Antietam. Full of falsehoods, accusations, and opinion, the document was a "blatant and disingenuous attempt to rescue his reputation." (*OR* 19 (1): 36)

1623. "Little Mac" challenged Abraham Lincoln for president as the Democratic candidate in the election of 1864. He won the electoral votes of only three states.

1624. McClellan served as governor of New Jersey from 1878 to 1881.

1625. The Young Napoleon's only visit to Sharpsburg after the battle came on Memorial Day, May 30, 1885. McClellan survived Antietam by 23 years, dying on October 29, 1885 at age 58, at Orange, New Jersey. He is buried in Riverview Cemetery in Trenton.

1626. Robert E. Lee became president of Washington College in Lexington, Virginia, after the war. He died on October 12, 1870.

1627. Ambrose E. Burnside reluctantly accepted command of the Army of the Potomac on November 7, 1862, following Lincoln's removal of McClellan. He informed General-in-Chief Halleck: "[You] will readily comprehend the embarrassments which surround me in taking command of this army, at this place, and at this season of the year. Had I been asked to take it, I should have declined; but being ordered, I cheerfully obey." Burnside suffered a disastrous defeat at Fredericksburg one month later, but regained some of his reputation by ably defending Knoxville against James Longstreet in the fall of 1863. Burnside suffered his final military exasperation in the battle of the Crater at Petersburg in July 1864. (*OR* 19 (2): 554)

1628. Burnside enjoyed a successful political career after the war. He was elected governor of Rhode Island three times (1866-1868), and in 1874, was elected a US Senator from Rhode Island. Burnside died 19 years after Antietam on September 13, 1881, at age 57, and is buried in Swan Point Cemetery in Providence.

1629. Ambrose Powell (A. P.) Hill, who stymied Burnside's final drive against Sharpsburg and stole victory away from McClellan, became Lee's third corps commander in June 1863. He was killed at Petersburg on April 2, 1865—one week before Lee's surrender at Appomattox.

1630. Joseph Hooker, commander of the First Corps that fought in The Cornfield and the East Woods, superceded Burnside as Commander of the Army of the Potomac in January 1863. He was defeated by Lee at Chancellorsville on May 1-4, 1863. Hooker resigned as army commander during the advance to Gettysburg. He was later transferred to the Western Theater, and won the battle of Lookout Mountain at Chattanooga on November 26, 1863.

1631. George Gordon Meade, division commander of the Pennsylvania Reserves at Antietam, led the Union army to victory at Gettysburg. He replaced Hooker at the helm of the Army of the Potomac on June 28, 1863—only three days before action commenced at Gettysburg. Meade remained commander of the Army of the Potomac until the end of the war.

1632. Thomas Jonathan "Stonewall" Jackson stopped Meade's advance at Fredericksburg on December 13, 1862, thus saving Lee's right in that Confederate victory. Nearly five months later, he was mortally wounded near Chancellorsville on the evening of May 2, after a flank march and attack that smashed Joe Hooker's right. Jackson was shot while reconnoitering between lines, and his right arm was amputated. He died eight days later from complications from pneumonia. Jackson is buried in Lexington, Virginia—his home before the war, and the subsequent home and final resting place of Robert E. Lee.

1633. The number of Union soldiers buried at the Antietam National Cemetery is 4,776. Of this number, 1,836—or 38 percent—are unknown.

1634. Aaron Good and Joseph Gill, both residents of Sharpsburg, were the first to identify the dead and locate graves on the Antietam battlefield beginning in 1862.

1635. Maryland passed legislation on March 10, 1864, to acquire land at Antietam to inter the remains of *both* Union and Confederate dead. Acquisition was delayed for a year due to a failure to obtain clear title to the land. New legislation in 1865 invited other states to appoint trustees for the cemetery. Eighteen states—all Union—joined the Antietam National Cemetery Corporation, contributing $90,000 for the cemetery.

1636. Despite Maryland's original intent to bury both Union and Confederate dead in the same cemetery—albeit in separate areas—no Confederates were interred in the National Cemetery at Antietam. The reason given for this change was that no Confederate state contributed money toward the establishment of the cemetery.

1637. Although originally created *only* for the dead of Antietam, the scope of the national cemetery changed to include Union dead from across the State of Maryland, as well as the Eastern Panhandle of nearby West Virginia. Hence, dead from South Mountain, Monocacy, Cumberland, and Harpers Ferry are also buried in the Antietam National Cemetery. The remains of eleven US soldiers were removed from Fulton County, Pennsylvania, and reinterred in the Antietam National Cemetery.

1638. Reinternment of Union dead in Maryland began in October 1866. Local day laborers and farmers were paid $1.00/day for discovery and disinternment of remains. Eleven months later, 4,695 soldiers had been re-interred in the cemetery. As additional remains were discovered in later years, another 81 bodies were added to the cemetery.

1639. Antietam National Cemetery was dedicated five years after the battle on September 17, 1867. President Andrew Johnson was a guest speaker at the dedication.

1640. No permanent headstones marked graves at the Antietam National Cemetery until 1873 when Congress authorized funding for such headstones. Prior to the use of stones, temporary wooden headboards marked the graves.

1641. According to the New York State Monument, New Yorkers suffered the greatest total of casualties at Antietam—3,765. The number killed was 689 (18.3 percent); wounded 2797 (74.3 percent); and missing 279 (7.4 percent).

1642. James Longstreet was the only Confederate major general at Antietam who survived into the twentieth-century. He served as a corps commander with Gen. Lee except during the fall of 1863 when he and his corps transfer to the Western Theater and helped win the battle of Chickamauga. Longstreet failed to dislodge Burnside during the siege of Knoxville, and returned to Lee's command in the spring of 1864. Longstreet was seriously wounded in the Wilderness on May 6 and was incapacitated until the fall. After the war, he became a Republican and a personal friend of U. S. Grant, who appointed him minister of Turkey. Longstreet was vilified by other Confederates, especially Jubal Early, in the post war period and was blamed for Lee's loss at Gettysburg. Longstreet died on January 2, 1904, and is buried at Gainesville, Georgia.

1643. John M. Bloss, discoverer of Special Orders 191, later served as an Indiana superintendent of schools and president of what is now Oregon State University. Bloss rose from sergeant to captain, commanding Company F, 27th Indiana Infantry. He was wounded four times during the war—Winchester, Antietam, Chancellorsville, and Resaca. Cpl. Barton Mitchell, another discoverer of the "Lost Order," was disabled by his leg wound at Antietam and assigned to the ambulance corps. He died in 1868 at age 51.

1644. Daniel Harvey Hill, defender of the gaps of South Mountain and Bloody Lane, assumed command of the Department of North Carolina in 1863. In the fall of that year, he transferred to the Western Theater to fight with Braxton Bragg at Chickamauga and Chattanooga, and became an outspoken critic of Bragg's generalship. After the war, he was president of the University of Arkansas from 1877-1884, and editor of a magazine entitled *The Lane We Love*. Hill spent much of his post-war career defending himself against charges that *he lost* the Lost Orders.

1645. John Brown Gordon, shot five times at Bloody Lane, rose through the ranks and eventually commanded Stonewall Jackson's corps during the last month of the war. After the surrender at Appomattox, he returned to his home state of Georgia. His political career included three elections to the US Senate and a term as governor. Gordon helped organize the United Confederate Veterans and served as its first commander-in-chief.

1646. Jacob D. Cox, temporary commander of the Ninth Corps, later directed a division of the Twenty-third Corps in the 1864 Atlanta Campaign and at Franklin and Nashville. He served as Governor of Ohio in 1866-67, and as President Grant's Secretary of Interior until the fall of 1870, during which time he was a strong proponent of civil service reform. Cox survived Antietam for nearly 38 years, dying on August 4, 1900, at age 71. He is interred at Spring Grove Cemetery in Cincinnati.

1647. Samuel D. Sturgis, whose division carried Burnside Bridge, was routed by Confederate cavalry chieftain Nathan Bedford Forrest at the battle of Brice's Cross Roads, Mississippi, in June 1864. Many consider this Forrest's greatest victory. Sturgis became colonel of the 7th US Cavalry in the Regular Army on May 6, 1869. His second in command was Lieut. Col. George Armstrong Custer. Sturgis was not present at The Little Big Horn when Custer met his end.

1648. John Frederick Hartranft, colonel of the 51st Pennsylvania—one of the two regiments that successfully seized Burnside Bridge—functioned as special provost marshal for the trial of the Lincoln assassination conspirators. After the war, he served two terms as governor of Pennsylvania.

1649. William B. Franklin, commander of the Sixth Corps, was elevated by Burnside to "Left Grand Division" commander (Sixth and First Corps) in the Fredericksburg Campaign. Franklin's miserable performance against the Confederate right at Fredericksburg triggered Burnside's demand that Franklin be cashiered. Franklin's Fredericksburg fiasco ended his career with the Army of the Potomac, but he did command the Nineteenth Corps in the ill-fated 1864 Red River Campaign.

1650. Franklin served for 22 years as general manager of the Colt's Fire Arms Manufacturing Company in Hartford, Connecticut. As a former engineer, he also supervised construction of the Connecticut capitol.

1651. Franklin was the last Antietam corps commander to die. He survived the battle by more than 40 years dying on March 8, 1903, in Hartford. He is buried in his hometown of York, Pennsylvania.

1652. The last Confederate general to die who fought at Antietam was Brig. Gen. Roger A. Pryor, who commanded R. H. Anderson's division in the fight at Bloody Lane. Pryor died on March 14, 1919—57 years after the battle—at the age of 91. Pryor is buried in Princeton, New Jersey.

1653. Boteler's or Blackford's Ford, the site of Lee's retreat from Antietam, was the river crossing used by the Confederate Second Corps during the third week of June 1863 while advancing into Maryland during the Gettysburg Campaign. Boteler's Ford also hosted the last Confederate invasion of the North, when Jubal Early's Second Corps waded across the Potomac during the last week of June 1864 en route to its march upon Washington.

1654. Repairs on the destroyed Baltimore & Ohio Railroad bridge, where it crossed the Monocacy River, began on September 17 and were finished by the 21st. (*OR* 19, pt. 2, 328, 342)

1655. The Frederick hospitals housed 5,353 patients—mostly wounded—as of September 30. One month later, only 2,603 remained in these hospitals. The vast majority (2,064) were sent to other hospitals, and only 403 were returned to duty. Of the 5,000-plus patients in Frederick, only 253 (4.7%) died during the month of October. (*OR* 19, pt. 1, p. 111)

Antietam and The Maryland Campaign Today

1656. The Antietam National Battlefield Site was established by Congress on August 30, 1890 as the second official Civil War area designated by the federal government. The first, also established in 1890, was the Chickamauga-Chattanooga National Military Park.

1657. The Antietam Battlefield Site was transferred from the jurisdiction of the War Department to the Department of Interior and the National Park Service on August 10, 1935.

1658. The Antietam National Cemetery was transferred from the board of trustees of the Antietam National Cemetery Association to the United States government on June 7, 1877.

1659. Eight United States presidents have visited Antietam while in office.

1660. The first president to travel to and to tour Antietam was Abraham Lincoln, October 2-4, 1862.

1661. The original "Lost Order" is part of the McClellan manuscript collection at the Library of Congress.

1662. D. H. Hill's copy of the "Lost Order"—the one he received from Stonewall Jackson—is housed at the North Carolina State Archives.

1663. Seven Union veterans served as superintendents at the Antietam National Cemetery between 1867-1909.

1664. The first superintendent at the Antietam National Cemetery was Hiram S. Seiss. He served three years in Company H, 1st Maryland Potomac Home Brigade. Seiss was removed by the War Department in 1879 after a 12-year tenure because he had not been wounded during the Civil War. The last Civil War soldier to serve as superintendent at the Antietam National Cemetery was Joshua V. Davis, formerly of the 66th Pennsylvania Infantry, who served from April 10, 1905-February 2,1909.

1665. Frank Barrows, a white lieutenant who served as an officer in the 30th US Colored Troops, was superintendent of the Antietam National Cemetery at the turn of the century, from March 1897 through May 1904.

1666. The first legislation recommending a federal presence at Antietam was introduced on June 7, 1890, by Representative Louis McComas, a Republican from Maryland. McComas' bill required the survey, location, and preservation of lines of battle.

1667. The first markers on the Antietam battlefield were temporary shingle stakes, installed by the Antietam Battlefield Board in 1892, that marked the positions of 43 different commands of the US Army.

1668. The Antietam Battlefield Board recommended replacing the wooden markers with stone tablets in June 1892. "Finding that such [wooden] markers were being destroyed or obliterated during the cultivation of fields," the frustrated Board reported, "we deemed it best to replace them . . . as soon as title to the land can be obtained." (Snell and Brown, "Antietam National Battlefield and National Cemetery: An Administrative History," p. 75)

1669. The first official report revealing characteristics and features of the battlefield changing since 1862 appeared in a June 10, 1892, report of the Antietam Battlefield

Board: " . . . country much changed by the disappearance of bodies of wood, now cultivated fields or orchards." (Snell and Brown, "Antietam National Battlefield and National Cemetery: An Administrative History," p. 76)

1670. The first recommendation that the government build roads to facilitate battlefield visitation came in a June 7, 1893 report from the Antietam Battlefield Board: "In justice to the farmers owning these fields, we think roadways should be constructed to enable visitors . . . to view and inspect these tablets without trampling upon and injuring growing crops, gardens, orchards, etc." (Snell and Brown, "Antietam National Battlefield and National Cemetery: An Administrative History," p. 78)

1671. Three military maps were researched and published by the Antietam Battlefield Board. The first, in August 1893, shows US and CS positions before the battle. The second, published in December 1893, shows the extreme advance of US forces. The final map shows troops positions after the battle ends.

1672. A "meagerness of reports" and missing reports (some 30 years after the battle) hampered the research and reconstruction of the events of September 17, 1862. To accumulate more information, the Antietam Battlefield Board sent letters to governors and adjutant generals throughout the country requesting documents and data on Antietam.

1673. The Antietam Battlefield Board requested, in 1894, that states send delegations "composed of intelligent officers who participated in the battle" to Antietam to physically locate their commands. (Snell and Brown, "Antietam National Battlefield and National Cemetery: An Administrative History," p. 83)

1674. Massachusetts and North Carolina were the first two states to send delegations to the Antietam battlefield to identify the locations of their troops during the battle.

1675. Landowners on the battlefield refused to sell isolated pieces or plots of ground to the government in 1894, but they would sell their entire farms.

1676. A new three-member Antietam Battlefield Board was appointed in 1894, consisting of two former Union officers and one Confederate. The Confederate member of the Board was Jedediah Hotchkiss, formerly the chief topographer for Stonewall Jackson. Hotchkiss was appointed as "expert topographer." Ezra Carmen, colonel of the 13th New Jersey Infantry at Antietam, was appointed to the Board as a "historical expert." Appointed President of the Antietam Battlefield Board in the fall of 1894 was Maj. George B. Davis, then Judge Advocate in the War Department.

1677. The "Antietam Plan" of battlefield preservation and interpretation was developed by Maj. Davis and Secretary of War Lamont in 1894-1895. This plan called for minimal land acquisition and the development of narrow avenues through the battlefield "along which the most severe fighting occurred." Upon these avenues, the government would "erect such tablets and markers as will clearly describe and explain the positions and operations" of the two armies. The "Antietam Plan" greatly reduced land acquisition costs at Civil War battlefields. The alternative, the "Chickamauga Plan"—where thousands of acres of battlefield were purchased by the government—had cost over $751,000 by June

30, 1896. Expenditures for Antietam—where 17 acres were purchased for avenues through the battlefield—was just under $63,000. (Snell and Brown, "Antietam National Battlefield and National Cemetery: An Administrative History," pp. 88-89, 91)

1678. Preservation of a battlefield in the "Antietam Plan" was predicated upon *indefinite agriculture*. "The portion of Maryland in which the battlefield is situated has always been an agricultural region and bids fair to continue so indefinitely," Secretary of War Lamont argued in a report to Congress in 1894. The Secretary's indefinite agricultural future for Washington County, Maryland, and Antietam did not envision a transportation revolution that would bring two interstate highways into the county (I-70 east/west and I-81 north/south)—placing the Antietam battlefield within one hour's drive of metropolitan Washington and Baltimore—and forcing it into the tentacles of urban sprawl, beginning in the 1970s. (Snell and Brown, "Antietam National Battlefield and National Cemetery: An Administrative History," p. 88)

1679. Implementation of the "Antietam Plan" for Antietam was substantially completed in 1896. Seventeen acres of land were purchased "in strips" for avenues that closely conformed to battle lines. Five miles of "substantial metaled roads" were constructed, and 200 iron tablets were erected to record the movements of the opposing armies. By the end of 1896, the total acreage owned by the US government at Antietam (excluding the National Cemetery) was 22 acres. This remained the land in government ownership until 1940.

1680. The threat of development at Antietam was first acknowledged in a November 4, 1947 memorandum from National Park Service Region One historian Appleman to the Regional Director: "Three new houses are under construction immediately east of Sharpsburg on the Harpers Ferry Road and adjacent to the park boundary. *This new construction is fair warning of what may be expected to take place in the vicinity of Sharpsburg at an increasing tempo* (emphasis added). . . . It is my belief that within a relatively few years the Sharpsburg area will be built up, either for permanent residences or for summer homes." (Snell and Brown, "Antietam National Battlefield and National Cemetery: An Administrative History," p. 230)

1681. Thirteen years passed from the initial 1947 warning of development pressures at Sharpsburg before the National Park Service was granted, in 1960 legislation, the authority to acquire land at Antietam.

1682. Other Civil War battlefield sites that originally adopted the "Antietam Plan" of limited land acquisition included Appomattox, Fort Donelson, Fredericksburg & Spotsylvania, Petersburg, Stones River, and Kennesaw Mountain.

1683. Originally, 383 cast iron tablets were placed on the Antietam, South Mountain, and Harpers Ferry battlefields that featured detailed battle narratives or directional signage. The text was researched and written by Civil War veterans under the sponsorship of the Antietam Battlefield Board. The cast iron tablets detailing the battles were produced by the Chattanooga Car & Foundry Company at a cost of $6,900.

1684. The original cast iron tablets at Antietam were divided as follows: 213 historical narratives; 20 locality narratives; and 150 directional guide markers. Cast iron markers on other battlefields in The Maryland Campaign were placed as follows: Harpers Ferry—five; Crampton's Gap—nine; Turner's Gap—six; and Shepherdstown Ford—five. Ezra Carmen, the Antietam Battlefield Board "historical expert," made changes to 18 cast iron markers in 1904 to "improve accuracy," and then improved two more in 1906. (Snell and Brown, "Antietam National Battlefield and National Cemetery: An Administrative History," pp. 109, 113)

1685. Fifteen detailed troop movement maps, researched by Ezra Carmen and drawn by Lieut. Col. E. B. Cope, were published by the Antietam Battlefield Board in 1904. After receiving new information, primarily offered by veterans who reviewed the 1904 edition and discovered errors, the 1904 troop maps—the most detailed maps in the history of Antietam—were revised in 1908, with corrections made by Carmen.

1686. The National Park Service counts 103 monuments on the battlefield. This includes two pillars at the entrance to Philadelphia Brigade Park and two small directional markers on Branch Avenue.

1687. The first monument at Antietam was the "Private Soldier," dedicated within the Antietam National Cemetery on September 17, 1880.

1688. Andrew Johnson was the second president to visit Antietam, and the first to be there on a battle anniversary—September 17, 1867. The cornerstone-laying ceremony for the monument that became the "Private Soldier" occurred in 1867 at the dedication of the National Cemetery, with President Johnson presiding.

1689. Before arriving in its permanent home at Antietam, the "Private Soldier" appeared on exhibit at the Philadelphia Centennial exposition of 1876. It returned to Stonington, Connecticut after the Centennial. The monument cost of $30,000 was not paid until 1879. The first four scheduled payments, between 1871-1873, amounted to $20,000. The final payment of $10,000 remained outstanding until 1879, when paid by the US government. (Charles Adams, *The Monuments at Antietam: Sharpsburg's Silent Sentinels*, p. 98; Snell and Brown, "Antietam National Battlefield and National Cemetery: An Administrative History," p. 24)

1690. The "Private Soldier" is composed of 27 separate pieces, collectively weighing 250 tons. The statue is granite and stands 21 and one half feet high. The statue sits atop a 23-foot pedestal. The entire height of the monument is 44½ feet.

1691. The sculptor of the "Private Soldier" was James W. Pollette of Westerly, Rhode Island. He sculpted the monument between 1871 and 1873.

1692. After the "Private Soldier" was shipped to Washington, it traveled via barge on the Chesapeake and Ohio Canal to Sharpsburg and was then pulled the 2½ half miles to town over a series of wooden rollers.

1693. " Old Simon" became the sobriquet for the "Private Soldier" statue at the Antietam National Cemetery.

1694. "Not for themselves, but for their country," is the only text engraved on the "Private Soldier."

1695. An early tourist attraction within the walls of the Antietam National Cemetery was "Lee's Rock." Local tradition claimed Gen. Lee directed much of the battle from this stone platform. Apparently offended by this Confederate bastion within the Union bivouac of the dead, the commission overseeing the cemetery destroyed the rock late in the nineteenth century.

1696. Prostitution became a problem within the Antietam National Cemetery in the early 1880s. According to Superintendent Walter A. Donaldson on July 23, 1883: "A prostitute from Washington has been living in Sharpsburg by the name of Martha Young—Her example has prompted others and that area of the National Cemetery is chosen for their vile proceedings." (Snell and Brown, "Antietam National Battlefield and National Cemetery: An Administrative History," pp. 48-49)

1697. The stone tower at the east end of Bloody Lane was constructed between 1896 and 1897 by the War Department as an observation tower for students of West Point and other visitors for the study of the battle.

1698. Four regimental monuments—two from Massachusetts, and one each from Maryland and Pennsylvania—were placed on each corner of Burnside Bridge near the turn of the twentieth century.

1699. The 20th New York monument was the first regimental memorial erected at Antietam. Dedicated on September 17, 1887—the 25th anniversary of the battle—it stands in the National Cemetery. It is the only marker with inscriptions written in both English and German. A second monument to the 20th New York stands just north of the Antietam Visitor Center on the ridge opposite the Dunker Church. Erected in 1910, it marks the regiment's farthest advance.

1700. Twelve states have monuments at Antietam.

1701. Corps badge insignia that appear on the monuments at Antietam were not designed or adopted until 1863.

1702. The Maryland legislature, in 1898, enacted a bill to "form a commission of nine persons, six of whom shall have served in the Union Army, and three of whom shall have served in the Confederate Army, and all of whom shall have participated in the battle of Antietam . . . for the erection of a State Monument to the Maryland soldiers of both sides engaged in said battle." (Adams, *The Monuments at Antietam: Sharpsburg's Silent Sentinels*, p. 18)

1703. The three former Confederates who served on the Maryland monument commission were Henry Kyd Douglas of Jackson's staff; Osmun Latrobe of Longstreet's staff; and William F. Dement, commander of the 1st Maryland Battery, CSA.

1704. The Maryland Monument, located just east of the Dunker Church, is the only monument on the battlefield to honor men of *both* North and South.

1705. President William McKinley dedicated the Maryland Monument on Memorial Day, May 30, 1900. Included within the presidential party were Gen. and Mrs. James Longstreet; former Confederate general and Spanish American War hero "Fighting Joe" Wheeler; and Secretary of War Elihu Root. Henry Kyd Douglas served as "Director of Ceremonies" for the dedication.

1706. William McKinley was the third president to visit Antietam, and the only one to be there on traditional Memorial Day (May 30).

1707. The only monument on the battlefield in honor of a US President is the McKinley Monument. Dedicated on October 13, 1903—two years and one month after McKinley's assassination in Buffalo, New York—the 33 foot, 6 inch monument memorializes McKinley's public service and his efforts to deliver hot coffee and food as a commissary sergeant in the 23rd Ohio at Antietam.

1708. The first superintendent at the Antietam National Battlefield Site, Charles W. Adams, was appointed June 14, 1900. Adams' jurisdiction was separate from the administration of the superintendent of the Antietam National Cemetery. Superintendent Adams was murdered by Charles Benner of Sharpsburg on June 6, 1912. One cause of the murder was that Benner believed his father-in-law had been cheated out of money when land had been acquired for the McKinley Monument. Benner later committed suicide.

1709. The second superintendent at the Antietam National Battlefield Site was George H. Graham. Graham was accused of "being almost continuously drunk"; patrolling the park avenues "with gun in hand"; and allowing his house to catch on fire, burning all the US government tools contained there. He was not easily dismissed because of the Civil Service laws that entitled him to hearings. Graham was finally fired after a raucous 18-month tenure from July 1912 to January 1914. (Snell and Brown, "Antietam National Battlefield and National Cemetery: An Administrative History," p. 125)

1710. The Gettysburg National Military Park has just over 1,300 monuments and memorials—13 times the number at Antietam.

1711. The 2nd Maryland Infantry Monument (USA) was originally mounted on the northeast corner of Burnside Bridge. The marker was moved to the east bank of Antietam Creek in 1964 during the Burnside Bridge restoration.

1712. Three monuments at Antietam honor infantry *companies*—the Company A & I monument, 5th Maryland Infantry, located near Bloody Lane; Company F, 1st US Sharpshooters, in the National Cemetery; and Companies E & H, 2nd US Sharpshooters, on Cornfield Avenue.

1713. The first Maryland monument erected at Antietam was the Company A & I monument, 5th Maryland Infantry, dedicated on September 17, 1890—constructed nearly ten years before the other Maryland monuments.

1714. The first monument placed at Antietam, within one month of its designation by the Congress as a federal battlefield site, was the Company A & I monument, 5th Maryland Infantry.

1715. Ten Maryland monuments commemorate the "Old Line State" at Antietam.

1716. Two Maryland monuments recognize Confederate Maryland units—Baltimore Light Artillery, located in Philadelphia Brigade Park and Dement's Battery, 1st Maryland Artillery.

1717. The only monument on the battlefield in the shape of a "minie ball" is the 21st Massachusetts Monument near Burnside Bridge. The 21st Massachusetts Monument was originally located on the southwest corner of Burnside Bridge. It was moved to a patio area along the east side of the Antietam Creek in 1964 as part of the Burnside Bridge restoration.

1718. Three granite cannon balls sit atop the 35th Massachusetts Monument. The monument was originally located on the northwest corner of Burnside Bridge but was moved in 1964 to the east side of the Antietam Creek as part of the bridge's restoration.

1719. The "Reclining Lion" monument of the 15th Massachusetts Infantry is the most original in concept at Antietam. The monument features a wounded lion, with its right paw poised and its mouth open in a roar, representing "defiant in death." Andrew O'Connor was the monument's sculptor. The monument stands on a rock shelf in the West Woods that denotes the regiment's most forward position and is clearly visible along the modern realignment of the Hagerstown Pike. Within the foundation of the monument is a copper box that contains Worcester, Massachusetts, papers, *A History of the Excursions of the 15th Massachusetts* by Capt. David Earle, and a list of the 15th regiment's members.

1720. Massachusetts has four monuments at Antietam—two at Burnside Bridge and two in or near the West Woods. All were dedicated in 1898, with the exception of the 15th Massachusetts "Reclining Lion," which was dedicated on September 17, 1900.

1721. President Theodore Roosevelt was the fourth president to visit Antietam. Roosevelt arrived on September 17, 1903, to dedicate the New Jersey monuments. The primary ceremony was held at the junction of Cornfield Avenue and the Hagerstown Pike. Accompanying the president was Governor Murphy of New Jersey who fought at Antietam as a 16-year-old.

1722. The only military unit with a monument at both South Mountain and Antietam is the 1st New Jersey Brigade. The brigade is the only brigade at Antietam to have two monuments in its honor. A metal-wire fence and gate separates the 1st New Jersey Brigade Monument from the Smoketown Road. According to the New Jersey office of the Adjutant General, the New Jersey monument commissioners purchased a plot back off the road because "during wet and stormy weather the monument would have been splashed with mud from the wagons passing by." (Adams, *The Monuments at Antietam: Sharpsburg's Silent Sentinels*, pp. 32-33)

1723. The nine-foot bronze statue atop the New Jersey State Monument represents Capt. Hugh C. Irish—the first soldier to fall in the 13th New Jersey Infantry. Irish's sister, Mrs. Sarah Hartwell, unveiled the monument at its dedication in 1903.

1724. Pennsylvania, New York, and Ohio collectively account for one-third of the monuments at Antietam.

1725. The southern-most monument on the battlefield is the 1st Battery, Ohio Light Artillery Monument located on Burnside Bridge Road about 500 yards south of the bridge. This monument has the not-so-eloquent sobriquet "Jackass Battery." It received this name because it was originally furnished with mules rather than horses for campaigning in the mountainous areas of western Virginia.

1726. The northern-most monument on the battlefield is the 7th Indiana Infantry Monument located on the Hagerstown Pike adjacent to the Joseph Poffenberger farm. The western-most monument at Antietam is the Lee headquarters marker located along the Shepherdstown Pike about three-quarters of a mile west of the Sharpsburg town square. The eastern-most monument on the battlefield is the 3rd Indiana Cavalry monument located on the Boonsboro Pike near the Middle Bridge.

1727. Only two monuments on the battlefield are dedicated to cavalry units—the 3rd Indiana Monument, located on the Boonsboro Pike near the Middle Bridge and the 12th Pennsylvania Cavalry on Mansfield Avenue in the East Woods. The only monument at Antietam depicting a cavalryman is the 12th Pennsylvania Monument. The cavalry soldier is not mounted, but instead standing with his right hand clasping the barrel of a cavalry carbine.

1728. Pennsylvania has the largest number of monuments on the battlefield—nineteen.

1729. Three of the Pennsylvania monuments depict specific individuals. Two are brigade commanders in the Ninth Corps; the third is a color sergeant. Brig. Gen. James Nagle, organizer and first colonel of the 48th Pennsylvania Infantry, is cast in bronze atop the pillar commemorating this Quaker State unit. The 50th Pennsylvania Monument displays a bronze cast statue of Col. Benjamin C. Christ, who commanded a brigade in Willcox's division of the Ninth Corps. Color Sergeant George A. Simpson is represented by the granite sculpture crowning the 125th Pennsylvania Monument located in the West Woods behind the Dunker Church. Simpson was killed at Antietam.

1730. The only soldier buried in the Antietam National Cemetery who has a monument depicting him on the battlefield is Sergeant Simpson.

1731. The first Pennsylvania monument was the Philadelphia Brigade Memorial, dedicated in the West Woods area on September 17, 1896.

1732. The imposing granite obelisk of the Philadelphia Brigade Memorial rises 73 feet, making it the tallest marker on the battlefield.

1733. The most monuments dedicated on any single day at Antietam occurred on September 17, 1904 when Pennsylvania commemorated its participation in the battle by unveiling 12 monuments. Six of the 12 represent Ninth Corps officers or units. Each of the 12 monuments cost $2,500. A thirteenth Pennsylvania monument was scheduled for dedication on September 17, 1904, but the 128th Infantry monument had not been finished and would not be installed until the following year on Cornfield Avenue.

1734. Four of the Pennsylvania monuments depict soldiers in various positions of loading a musket.

1735. The 132nd Pennsylvania Monument, a dramatic statue at Bloody Lane, features a color bearer waving the colors at the moment the lower staff was shot away. The monument actually illustrated an incident that occurred at the battle of Fredericksburg on December 13, 1862.

1736. The monument with the highest regimental designation at Antietam is the 137th Pennsylvania Monument, located on Cornfield Avenue.

1737. The only monument at Antietam featuring the shape of a drum is the 51st Pennsylvania Infantry Monument near Burnside Bridge. The 51st Pennsylvania Monument was originally located on the southeast corner of Burnside Bridge. It was removed to the east side of Antietam Creek in 1964 during restoration of the bridge.

1738. Two years after unveiling 12 monuments, Pennsylvania returned on September 17, 1906 to dedicate four stone monuments in honor of four Pennsylvania reserve regiments. These monuments are located on Mansfield Avenue in the vicinity of the North Woods site and the Joseph Poffenberger farm.

1739. The only monument at Antietam depicting a cannoneer is Durell's Independent Battery D, Pennsylvania Artillery. The granite statue, located on Branch Avenue, represents an artilleryman, with sponge staff in his left hand, and his right hand raised to shade his eyes as he scans the enemy's position for the effect of his last projectile.

1740. One Pennsylvania monument erected at Antietam no longer stands. The 90th Pennsylvania Monument, built sometime in the late nineteenth century, was three stacked rifles, bayonets affixed, and a camp bucket suspended from the rifle tripod. This fragile memorial did not last, but parts of the monument are stored in the park's curatorial collection.

1741. New York and Maryland share the distinction of having the second highest number of monuments on the battlefield—ten.

1742. New York is the only state that had 10 monuments placed at Antietam over a 33-year period—from 1887 to 1920.

1743. The first two regimental monuments erected at Antietam honor New York regiments—the 4th New York Infantry and the 20th New York Infantry. Both were placed in the National Cemetery in 1887.

1744. The New York State Monument sits on high ground east of the Dunker Church, adjacent to the modern National Park Visitor Center, and is visible from most parts of the battlefield with the exception of the southern end. New York acquired seven acres for its state memorial in 1907 at an exorbitant rate of $200.00 per acre from Rezin and Emma Fisher—the first land speculators at Antietam. The seven-acre New York State "reservation" was originally fenced with cement posts and three tiers of iron pipe railing.

1745. Lieut. Gen. Nelson A. Miles, commander of the Army, was the keynote speaker at the dedication of the New York State Monument.

1746. The last state monument erected from the North was the New York State Monument, dedicated on September 17, 1920. The second highest monument at Antietam, the monument stands 58 feet tall. The second most expensive monument at Antietam prior to 1997 was this monument at a cost of $29,022.06. The "Private Soldier" in the National Cemetery cost $30,000.

1747. The 9th New York Infantry Monument (Hawkins' Zouaves), located at the southern end of the battlefield near the Harpers Ferry Road, represents the high-water mark of Burnside's attack. The highest monument at the southern end of the battlefield is this memorial—a granite obelisk on a tiered platform standing 52 feet high.

1748. Text inscribed on the 34th New York Monument, located behind the Dunker Church, notes that two geographic landmarks—both the East Woods and West Woods—were "extinct" when the monument was dedicated on September 17, 1902.

1749. U. S. Grant was the fifth president to visit Antietam. He toured the battlefield with Gen. William T. Sherman on October 15, 1869.

1750. The only stone monument at Antietam in memory of a major general is the Mansfield Monument. Dedicated in May 1900, the monument stands along the Smoketown Road in the East Woods, within yards of the site of Union Maj. Gen. Joseph F. K. Mansfield's mortal wounding.

1751. Four Connecticut monuments stand at Antietam, each dedicated on October 8, 1894. The 11th Connecticut Infantry Monument features a bronze bas-relief representing the regiment's ill-fated charge at Burnside Bridge.

1752. Delaware has three monuments at Antietam, each erected during the Civil War Centennial. Two of the monuments are at Bloody Lane—1st and 2nd Delaware—and the 3rd Delaware is in the West Woods.

1753. Six Indiana monuments commemorate the Hoosier state at Antietam, all constructed in 1910.

1754. The first monument erected on the South Mountain Battlefield was at Fox's Gap in honor of Union Maj. Gen. Jesse L. Reno. The Reno Monument is located on a one-tenth acre plot in Wise's Field. Acquisition cost for the land was $50.00 and the monument cost $443.93. The featured speaker for the dedication, before nearly 1,000 people on a damp and dreary September 14, 1889, was former Ninth Corps division commander Orlando B. Willcox.

1755. Peter Beachley, the great-great-great-great grandfather of the author Dennis E. Frye, owned a farm on the east side of South Mountain that constituted a large portion of the Fox's Gap battlefield in 1862.

1756. Former President Rutherford B. Hayes, who was wounded at Fox's Gap, contributed ten dollars toward the Reno Monument.

1757. Reno, Nevada, is named after Jesse L. Reno.

1758. Ohio has nine monuments on the battlefield, all erected in 1903.

1759. The Piper barn, located just south of Bloody Lane, was substantially enlarged in 1898 by a 60 by 44-foot addition built onto the north end of the structure.

1760. The Norfolk and Western Railroad, which runs west of Sharpsburg and the battlefield, did not arrive in the area until 1879-1880. No railroad serviced Sharpsburg during the Civil War.

1761. A "Cannon" monument was erected at the Antietam train station by the Antietam Battlefield Commission board by 1898. The monument was composed of eight parrot cannon, set breech down on a granite block, with the guns leaning against each other at their muzzles. Atop the muzzles was a cast iron plate with a pyramid of cannonballs. Nothing remains of the "Cannon" monument at the Antietam train station except the base.

1762. The first macadamized road in Sharpsburg was constructed by the US Government in 1891. It ran from the gate of the Antietam National Cemetery along Main Street through Sharpsburg and to the Antietam Station on the N&W Railroad in 1891. The road was 9300 feet in length. Three hundred Norway maples were planted by the federal government in November 1894 astride the macadamized road—named after Maryland US Senator Louis E. McComas. None of the trees were less than eight feet high and were furnished by a nursery in West Chester, Pennsylvania.

1763. Six mortuary cannon, installed by the Antietam Battlefield Commission in 1897, identify the locations where Union and Confederate generals were killed or mortally wounded at Antietam. The mortuary cannon—three Union and three Confederate—consist of a masonry foundation in which are set an inverted 12-pounder Napoleon tube. About 18 inches of the tube is embedded in the foundation. A bronze plate on each tube names the general and gives precise directions to the spot where he was killed or mortally wounded.

1764. Two mortuary cannon—one each for North and South—stand in each of the three phases of the battle. In Phase I are the markers for Gen. Mansfield (East Woods) and Gen. Starke (West Woods). Phase II reveal the locations of Gen. Richardson and Gen. G. B. Anderson at Bloody Lane. Phase III show the positions of Gen. Rodman and Gen. Branch at the south end of the field.

1765. The first preservation battle at Antietam occurred in 1928 when the Chesapeake and Potomac phone company requested permission from the War Department to install telephone polls adjacent to the Antietam National Cemetery. The War Department refused: "[I]f the trees along the edge of the National Cemetery were trimmed, their beauty would be permanently marred, and it would be detrimental to the government to place the poles on the side of the front of the cemetery." (Snell and Brown, "Antietam National Battlefield and National Cemetery: An Administrative History," p. 64)

1766. The end of an era occurred in September 1929 when the Antietam National Cemetery's mule—no longer able to work—was surveyed and shot, replacing animal-powered mowers with gasoline-powered mowers.

1767. The first telephone was installed at the Antietam National Cemetery lodge in November 1929.

1768. At the 73rd Antietam anniversary banquet, held at the Hotel Alexander in downtown Hagerstown, the invited guests included Lieut. Col. George B. McClellan, Jr., and Dr. George Bowling Lee. The menu featured "Hooker-Hood cocktail"; "chicken a-la-shrapnel"; "grape and canister peas"; "bloody cornfield salad"; "artillery horses—cold cut"; and "Sgt. McKinley coffee."

1769. Franklin Delano Roosevelt was the sixth president to visit Antietam. FDR arrived on the battle's 75th anniversary (September 17, 1937) and addressed a crowd estimated at 50,000. Roosevelt was the last president to be at Antietam on the battle's anniversary date. FDR was the only president to visit the battlefield twice. In addition to his 75th anniversary appearance in 1937, he returned on May 28, 1944, for a brief visit to the Bloody Lane observation tower area.

1770. The first large-scale reenactment of Antietam occurred on Friday, September 17, 1937, as part of the 75th anniversary activities. The reenactment of the action at Bloody Lane, which occurred on the original site, featured national guardsmen serving in the 29th Division National Guard from Maryland, Virginia, Pennsylvania, and the District of Columbia.

1771. In June 1937, the 75th Congress authorized the minting of 50,000 special half dollars to mark the 75th anniversary of Antietam. On one side of the coin were the profiles of Lee and McClellan while the reverse side featured Burnside Bridge.

1772. The superintendent of the Antietam Battlefield and National Cemetery at the time of the battle's 75th anniversary was John K. Beckenbaugh, nephew of Henry Kyd Douglas. Beckenbaugh was appointed superintendent on October 10, 1933.

1773. Nine massive oak trees in the original West Woods were cut and hauled away for lumber in 1940. One of the trees measured 66 inches in circumference and showed rings totaling 300 years.

1774. The Washington County Historical Society acquired 125 acres of the Spong farm in 1937. The Spong farm was the Confederate position overlooking Burnside Bridge on the west bank of Antietam Creek. The historical society could not donate the property because the battlefield had no authority to receive donated lands.

1775. Congress adopted legislation in 1940 that allowed the Antietam National Battlefield Site to accept gifts of land, such as the Spong farm at Burnside Bridge. The total acreage of the battlefield under National Park Service jurisdiction in 1943 was 128.588 acres. The battle encompassed over 8,000 acres. The acreage ceiling at Antietam was expanded to 1,800 acres in 1960 legislation. Between 1960-1964, the park added 592 acres, including the Piper farm.

1776. The Dunker Church is not the original building. A severe hail and windstorm destroyed the church on May 23, 1921.

1777. The Washington County Historical Society acquired the original Dunker Church site in April 1951 and donated the site to the NPS in 1953. The State of Maryland donated $35,000 to the National Park Service in February 1961 to rebuild the Church. The present Dunker Church was rebuilt on its original location—being completed in January 1962. Parts of the church are original, including the first 13 floorboards at the east entrance and 3,000 bricks surrounding the east entrance. National Park Service architect Archie Franzen researched, designed, and supervised construction of the rebuilt Dunker Church.

1778. The Hagerstown Civil War Round Table gave new members "sections" of brick from the original Dunker Church for 20 years, when its supply was depleted. Each rectangular brick section, cut from a larger brick, measured one inch by three inches.

1779. The three-arch stone bridge known as the Middle Bridge, located on the Boonsboro-Sharpsburg Pike, was destroyed in the 1889 "Johnstown [Pennsylvania] Flood."

1780. Construction of the modern visitor center at Antietam began on January 18, 1962. Construction was completed in October of that year and the visitor center was opened in mid-January 1963.

1781. Two monuments stand on locations that identify where an individual soldier (other than a general) was killed or mortally wounded. The Lieut. Col. John L. Stetson monument (59th New York Infantry) is in the West Woods just south of the "Reclining

Lion" of the 15th Massachusetts. It was erected by his brother in 1920. Col. James H. Childs's marker (4th Pennsylvania Cavalry) is near the Middle Bridge on the Boonsboro Pike.

1782. Until the year 2003 no equestrian monuments stood at Antietam, though statues portraying Generals Lee, Jackson, and Stuart had been proposed by the owner of the Newcomer property in 1999. Historians were concerned about the appropriateness of this proposal since the Newcomer property was in Union territory before, during, and after the battle. Because the Newcomer property is private property, the owner went ahead with his plans and erected an equestrian statue to Gen. Lee in 2003.

1783. The first Confederate memorial—and only monument placed by Confederate veterans at Antietam—reads: "A.N.V. Near this spot an abandoned Confederate gun manned by a Second Lieutenant of the 6th Virginia Infantry, Mahone's Brigade, and two Infantry Volunteers from Anderson's Georgia Brigade, was placed in action here September 17, 1862."

1784. The placement of the first Confederate monument at Antietam was described in a 1918 issue of *The Confederate Veteran*. Washington Camp No. 171, United Confederate Veterans, placed the memorial in honor of Lt. W. W. Chamberlaine of the 6th Virginia. Chamberlaine rallied a few men and turned an abandoned cannon against federals advancing on the Piper Farm following the Confederate withdraw from Bloody Lane.

1785. Four monuments were erected at Antietam during the centennial. Three are state monuments—Georgia, Texas, and Delaware—and the other is the Clara Barton monument. Georgia erected its monument on September 20, 1961. Texas selects Veterans' Day 1964, as its dedication day.

1786. Only four Confederate monuments stand on the Antietam Battlefield. Two are state monuments—Georgia and Texas—erected along Cornfield Avenue. The third is a private memorial located along the Hagerstown Pike near the Piper Lane entrance. The fourth recognizes the site of Gen. Robert E. Lee's headquarters just west of Sharpsburg.

1787. Gen. Lee's headquarters site, located in an oak grove on a ridge north of the Shepherdstown Pike, was "purchased, restored, and marked" by the West Virginia Division, United Daughters of the Confederacy. The monument denoting this site was unveiled on September 17, 1936.

1788. The Clara Barton Monument, located just south of the Joseph Poffenberger farmstead, was dedicated on September 9, 1962, by Gen. Alfred Gruenther, president of the American Red Cross. The "red cross" featured on the boulder of the Clara Barton Monument was made from red brick extracted from the chimney of Barton's birthplace in North Oxford, Massachusetts.

1789. The man credited as the first regular tour guide at Antietam was Oliver T. "O.T." Reilly of Sharpsburg. Reilly was 5½ years old at the time of the battle, but in adulthood, he made a living as a guide, charging between $1.50 and $2.00 "for an auto or carriage load making a ten-mile run that takes in about all of the historic points of interest; about one hour and a quarter time, to autos." Reilly gave tours at Antietam to generals Joseph Hooker and James Longstreet.

1790. Reilly published a souvenir booklet in 1903 featuring photos and a section entitled "Stories of Antietam: As Told to Mr. Reilly by Veterans and Eye-Witnesses of the Battle." This booklet remains in print as of 2003 and continues to sell well at the battlefield bookstore.

1791. In 1927, six years after the Dunker Church was destroyed by a storm, Reilly erected a monument near the original foundation, with the inscription: "To the memory of the old Dunkard Church, the oak tree that stood in front, and the Union Civil War Veterans of Sharpsburg, Md." The monument still stands in 2003 on private property just west of the visitor center.

1792. George Alfred Townsend financed his War Correspondents Memorial at Crampton's Gap by sending letters of appeal to prominent men, newspapers, and businesses in December 1895. He raised over $5,000, including donations from Thomas Edison, J. P. Morgan, George Pullman, and Joseph Pulitzer.

1793. The War Correspondents Memorial Arch was dedicated on October 16, 1896—the 37th anniversary of the John Brown Raid at Harpers Ferry. CNN television reporter Peter Arnett gave the keynote address at the 100th anniversary rededication of the War Correspondents Memorial on September 18, 1996.

1794. The seventh president to visit Antietam was John F. Kennedy, touring the field on April 3, 1963, in an open convertible. Edward Kennedy and his wife Joan joined JFK during his presidential visit.

1795. The last monument built at Antietam was the Irish Memorial at the east end of Bloody Lane, dedicated in October, 1997. The Irish ambassador to the United States attended the Irish Brigade Monument dedication. The monument is a 20-ton tablet of gray Irish granite imported from the Ballyknockan quarry in County Wicklow, Ireland.

1796. The most expensive monument at Antietam is the Irish Brigade Monument—at a cost of $170,000—nearly six times the cost of the previous most expensive, the "Private Soldier" in the National Cemetery ($30,000 in the 1870s). Inflation!

1797. National Park Service historian Dennis Frye learned of the discovery of Irish Brigade soldiers' remains following a presentation to the Cleveland Civil War Round Table in the spring of 1988. The relic hunter who made the discovery on the privately-owned Roulette farm was a cooperative informant. Frye organized an archeological excavation of the Irish Brigade remains' site in August 1988. The principal investigators were Dr. Stephen Potter, regional archeologist for the park service's National Capital Region, and Dr. Doug Owsley, physical anthropologist with the Smithsonian. The discoverer of the remains assisted throughout the excavation.

1798. No skulls or long bones were discovered during the excavation of the Irish Brigade remains' site. Collapsed rib cages and incomplete hand and foot extremities were found, including one foot with a leather shoe still attached. Smashed bullets were removed from interior chest cavities. The failure to discover skulls and long bones strongly suggested that the graves had been previously disturbed—most likely during the original national cemetery re-internment effort in 1865-1866.

1799. The internment of the Irish Brigade remains in the Antietam National Cemetery in September 1989 was organized and coordinated by Dennis Frye. Battlefield Superintendent Richard Rambur officiated at the ceremony and Colin McDonald led the reconstituted 28th Massachusetts (Irish Brigade) reenactment group as the honor guard and burial detail.

1800. The Hagerstown-Sharpsburg Turnpike was widened in 1952. The stone wall bordering the Piper Farm was moved and rebuilt at this time.

1801. The Hagerstown Pike was relocated off the original road in 1965 when a 1½ mile bypass was constructed beginning south of the Dunker Church that continued north to the Joseph Poffenberger farm. The bypass runs through the western edge of the West Woods.

1802. Washington County deeded Burnside Bridge to the National Park Service on November 20, 1945. Modern vehicular traffic continued to utilize the original Burnside Bridge as an Antietam Creek crossing until 1965 when a county bypass was completed to the north and east. The Burnside Bridge overlook was completed in 1962. The Bloody Lane bypass was opened in 1965.

1803. White's Ferry, where the ferry boat *Jubal Early* crosses the Potomac River today, is *not* the site of White's Ford, where Lee's Confederates splashed north to open The Maryland Campaign. White's Ferry is the wartime location of Conrad's Ferry. Via the river and the C & O Canal, White's Ford is six miles north and west of White's Ferry.

1804. The Appalachian National Scenic Trail passes through the South Mountain battlefields of Crampton's, Fox's, and Turner's Gaps.

1805. Dr. Walter H. Shealy, a Sharpsburg physician who served as President of the Antietam-South Mountain Centennial Association—the organization responsible for the 100th anniversary commemoration of Antietam—is the doctor who delivered Dennis E. Frye, chairman of the Antietam Commemoration Committee, that produced all events associated with Antietam's 135th anniversary.

1806. The last reenactment on the original Antietam Battlefield occurred during the centennial in September 1962. Nearly 18,000 visitors attended the two-day reenactment that featured 2,000 troops from 17 different states. The National Park Service banned reenactments at its Civil War sites following the Antietam centennial reenactment. This ban has remained in place since 1962.

1807. The eighth president to visit Antietam was Jimmy Carter in July 1978. He was accompanied by his wife Rosalynn and historian Shelby Foote. En route from Antietam to Harpers Ferry, President Carter's motorcade was delayed for nearly 20 minutes by dairy cattle crossing West Virginia Rt. 230 about three miles south of Shepherdstown. The cows were making their way from their grazing field to the milking parlor.

1808. Harpers Ferry National Monument was established on June 30, 1944—24 days after "D-Day" and the allied invasion of Europe during World War II.

1809. Dr. Henry T. McDonald, president of Storer College in Harpers Ferry from 1890-1944, began advocating the establishment of Harpers Ferry as a national park site in the early 1930s. Representative William Jennings Randolph of West Virginia (who later became a US Senator) spearheaded legislation in the US Congress that established Harpers Ferry as a national monument.

1810. The State of West Virginia acquired Lower Town Harpers Ferry (Shenandoah Street and portions of High and Potomac Streets) during the early 1950s and donated the site to the National Park Service in the mid-1950s. The State of West Virginia also acquired acreage on Loudoun Heights and Bolivar Heights. The State of Maryland acquired 763 acres on Maryland Heights that was donated to Harpers Ferry Park in 1963.

1811. Congress changed the designation of Harpers Ferry from a national monument to Harpers Ferry National Historical Park in 1963.

1812. The National Park Service acquired the former Storer College campus on Camp Hill in 1960. Included in the purchase was the relocated "John Brown Fort" and the US Armory superintendent's quarters—known as "Barbour's House" during Jackson's siege—which was redeveloped into the administrative building of Storer College in 1884.

1813. One hundred years after Jackson's siege, "Barbour's House" on Camp Hill opened in 1962 as the Stephen T. Mather Training Center, a National Park Service training facility.

1814. During the first 18 years of its operation as a national park site, almost no emphasis was placed upon the role of Harpers Ferry in the Civil War. The primary emphasis was on John Brown. The first living history effort to interpret the Civil War at Harpers Ferry began in 1973 when a US "Recruiting Office" was established on Shenandoah Street. Although entertaining for visitors, the "Recruiting Office" had little historical relevance, and it was modified in 1980 into a more appropriate "Provost Marshal's Office."

1815. Donald W. Campbell began serving as superintendent of Harpers Ferry National Historical Park in 1979. Twenty-four years later in 2003, he continues as Harpers Ferry's park superintendent—longer than any other manager in the history of the park.

1816. A Maryland Heights historical and archeological survey in the mid 1980s discovered seven Civil War fortifications within the Harpers Ferry park boundary on the heights. The best preserved and most imposing and unique fortification on Maryland Heights today is the "Stone Fort," built on the crest in 1862 by Union forces. Thirteen powder magazines were located by archeologists in or near the Maryland Heights fortifications. Thirteen Civil War campgrounds, encompassing nearly 60 acres, were also identified on Maryland Heights. Within these campgrounds, archeologists discovered 319 different features, ranging from stone foundations to cooking areas to tent platforms.

1817. The National Park Service proposed in 1973 the construction of a radio transmitter on top of Maryland Heights to provide uninterrupted radio service for rangers in the Chesapeake & Ohio Canal National Historical Park. John C. Frye, father of the author, killed the proposal as a member of the first federal C & O Canal Commission.

1818. A cable television tower threatened the integrity of the Bolivar Heights skyline from 1987 to 1989. The original proposal was defeated by a coalition led by Scot Faulkner, president of Friends of Harpers Ferry Park, NPS historian Dennis Frye, and

Harpers Ferry Park superintendent Donald W. Campbell. A compromise tower that is painted dark green was erected below the tree line making the tower invisible from the surrounding area.

1819. A cable television tower, adorned with satellite dishes, threatened the integrity of the Antietam National Battlefield those same years, 1987-1989. The same company proposing the tower on Bolivar Heights was attempting to build another tower on Red Hill near Antietam.

1820. The Save Historic Antietam Foundation allied with the Friends of Harpers Ferry Park and the National Park Service leadership at Antietam and Harpers Ferry in 1988, filing an injunction with the Federal Communications Commission to review cable television towers affecting the two battlefields.

1821. The first invocation of NEPA—the National Environmental Protection Act—to fight cable television towers having a detrimental effect on Civil War battlefields occurred in 1988. The Red Hill cable television tower was constructed, but only after the company agreed to lower its height by nearly one half and promised not to attach any satellite dishes on the tower frame which would be visible from the Antietam Battlefield.

1822. Bolivar Heights was threatened by the installation of a 190 foot cellular telephone tower in 1998-1999. The Friends of Harpers Ferry Park, along with the Harpers Ferry Conservancy and the leadership of Harpers Ferry National Historical Park, developed a compromise with the company that placed an 80 foot tower—nearly invisible from the surrounding area—at the crest of the heights.

1823. School House Ridge, a critical Confederate position during Jackson's 1862 siege of Harpers Ferry—is not within the national park boundary as of 2003.

1824. A 1989 Special Boundary Study conducted by the National Park Service for Harpers Ferry Park identified over 1,000 acres of battlefield outside of, but adjacent to, the park boundary—most of it Confederate positions on School House Ridge and the Chambers' Farm.

1825. A Jefferson County, West Virginia, commissioner, who was an avid opponent of battlefield preservation at Harpers Ferry, at one point informed NPS historian Dennis Frye—this was during the opening conference on the park's Special Boundary Study in December 1988. "Nothing happened here, 'boy,' nothing happened here." Frye showed the commissioner Volume 19 of the *Official Records* to refute the official's statement.

1826. Jefferson County, West Virginia, during enactment of the first county zoning ordinance in 1988, zoned School House Ridge and the Chambers' Farm for high-density residential and light commercial development. The National Park Service had requested the area be zoned agricultural, reflecting its current usage in 1988.

1827. The first and only monuments erected on School House Ridge and on Bolivar Heights were installed between 1910 and 1911 by Confederate veterans from Jefferson County, [West] Virginia. They identified the actions surrounding the siege and capture of Harpers Ferry. The monuments, which are numbered obelisks that accompany a guidebook, still stand today.

1828. The first land acquisition by the newly organized Civil War Trust occurred in 1993 when the Trust acquired 52 acres of battlefield between School House Ridge and Bolivar Heights. The property had been subdivided for nearly 300 town houses. The Civil War Trust donated the property to Harpers Ferry National Historical Park in October 1998.

1829. The first national Civil War publication to give notoriety to Jackson's siege and capture of Harpers Ferry is *Blue and Gray Magazine*. The magazine's cover and feature article in its September 1987 edition—published at the time of the 125th anniversary of the siege—was written by this volume's author, with an accompanying tour by publisher David Roth.

1830. Official National Park Service records housed at the battlefield were destroyed by Superintendent W. Dean McClanahan in 1967 when Antietam was placed under the administration of the Chesapeake & Ohio Canal national park area. The records destroyed spanned the era from 1933 to 1965. The Antietam Battlefield records were destroyed because space was required in the park visitor center for the staff of the Chesapeake & Ohio Canal park.

1831. A 500,000 volt power line threatened the Antietam Battlefield in 1967. The line was planned by the Potomac Edison Company without consultation with local officials or the National Park Service.

1832. The power line threat was first uncovered by John C. Frye, supervisor of the Washington County Property Map Department, where all deed transactions are recorded. Frye first learns of the power line and its proposed route through right-of-way acquisitions by Potomac Edison. John Frye plot maps showed the power line not only threatened the Antietam Battlefield, but also Civil War sites at South Mountain, Pleasant Valley, Solomon's Gap on the Elk Ridge, and the Chesapeake & Ohio Canal. Frye notified Washington County commissioner president Lem E. Kirk of the power line proposal, and Kirk activated the local, state, and federal political process to defeat the power line or alter its location.

1833. Bernard Hillenbrand, executive director of the National Association of Counties in Washington, D.C., joined the fight against the power line when he discovered his eighteenth century farm near the mouth of Antietam Creek was included within the power line's 200-foot right-of-way. Hillenbrand purchased two shares of stock in Potomac Edison and attended the annual stockholders meeting in New York City where he publicly censured the power company for a plan that would despoil unique historic resources.

1834. The power line controversy made headline news in the Washington *Post* on May 22 and May 23, 1967, bringing national attention to the controversy. The National Trust for Historic Preservation announced its official opposition to the power line on June 10, 1967.

1835. Secretary of Interior Stewart Udall forced Potomac Edison to consider alternative routes in October 1967 by withholding a permit allowing the company to cross the C & O Canal.

1836. The "Second Battle of Antietam," as the press labeled the power line controversy, ended in May 1968 when Potomac Edison agreed to an alternative route, about four miles north of the battlefield, making the transmission line virtually invisible from battlefield.

The new route of the power line crosses South Mountain at the extreme southern end of Fox's Gap. The transmission towers were painted dark green to better blend into the environment, and the right-of-way followed a "switch back" pattern over the mountain, thus reducing visible scars to the landscape.

1837. Antietam was the first National Park Service battlefield to permit women to portray male soldiers in government-sanctioned living history programs. Beginning in 1977, women rangers began dressing as male soldiers to portray artillerymen during the park's cannon-firing demonstrations.

1838. The 125th anniversary commemoration of Antietam in September 1987 featured a reenactment that attracted over 6,000 troops. The two-day weekend event, sponsored by a national organization known as The American Civil War Commemoration Committee (ACWCC) was staged on a farm off Maryland Route 68 just north and west of Boonsboro.

1839. The first live radio broadcast of a reenactment occurred in September 1987 for the 125th anniversary reenactment of Antietam. The author, and radio personality and historian Roger Keller, broadcast the Cornfield and Bloody Lane battles over a Hagerstown radio station. Keller provided the "play by play" tactical analysis and Frye offered the "color commentary" about Antietam's historic personages.

1840. The 135th anniversary of Antietam included a reenactment that attracted nearly 13,000 reenactors and nearly 100,000 spectators.

1841. The Save Historic Antietam Foundation, Inc. (SHAF) was established in 1986—two years prior to the 1988 "Don't mall the battlefield" fight at Manassas. SHAF's mission was to preserve unprotected properties on the Antietam Battlefield and in the adjoining Antietam valley.

1842. The organizers of the Save Historic Antietam Foundation were Dennis Frye, Tom Clemens, and John Schildt. Frye suggested the foundation's name, and the IRS conferred non-profit charity status upon the organization. The first president of SHAF was Frye, serving from 1986-1989. Tom Clemens succeeded Frye, and continues as president as of 2003.

1843. An August 1985 rezoning of the historic Grove Farm by the Washington County Commissioners was the impetus for the formation of the Save Historic Antietam Foundation, Inc. The Grove Farm was the site where the famous Lincoln-McClellan photographs were taken in October 1862. The commissioners rezoned the property from agricultural to business general.

1844. The Save Historic Antietam Foundation claimed the Grove Farm rezoning was illegal because it did not meet two tests: 1) an original mistake in the zoning—the property was a farm in 1985 and appropriately was zoned agricultural; and 2) a change in the character of the neighborhood—nothing has changed at the site since the original 1973 zoning. A Washington County circuit court judge overturned the Grove Farm rezoning in 1988 after SHAF challenged Washington County's decision in court. The property reverted to agricultural zoning. The Maryland Court of Appeals overturned the circuit court ruling, however—on a technicality. The appeals court agreed the county committed an illegal action, but since the appeal was not filed in the prescribed 30 days, the business general zoning remained in place.

1845. Plans for a shopping center on the Grove Farm were presented by a developer in 1988, but an economic recession forestalled its construction and eventually resulted in the cancellation of the project.

1846. Washington County became the first county in the United States—as a result of the Grove Farm battle and its heightened awareness of its unique heritage—to establish a historic preservation overlay zone to protect approaches to the Antietam National Battlefield. The local ordinance was enacted in 1989. Washington County established a Historic District Commission to review construction or development activities within the Antietam overlay approach zones.

1847. The Save Historic Antietam Foundation acquired 40 acres of the Grove Farm in 1991 at a cost of $325,000.

1848. The Antietam National Battlefield was listed on the very first Endangered Top Eleven listing of the National Trust for Historic Preservation issued in 1988. Antietam remained on the top endangered list for the next four consecutive years.

1849. The first donation for land acquisition to a battlefield organization from the Civil War Trust occurred in 1993 with a $100,000 donation to the Save Historic Antietam Foundation as a matching grant toward SHAF's 40-acre purchase on the Grove Farm.

1850. The famous Cornfield and North Woods remained private property until 1990. They were then acquired by a gift provided by the Richard King Mellon Foundation, through a transaction negotiated by the Conservation Fund. The property was donated to the National Park Service. Much of the West Woods was acquired in 1995 also through a Mellon Foundation gift. The Roulette Farm, over which the federals in the Second Corps attacked Bloody Lane, was acquired in 1998 through a gift provided again by the Mellon Foundation. These properties were also donated to the NPS.

1851. Maryland was the first state to utilize ISTEA dollars—an acronym for a federal transportation bill passed in 1991—to acquire Civil War battlefields.

1852. Maryland expended nearly $15 million between 1992 and 2001 to acquire property or purchase easements on over 4,000 acres at Antietam, South Mountain, and Monocacy battlefields. One half of the acquisition money came from federal transportation enhancement programs, and the other half from the state's Open Space program.

1853. Maryland established South Mountain State Battlefield Park during the 2000 legislature through the leadership of Delegates Chris Shank from Washington County, Louise Snodgrass from Frederick County, and Washington County Senator Don Munson. This represented Maryland's first official battlefield park.

1854. The first Antietam National Battlefield illumination occurred in 1989. Nearly 800 volunteers set out 23,110 candles to represent the casualties of Antietam. The event was held the first Saturday in December and was organized by Ms. Georgene Charles.

1855. Burkittsville, site of the battle of Crampton's Gap at South Mountain, became nationally famous as home of the Blair Witch in the 1999 movie *The Blair Witch Project.*

October 1862 Signal Station (*USAMHI*)

The Blair Witch does not exist—and never has existed—at Burkittsville. Virtually none of the movie *The Blair Witch Project* was filmed at Burkittsville.

1856. Antietam National Battlefield completed a General Management Plan in 1992 that recommended restoring, to the maximum extent possible, the 1862 battlefield landscape.

1857. Approximately 345 acres of woods existed within the present park boundary at the time of the battle. No woods existed in the North Woods (originally 19 acres) in 1998, but a reforestation project has begun there. Few trees existed in the West Woods (originally 75 acres), but reforestation began there in 1995. The East Woods (39 acres at battle time) remains in private ownership and is the most forested area of the three famous woodlots as of 2003. The American Civil War Round Table of the United Kingdom donated $600.00 toward the restoration of the West Woods in 2001.

1858. In 2001 the Save Historic Antietam Foundation acquired the post-battle signal station site where the famous log-cribbing signal tower photos were taken in October 1862. The original square foundation of the signal station still remains, visibly outlined in the ruins of an old charcoal hearth. The site was discovered by the author.

1859. The Prime Minister of Israel, Ehud Barak, visited the Antietam National Battlefield on January 9, 2000—taking a break from Israeli-Palestinian peace talks in nearby Shepherdstown, West Virginia. Accompanying the prime minister was his wife and then Secretary of State Madeline Albright. The tour guide for the party was Antietam Ranger-historian Paul Chiles.

1860. The Mumma Cemetery on the Antietam Battlefield, adjacent to the Mumma farmstead, includes approximately 336 internments. The stone wall that surrounds the graveyard today did not exist at the time of the battle but was built in the 1870s.

1861. "The Cornfield" battle that appears in the Hollywood movie *Gods and Generals* is actually a field of corn located in the Shenandoah Valley midway between Staunton and Lexington, Virginia. The production company filmed the Antietam portion of the movie in mid-September 2001.

1862. Lower Town Harpers Ferry served as the setting for the Fredericksburg street-scene fighting portrayed in the movie *Gods and Generals*. Associate Producer Dennis Frye negotiated with the Harpers Ferry Park Superintendent for use of the national park buildings and streets. The production company also constructed seven facade buildings along Shenandoah Street to complement the actual historic structures.

1863. The State of Maryland inaugurated its first "Civil War Trail" driving tour in September 2002, in conjunction with the 140th anniversary of the battle of Antietam. The Trail begins in Leesburg, Virginia, and then follows the original routes used by Union and Confederate armies as they marched through Washington, Frederick, and Montogomery counties during The Maryland Campaign. Marci Ross spearheaded the effort on behalf of the Maryland Office of Tourism Development. Mitch Bowman, Executive Director of Virginia Civil War Trails, coordinated the project.

1864. The Antietam National Cemetery includes 5,022 graves—4,776 of which are Union soldiers. The remaining graves are veterans who served in wars after the Civil War. The national cemetery was closed to further burials (with the exception of veteran's wives who had reserved a plot with their husbands) on June 17,1953.

1865. The last burial in the Antietam National Cemetery was for US Navy Fireman Apprentice Patrick Roy, a Keedysville native, who was killed in the terrorist attack against the USS *Cole* in Yemen in October 2000.

Fireman Apprentice Patrick Roy's gravestone
Antietam National Cemetery (*CWH*)

Bibliography

Articles, Periodicals & Manuscripts

Alexander, Ted. "Destruction, Disease, and Death: The Battle of Antietam and the Sharpsburg Civilians." *Civil War Regiments*, 6, No. 2 (1998), pp.143-173.
_____. "Forgotten Valor: Off the Beaten Path at Antietam." *Blue and Gray Magazine*, 13, No. 1 (1995), pp. 8-19; 48-64.
Antietam Battlefield folders. Vertical files. Western Maryland Room, Washington County Free Library, Hagerstown, MD.
Battle of Antietam Centennial and Hagerstown Bicentennial Official Program and Historical Guide. Hagerstown: Antietam-South Mountain Centennial Assn., Inc., 1962.
Chiles, Paul. "Artillery Hell! The Guns of Antietam." *Blue and Gray Magazine*, 16, No. 2 (1998), pp. 6-25; 41-65.
Coffin, Charles C. "Antietam Scenes." In *Battles and Leaders of the Civil War*. edited by Robert U. Johnson and Clarence C. Buel. 2:682-685.
Colgrove, Silas. "The Finding of Lee's Lost Order." In *Battles and Leaders of the Civil War*. edited by Robert U. Johnson and Clarence C. Buel. 2:603.
Cox, Jacob D. "Forcing Fox's Gap and Turner's Gap." In *Battles and Leaders of the Civil War*. edited by Robert U. Johnson and Clarence C. Buel. 2:583-590.
_____. "The Battle of Antietam." In *Battles and Leaders of the Civil War*. edited by Robert U. Johnson and Clarence C. Buel. 2:630-660.
Franklin, William B. "Notes on Crampton's Gap and Antietam." In *Battles and Leaders of the Civil War*. edited by Robert U. Johnson and Clarence C. Buel. 2:591-597.
Frye, Dennis E. "Drama between the Rivers: Harpers Ferry in the 1862 Maryland Campaign." In *Antietam: Essays on the 1862 Maryland Campaign*. Gary W. Gallagher. ed. Kent: Kent State University Press, 1989, pp. 14-34.
_____. "Harpers Ferry, West Virginia." In *Encyclopedia of the Confederacy*. Richard N. Current. ed. New York: Simon & Schuster, 1993, pp. 738-744.
_____. "Stonewall Attacks: The Siege of Harpers Ferry." *Blue and Gray Magazine*, 5, No. 1 (1987), pp. 8-27; 47-63.
_____. "Stuart's Raids." In *Encyclopedia of the Confederacy*. Richard N. Current. ed. New York: Simon & Schuster, 1993, pp. 1154-1556.
Frye, Dennis E. & Susan W. Frye. "Maryland Heights: Archeological & Historical Resources Study." 1989. Document on file at Harpers Ferry National Historical Park Library. Note: This document is restricted to protect sensitive archeological resources.

Heysinger, Isaac W. "The Cavalry Column from Harper's Ferry in the Antietam Campaign." In *The Morningside Notes.* 22. Dennis E. Frye. ed. Dayton: Morningside Press, 1987, pp. 5-19.

Hill, Daniel Harvey. "The Battle of South Mountain, or Boonsboro: Fighting for Time at Turner's and Fox's Gaps." In *Battles and Leaders of the Civil War.* edited by Robert U. Johnson and Clarence C. Buel. 2:559-581.

Holsworth, Jerry W. "Uncommon Valor: Hood's Texas Brigade in the Maryland Campaign." *Blue and Gray Magazine,* 8, No. 6 (1996), pp. 6-20; 50-62.

David A. Lilley Collection. Western Maryland Room, Washington Country Free Library, Hagerstown, MD.

Longstreet, James. "The Invasion of Maryland." In *Battles and Leaders of the Civil War.* edited by Robert U. Johnson and Clarence C. Buel. 2:663-674.

Mitchell, Mary Bedinger. "A Woman's Recollections of Antietam." In *Battles and Leaders of the Civil War.* edited by Robert U. Johnson and Clarence C. Buel. 2:687-695.

Official Program and Historical Guide of the National Antietam Commemoration: Commemorating 75th Anniversary of the Battle of Antietam. Hagerstown: Washington County Historical Society, 1937.

Otott, George E. "Clash in the Cornfield: The 1st Texas Volunteer Infantry in the Maryland Campaign." *Civil War Regiments,* 5, No. 3 (1997), pp. 73-123.

Pfanz, Harry W. "Troop Movement Maps, 1862." Special History Report, National Park Service, 1976. Document on file at Harpers Ferry National Historical Park.

Reese, Timothy J. "Howell Cobb's Brigade at Crampton's Gap." *Blue and Gray Magazine,* 15, No. 3 (1998), pp. 6-21; 47-61.

Scott, Gary. "The Philip Pry House: Headquarters of General George B. McClellan." 1980. Manuscript at Antietam National Battlefield library.

Sherlock, Scott. "The Lost Order and the Press." *Civil War Regiments.* 6, No. 2 (1998), pp. 174-176.

Snell, Charles W. and Sharon A. Brown. "Antietam National Battlefield and National Cemetery: An Administrative History." National Park Service, 1986. Document on file at Antietam National Battlefield Library.

Snell, Mark A. "Baptism of Fire: The 118th Pennsylvania ('Corn Exchange') Infantry at the Battle of Shepherdstown." *Civil War Regiments,* 6, No. 2 (1998), pp. 119-142.

Trimpi, Helen. "Lafayette McLaws' Aide-De-Camp: The Maryland Campaign Diary of Captain Henry Lord Page King." *Civil War Regiments,* 6, No. 2 (1998), pp. 23-57.

Walker, John G. "Jackson's Capture of Harper's Ferry." In *Battles and Leaders of the Civil War.* edited by Robert U. Johnson and Clarence C. Buel. 2:604-611.

White, Julius. "The Surrender of Harper's Ferry." In *Battles and Leaders of the Civil War.* edited by Robert U. Johnson and Clarence C. Buel. 2:612-615.

Books

Adams, Charles S. *The Monuments at Antietam: Sharpsburg's Silent Sentinels.* Shepherdstown: privately printed, 2000.

After the Dunker Church: A Century of Faithful Service—The Sharpsburg Church of the Brethren, 1899-1999. privately printed, 1999.

Alexander, Charles Ted & William P. Conrad. *When War Passed This Way.* Shippensburg: Biedel Printing House, 1982.

Alexander, E. P. *Fighting for the Confederacy: The Personal Recollections of General Edward Porter Alexander.* edited by Gary W. Gallagher. Chapel Hill: University of North Carolina Press, 1989.

_____. *Military Memoirs of a Confederate.* New York: Charles Scribner's Sons, 1907.

Allan, William. *The Army of Northern Virginia in 1862.* Boston: Houghton Mifflin & Company, 1892.

Antietam Battlefield Board. *Atlas of the Battlefield of Antietam.* Washington, D.C.: War Department, Chief of Engineers, 1904, 1908.

Bailey, Ronald H. *The Bloodiest Day: The Battle of Antietam.* Alexandria: Time-Life Books, 1984.

Blackford, W. W. *War Years with Jeb Stuart.* New York: Charles Scribner's Sons, 1945.

Bridges, Hal. *Lee's Maverick General: Daniel Harvey Hill.* New York: McGraw-Hill, 1961.

Caldwell, J. F. J. *The History of [Gregg's] Brigade of South Carolinians.* Philadelphia: King & Baird, 1866.

Chambers, Lenoir. *Stonewall Jackson.* 2 vols. New York: Morrow, 1959.

Cox, Jacob D. *Military Reminiscences of the Civil War.* 2 vols. New York: Charles Scribner's Sons, 1900.

Cunningham, D. & W. W. Miller. *Report of Ohio Antietam Battlefield Commission.* Springfield: Springfield Publishing Co., 1904.

Dedication of New York State Memorial on the Battlefield of Antietam. Albany: J. B. Lyon, 1923.

Dickert, D. Augustus. *History of Kershaw's Brigade.* Newberry: Elbert H. Hull, Co., 1899.

Douglas, Henry Kyd. *I Rode with Stonewall.* Chapel Hill: University of North Carolina Press, 1940.

Early, Jubal A. *War Memoirs.* edited by Frank Vandiver. Bloomington: University of Indiana Press, 1960.

Eby, Cecil B., Jr., ed. *A Virginia Yankee in the Civil War: The Diaries of David Hunter Strother.* Chapel Hill: University of North Carolina Press, 1961.

Ernst, Kathleen A. *Too Afraid to Cry: Maryland Civilians in the Antietam Campaign.* Mechanicsburg: Stackpole Books, 1999.

Fishel, Edwin C. *The Secret War for the Union: The Untold Story of Military Intelligence in the Civil War*. Boston: Houghton Mifflin & Company, 1996.

Frassanito, William A. *Antietam: The Photographic Legacy of America's Bloodiest Day*. New York: Charles Scribner's Sons, 1978.

Freeman, Douglas Southall. *Lee's Lieutenants*. 3 vols. New York: Charles Scribner's Sons, 1942-44.

Frye, Dennis E. *2nd Virginia Infantry*. Lynchburg: H. E. Howard, Inc., 1984.

_____. *12th Virginia Cavalry*. Lynchburg: H. E. Howard, Inc., 1988.

Gallagher, Gary W., ed. *Antietam: Essays on the 1862 Maryland Campaign*. Kent: Kent State University Press, 1989.

_____. *The Antietam Campaign*. Chapel Hill: University of North Carolina Press, 1999.

Gibbon, John. *Personal Recollections of the Civil War*. New York: Putnam's, 1928.

Gordon, John Brown. *Reminiscences of the Civil War*. New York: Charles Scribner's Sons, 1903.

Gordon, Paul, and Rita Brown. *Frederick County, Maryland: A Playground of the Civil War*. Frederick: M & B Printing, 1994.

Gould, John M. *History of the First—Tenth—Twenty-ninth Maine Regiment*. Portland: Stephen Berry, 1871.

Harsh, Joseph L. *Confederate Tide Rising: Robert E. Lee and the Making of Southern Strategy 1861-1862*. Kent: Kent State University Press, 1998.

_____. *Sounding the Shallows: A Companion for the Maryland Campaign of 1862*. Kent: Kent State University Press, 2000.

_____. *Taken at the Flood: Robert E. Lee & Confederate Strategy in the Maryland Campaign of 1862*. Kent: Kent State University Press, 1999.

Hassler, Warren W., Jr. *General George B. McClellan: Shield of the Union*. Baton Rouge: Louisiana State University Press, 1957.

Henderson, G. F. R. *Stonewall Jackson and the American Civil War*. New York: Longmans, Green, & Co., 1898.

Heitman, Francis B. *Historical Register & Dictionary of the United States Army*. 2 vols. Washington, D. C.: Government Printing Office, 1903.

Heysinger, Isaac W. *Antietam and the Maryland and Virginia Campaigns of 1862*. New York: Neale, 1912.

Hood, John Bell. *Advance and Retreat*. edited by Richard N. Current. Bloomington: University of Indiana Press, 1959.

Jamieson, Perry D. *Death in September: The Antietam Campaign*. Fort Worth: Ryan Place Publishers, 1995.

Johnson, Robert U., and Clarence C. Buel, eds. *Battles and Leaders of the Civil War*. 4 vols. New York: Century Company, 1884-1889.

Jones, Wilbur D., Jr. *Giants in the Cornfield: The 27th Indiana Infantry*. Shippensburg: White Mane Publishing Co., 1997.

Keller, S. Roger. *Events of the Civil War in Washington County, Maryland.* Shippensburg: Burd Street Press, 1995.

Krick, Robert K. *Lee's Colonels: Biographical Register of the Field Officers of the Army of Northern Virginia.* Dayton: Press of Morningside Bookshop, 1984.

_____. *9th Virginia Cavalry.* Lynchburg: H. E. Howard, Inc., 1982.

Lee, Robert E. *Recollections and Letters of Robert E. Lee by his son, Captain Robert E. Lee.* New York: Doubleday, Page & Co., 1904.

Livermore, Thomas L. *Numbers and Losses in the Civil War in America, 1861-1865.* Boston: Houghton Mifflin & Company, 1902.

Longstreet, James. *From Manassas to Appomattox.* Philadelphia: Lippincott, 1896.

Luvaas, Jay & Harold W. Nelson, eds. *The U. S. Army War College Guide to the Battle of Antietam: The Maryland Campaign of 1862.* Carlisle: South Mountain Press, 1987.

Marvel, William. *Burnside.* Chapel Hill: University of North Carolina Press, 1991.

McAfee, Michael J. *Zouaves: The First and The Bravest.* Gettysburg: Thomas Publications. 1991.

McClellan, George B. *McClellan's Own Story.* New York: Webster, 1887.

_____. *Report on the Organization of the Army of the Potomac, and of Its Campaigns in Virginia and Maryland.* Washington, D.C.: Government Printing Office, 1864.

McClellan, H. B. *I Rode with Jeb Stuart.* edited by Burke Davis. Bloomington: University of Indiana Press, 1958.

Meade, George G. *The Life and Letters of George Gordon Meade.* 2 vols. New York: Charles Scribner's Sons, 1913.

Murfin, James V. *The Gleam of Bayonets: The Battle of Antietam and the Maryland Campaign.* New York: A. S. Barnes & Co., 1965.

Naisawald, L. Van Loan. *Grape and Canister: The Story of the Field Artillery of the Army of the Potomac, 1861-1865.* New York: Oxford University Press, 1960.

Nolan, Alan T. *The Iron Brigade: A Military History.* Ann Arbor: Historical Society of Michigan, 1983.

Oates, Stephen B. *A Woman of Valor: Clara Barton and the Civil War.* New York: The Free Press, 1994.

Palfrey, Francis Winthrop. *The Army in the Civil War: The Antietam and Fredericksburg.* New York: Charles Scribner's Sons, 1882.

Palmer, Michael A. *Lee Moves North: Robert E. Lee on the Offensive.* New York: John Wiley & Sons, 1998.

Pennsylvania at Antietam. Report of the Antietam National Battlefield Memorial Commission of Pennsylvania. Harrisburg: Harrisburg Publishing Company, 1906.

Pettengill, Samuel B. *The College Cavaliers.* Chicago: Ft. McAllister & Co., 1883.

Poague, William T. *Gunner with Stonewall.* edited by Monroe F. Cockrell. Wilmington: Broadfoot Publishing Co., 1987.

Priest, John Michael. *Before Antietam: The Battle for South Mountain.* Shippensburg: White Mane Publishing Co., 1992.
_____. *Antietam: The Soldiers' Battle.* Shippensburg: White Mane Publishing Co., 1989.

Quaife, Milo M., ed. *From the Cannon's Mouth: The Civil War Letters of General Alpheus S. Williams.* Detroit: Wayne State University Press, 1959.

Quigley, Robert D. *Civil War Spoken Here: A Dictionary of Mispronounced People, Places and Things of the 1860's.* Collingswood: C.W. Historicals, 1993.

Reese, Timothy J. *Sealed with Their Lives: The Battle for Crampton's Gap.* Baltimore: Butternut & Blue, 1998.

Reilly, Oliver T. *The Battlefield of Antietam.* Hagerstown: Hagerstown Printing Co., 1906.

Robertson, James I., Jr. *General A. P. Hill: The Story of a Confederate Warrior.* New York: Random House, 1987.
_____. *Stonewall Jackson: The Man, The Soldier, The Legend.* New York: Simon & Schuster, 1997.
_____. *The Stonewall Brigade.* Baton Rouge: Louisiana State University Press, 1963.

Schildt, John W. *Antietam Hospitals.* Chewsville: Antietam Publications, 1987.
_____. *Drums Along the Antietam.* Parsons: McClain Printing Co., 1972.
_____. *Four Days in October.* privately printed, 1978.
_____. *Monuments at Antietam.* Frederick: Great Southern Press, 1991.
_____. *Roads to Antietam.* Chewsville: Antietam Publications, 1985.

Sears, Stephen W. *George B. McClellan: The Young Napoleon.* New York: Ticknor & Fields, 1988.
_____. *Landscape Turned Red: The Battle of Antietam.* New York: Ticknor & Fields, 1983.
_____. ed. *The Civil War Papers of George B. McClellan: Selected Correspondence, 1861-1865.* New York: Ticknor & Fields, 1989.

Sorrel, G. Moxley. *Recollections of a Confederate Staff Officer.* New York: Neale, 1905.

Sparks, David S. ed. *Inside Lincoln's Army: The Diary of Marsena Rudolph Patrick, Provost Marshal General, Army of the Potomac.* New York: Thomas Yoselof, 1964.

Stackpole, Edward J. *From Cedar Mountain to Antietam.* Harrisburg: The Stackpole Company, 1959.

Stotelmyer, Steven R. *The Bivouacs of the Dead: The Story of Those Who Died at Antietam and South Mountain.* Baltimore: Toomey Press, 1992.

Swinton, William. *Campaigns of the Army of the Potomac.* New York: Charles Scribner's Sons, 1882.

Taylor, Walter H. *Four Years with General Lee.* edited by James I. Robertson, Jr., Bloomington: University of Indiana Press, 1962.

Tilberg, Frederick. *Antietam National Battlefield Site*. Washington, D.C.: National Park Service Historical Handbook Series No. 31, 1960.

U. S. War Department. *The War of the Rebellion: A Compilation of the Official Records of the Union and Confederate Armies*. 128 vols. Washington, D.C.: U. S. Government Printing Office, 1880-1901.

Warner, Ezra J. *Generals in Blue: Lives of the Union Commanders*. Baton Rouge: Louisiana State University Press, 1964.

_____. *Generals in Gray: Lives of the Confederate Commanders*. Baton Rouge: Louisiana State University Press, 1959.

Williams, Kenneth P. *Lincoln Finds a General: A Military Study of the Civil War*. 5 vols. New York: The Macmillan Company, 1949-1959.

Williams, T. Harry. *Lincoln and his Generals*. New York: Alfred A. Knoff, 1952.

Wise, Jennings C. *The Long Arm of Lee: The History of the Artillery of the Army of Northern Virginia*. New York: Oxford University Press, 1959.

Wyckoff, Mac. *A History of the 2nd South Carolina Infantry*. Fredericksburg: Sgt. Kirkland's Museum and Historical Society, 1994.

Index

Patrick Marsena, 56, 80, 83, 87.
Pendleton, William, 37, 38, 64, 65, 75, 138, 154.
Pennsylvania Reserves, 70, 76, 77, 79, 83, 161.
Piper Farm, 100, 104, 107, 109-113, 145, 174, 176, 177, 179.
Pleasant Valley, 27, 28, 37, 45, 46, 47, 48, 50, 59, 60, 61, 62, 65, 72, 93, 150, 182.
Pleasonton, Alfred, 45, 50, 63, 137, 138, 139, 148, 156, 160.
Poffenberger Farm, Joseph, 71, 75, 129, 171, 173, 177, 179.
Porter, Fitz John, 11, 42, 67, 68, 117, 125, 138, 139, 148, 153, 158, 160.
Potomac River, 1-6, 9-15, 17, 19, 21, 23, 24, 25, 27, 33, 34, 36, 37, 39, 45, 60, 64, 65, 69, 75, 123, 127, 128, 135-141, 146, 148, 149, 150, 156, 159, 160, 164, 179.
Presidential Visits, 165, 168, 169, 171, 173, 175, 178, 179.
Pry House, 67, 68, 90, 110, 113, 134, 145, 153.

Red Hill, 68, 128, 181.
Reno, Jesse L., 14, 52, 58, 174.
Reynolds, John F., 63, 140, 155.
Richardson, Israel B., 23, 66, 91, 106, 112, 113, 145, 153, 175.
Richmond, VA, 3, 6, 12, 21, 94, 141, 151, 159.
Ricketts, James, B., 54, 55, 57, 70, 75, 76, 77, 79-83, 85, 91.
Ripley, Roswell, 52, 81, 87, 88, 89, 100.
Rodes, Robert, 54, 55, 56, 63, 97, 100, 101, 103, 104, 109, 110, 112.
Rodman, Isaac P., 52, 119, 120, 122, 124, 126, 127, 129, 130, 132, 175.
Roulette Farm, 100, 101, 102, 105, 111, 114, 136, 150, 178, 184.

School House Ridge, 21, 24, 28, 32, 33, 34, 38, 39, 181, 182.
Second Corps, (Army of the Potomac), 10, 66, 86, 90, 91, 101, 105, 106, 150, 152, 184.
Sedgwick, John, 23, 91-94, 96, 97, 101, 102, 104, 105.
Semmes, Paul J., 48, 61, 93, 96, 97.
Sharpsburg, MD, 1, 2, 14, 15, 36, 37, 43, 46, 47, 57, 59, 60, 62-68, 71, 77, 78, 92, 93, 97, 99, 100, 104, 115, 120, 124-128, 132, 133, 134, 136, 140-145, 149-153, 158, 160, 161, 162, 167, 168, 169, 170, 171, 174, 177, 178, 179.
Shenandoah River, 15, 21, 23, 32, 36, 39, 149.
Shenandoah Valley, 9, 12, 13, 15, 22, 24, 26, 28, 64, 105, 142, 149, 151, 156, 157, 159, 186.
Sherrick Farm, 125, 126, 144.
Shepherdstown (WV), 1, 2, 36, 39, 59, 63, 64, 65, 75, 132, 137, 138, 140, 179, 185.
Showman Farm, 149, 150, 152, 153.
Sixth Corps, (Army of the Potomac), 10, 34, 37, 45, 47, 60, 62, 72, 93, 113, 135, 153, 160, 164.
Smoketown Road, 70, 71, 86, 90, 94, 147, 171, 174.
Snavely's Ford, 115, 119, 120, 122, 132.
South Mountain, 2, 14, 27, 34, 45, 46, 48, 50, 51, 53, 54, 55, 57-63, 68, 77, 89, 90, 148, 149, 153, 156, 162, 163, 167, 171, 174, 179, 182, 183, 184.
Special Order 191, 13, 14, 15, 17, 18, 19, 27, 32, 45, 46, 47, 50, 87, 163.
Stanton, Edwin M., 3, 4, 11, 24, 38, 151, 157.
Stuart, James E. B., 6, 12, 34, 36, 37, 57, 60, 61, 62, 77, 91, 92, 111, 135, 136, 138, 155, 156, 157, 177.

Solitary Grave of John Marshall (28th Pennsylvania Infantry)
on the Samuel Mumma Farm (*USAMHI*)

Dennis E. Frye is the former Chief Historian of the Harpers Ferry National Historical Park and is a founder and past president of the Association for the Preservation of Civil War Sites. He is also a founder and the first president of the Save Historic Antietam Foundation. Dennis grew up astride South Mountain and began his National Park Service career as a teenage volunteer at the Antietam National Battlefield. Dennis has written and lectured extensively on the Maryland Campaign for the past two decades. He has also restored and currently resides in General Ambrose Burnside's post-Antietam headquarters.

Donations and memberships for the **Save Historic Antietam Foundation, Inc.** may be made by contacting the Foundation at PO Box 550, Sharpsburg, MD 21783.
301-432-2996